BOMBING EUROPE

The Illustrated Exploits of the Fifteenth Air Force

KEVIN A. MAHONEY

ZENITH
PRESS

First published in 2015 by Zenith Press, an imprint of Quarto Publishing Group USA Inc., 400 First Avenue North, Suite 400, Minneapolis, MN 55401 USA

Zenith Press titles are also available at discounts in bulk quantity for industrial or sales-promotional use. For details write to Special Sales Manager at Quarto Publishing Group USA Inc., 400 First Avenue North, Suite 400, Minneapolis, MN 55401 USA.

To find out more about our books, visit us online at www.zenithpress.com.

ISBN: 978-0-7603-4815-4

Library of Congress Cataloging-in-Publication Data

Mahoney, Kevin A.
Bombing Europe : the illustrated exploits of the Fifteenth Air Force / Kevin A. Mahoney.
    pages cm
 Includes bibliographical references.
 ISBN 978-0-7603-4815-4 (hc w/ jacket)
 1. United States. Army Air Forces. Air Force, 15th. 2. World War, 1939-1945—Aerial operations, American. 3. World War, 1939-1945—Campaigns—Europe. I. Title.
 D790.2215th .M34 2015
 940.54'4973--dc23
                                        2014047975

Acquisitions Editor: Elizabeth Demers   Cover Designer: Andrew Brozyna
Project Manager: Madeleine Vasaly   Layout Designer: Lee Ann McKevitt
Art Director: James Kegley

On the front cover: "Bombs away!" from B-24 Liberators of the 464th Bomb Group
    over Vienna on March 22, 1945.
On the back cover: Bombs fall as others have already hit their target at Regensburg,
    Germany, during the raid by B-17s of the 5th Bomb Wing on December 25, 1944.
Opposite page: A flight of Mustangs of the 31st Fighter Group in formation.

Printed in China

10 9 8 7 6 5 4 3 2

CONTENTS

FIFTEENTH AIR FORCE AREA OF OPERATIONS 1943–1945
1937 BORDERS

PREFACE

Unlike my previous work, *Fifteenth Air Force against the Axis,* this book is not a history of the Fifteenth Air Force. Rather, it attempts to portray the combat experienced by these aircrews, in the air and on the ground, in southern and central Europe. Most of these stories are based on contemporary reports, recorded at the time or shortly after the events occurred. All quotations are taken from these documents. None have been reconstructed or enhanced, as the contemporary words of the participants themselves are the most accurate record of these events.

—Kevin A. Mahoney
2015

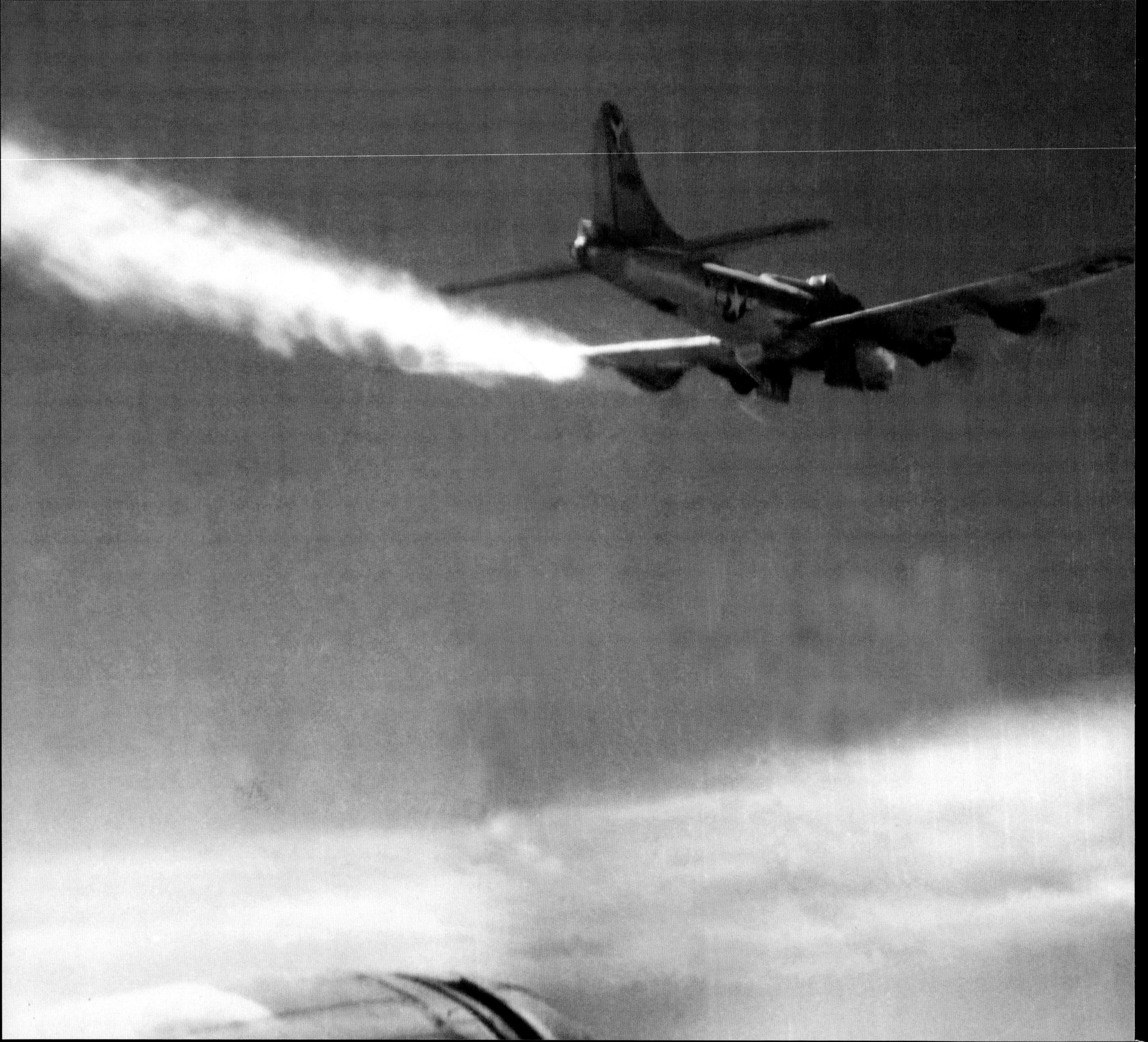

CHAPTER 1

SUPREME SACRIFICE

As the Allies thrust deep into Germany in late April 1945—the Soviet Army from the east and the American, British, and French armies from the west— the American Fifth and British Eighth Armies drove into northern Italy. By April 20, as the Russian army entered the suburbs of Berlin, the Fifth and the Eighth had fanned out over the Po River plain. A few days earlier, the Fifteenth Air Force, the American strategic air force that bombed the Axis in southern and central Europe, ended its strategic air campaign and concentrated on support of Allied ground troops in Italy. Railway marshalling yards were some of the prime targets as their destruction would impede the movement of supplies and troops to the beleaguered German and Italian troops trying to stem the Allied advance.

Opposite page: This flak-damaged 463rd Bomb Group Flying Fortress on fire over Fortezza on April 20, 1945, is believed to be the plane piloted by Lt. John Cunningham.

Above right: The insignia of Cunningham's squadron, the 772nd Bomb Squadron.
Kevin A. Mahoney

On April 20, B-17 Flying Fortresses from the Fifteenth attacked the marshalling yards at Fortezza, near the Po River. Over the target, flak (German antiaircraft artillery) slammed a 463rd Bomb Group Fortress, *Magnificent Malfunction*, flown by 2nd Lt. John Cunningham. Just after the bombardier had called "bombs away," more flak hit two engines, knocked out the intercom, and ravaged the center portion of the fuselage, including the radio compartment. Shrapnel killed the radio operator instantly, hitting him in the throat. The same burst practically decapitated the ball-turret gunner nearby, who had just gotten out of his turret. A waist gunner, Staff Sgt. James Wolfgang, was wounded in the knee, and the navigator, 2nd Lt. James Millar, was severely wounded in the stomach. Two crewmen unsuccessfully attempted to revive the radioman with oxygen. They also moved Lieutenant Millar from the nose of the ship to the partially destroyed radio compartment.

The plane struggled on for about twenty minutes as the fuselage began to burn and smoke filled the cockpit. The flight engineer, Sgt. Conrad Bailey, later reported: "I asked him [Cunningham] if we could make it back [to base]. He didn't know." Lieutenant Cunningham then told Bailey to pass the word to the crew that it was time to bail out. Millar later recalled: "When I reached the radio room, I could see that the whole ship was empty, except for me, the pilot, and co-pilot." He soon passed out from his wounds, and it was obvious that he could not bail out, or be bailed out, and survive. On the very slim chance that either radio operator or ball-turret gunner might still be alive, both were bailed out of the stricken ship with a static line to open their chutes once they had cleared the badly damaged bomber. Afterward the remaining crewmen also began to bail out.

The bombardier, 2nd Lt. Alfred Baldwin, passed Cunningham and the copilot, 2nd Lt. Arthur Hall, at the controls in the cockpit as he passed through on the way to the waist of the aircraft to bail out. Hall followed him, but Cunningham heroically remained at the controls. He planned to ditch the rapidly disintegrating B-17 in the Po River to save the life of the navigator.

The stricken bomber never made it to the river, but crashed nearby. Lieutenant Baldwin later reported: "After I landed I saw a thin column of black smoke rising several hundred feet in the air."

III - AWARD OF DISTINGUISHED FLYING CROSS (POSTHUMOUS)

By direction of the President, under the provisions of Army Regulations 600-45, as amended, the Distinguished Flying Cross was posthumously awarded by the Theater Commander to the officer named below:

JOHN G. CUNNINGHAM, O817170, Second Lieutenant, 772d Bombardment Squadron, 463d Bombardment Group, for extraordinary achievement while participating in aerial flight in Italy on 20 April 1945. As pilot of a B-17 type aircraft on a bombing mission against the enemy marshalling yards at Fortezza, Italy, Second Lieutenant Cunningham, although his plane was hit several times by antiaircraft fire, held his position in formation and completed a successful bomb run. Just after the bombs were away, his plane was riddled by antiaircraft fire, rendering the plane almost unmaneuverable. Through extreme effort and outstanding skill Second Lieutenant Cunningham was able to return to the formation. Upon nearing the Po river the plane was further damaged by flak which started a fire in the nose. When the crew was ordered to bail out Second Lieutenant Cunningham saw

1

Hq MTOUSA General Orders Number 88 (Cont'd)

that the navigator was too seriously wounded to do so. Staying with the wounded man and trying to fly the seriously damaged plane, he made an unsuccessful attempt to ditch the plane in the Po River. The outstanding devotion to duty displayed by Second Lieutenant Cunningham was in keeping with the highest traditions of the military service.

The crash unfortunately killed Cunningham, but his attempt to save the life of navigator Millar was successful, although Millar's back was broken in the crash.

All the surviving crewmen were immediately taken prisoner by German troops. Navigator Millar was taken to a German hospital, and the Germans found and buried the bodies of the two dead men who had been bailed out. Lieutenant Millar provided a suitable epitaph for Cunningham: "[He] landed the ship to save me." His selfless conduct led to recommendation for gallantry. Earlier if the war, he most likely would have been awarded the Distinguished Service Cross, but in 1946 the army's Mediterranean Theater of Operations posthumously awarded him the Distinguished Flying Cross.[i]

The Fifteenth Air Force, of which Cunningham was a member, bombed strategic targets in Europe during World War II along with the more famous Eighth Air Force. The Eighth, based in the England, bombed targets in Germany and northwestern Europe. Half the size of the Eighth, the Fifteenth operated over a wide geographical area, attacking targets in eleven different countries, from France to Bulgaria. Created in November 1943 from portions of the American Ninth and Twelfth Air Forces that had fought in the Mediterranean since the summer of 1942, its B-17 Flying Fortress and B-24 Liberator bombers, escorted by P-38 Lightning, P-47 Thunderbolt, and P-51 Mustang fighters, took the air battle against the Axis to areas Allied bombers based in England could not reach in central and eastern Europe, including the oil refineries at Ploesti, Romania, vital to Germany's war effort. Its crews fought weather, as well as the enemy, by flying over the Alps to reach many of their targets and made a significant contribution to the victory over Germany.

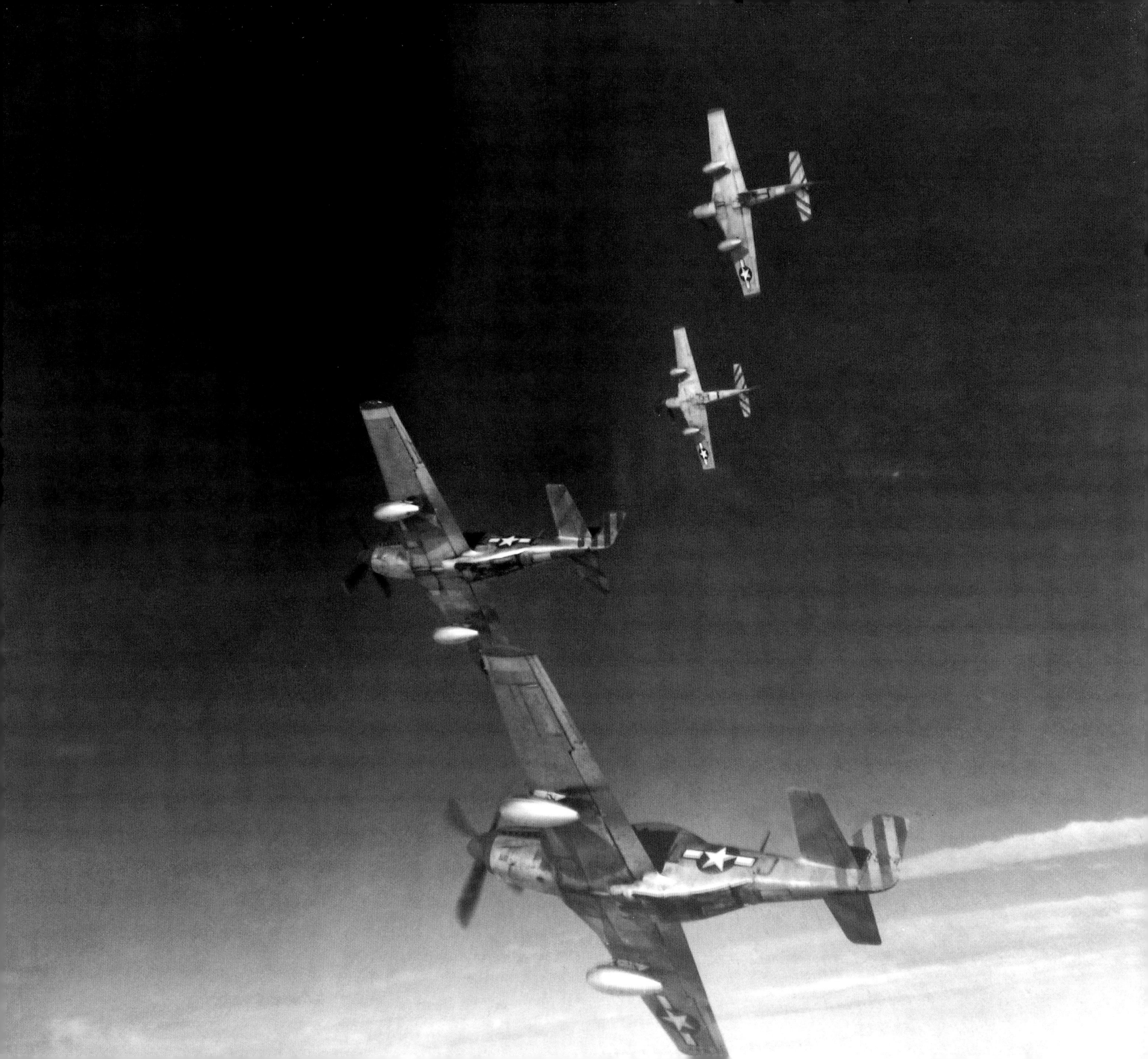

CHAPTER 2

DOGFIGHTS

When the Fifteenth Air Force began operations on November 1, 1943, it possessed six heavy bomb groups, five medium bomb groups, and four fighter groups. The medium bomber groups transferred to the tactical air force in Italy, the Twelfth, within weeks, leaving the heavy bombers and fighters, all combat veterans, to carry out offensive operations. Some of the fighter groups had been flying in combat for almost a year, since the invasion of North Africa in November 1942. The 1st, 14th, and 82nd flew the two-engine Lockheed Lightning, while the 325th Fighter Group, operational with the Fifteenth in December, flew P-47B Thunderbolts. When the Fifteenth moved from North African bases to Italy at the end of 1943, neither aircraft had the range to escort the fledgling bomber force over the Alps, to targets in Germany and Austria. The Lightnings could, however, escort the bomber force of the Fifteenth to targets in Italy, southern France, and Greece. The Thunderbolts had a more limited range and usually escorted bombers on the outbound or homebound portions of a mission, often

Opposite page: A flight of Mustangs of the 31st Fighter Group in formation.

splitting into two flights for his purpose. The major hazards they encountered were flak, enemy fighters, and engine failure, the latter a constant concern during missions for both aircraft. Although the Lightnings had two engines, they could be temperamental, and the failure of even one could lead to the loss of the aircraft, often over enemy territory.[ii]

During the first nine months of Fifteenth Air Force operations, its fighters often tangled with enemy fighters attacking bomber formations. Just as long-range fighter types, the P-51 and long-range P-38J, arrived at the Fifteenth in April, Luftwaffe fighters began to directly engage the fighter escort as well. "Destroyer" Messerschmitt Me 109s and Focke-Wulf Fw 190s, equipped with light and heavy machine guns, fought with the American fighter escort, while Me 109s and Fw 190s equipped with both cannons and machine guns attacked the bombers. The German formations could be massive; one hundred to three hundred fighters attacked in "flying wedges" or waves that could last for a half hour or longer. As American fighters gained supremacy in the air during the spring of 1944, however, Luftwaffe fighters would make one pass against an American formation, often a bomber formation separated from the mass of bombers in the bomber column, then break away to find lone bomber stragglers, the preferred targets of German fighters.[iii]

The inexperience of Luftwaffe fighter pilots committed to combat became evident in the spring of 1944, the result of high losses in pilots in the previous few months, most shot down by American fighters. The aircraft lost were replaced, but experienced pilots were not. Training of new pilots suffered, and they often entered combat with limited flight and tactical training that emphasized attacking bombers, not dogfighting with fighters. This, in combination with their inexperience, led to a reasonable fear of encountering American fighters Luftwaffepilots called *Jaeger Schreck*.[iv]

Despite this inexperience many Luftwaffe fighter pilots continued to defend their homeland vigorously. During the mission to Wiener Neustadt on April 12, the 325th Fighter Group fought with more than fifty German fighters just before "bombs away." The 325th bagged six enemy fighters in the dogfight, the first destroyed by Capt. Raymond Hartley, whom we will meet again later, earlier in the year. Near the target, he spotted a small group of Me 109s. As one flew underneath him, he got on its tail and fired, scoring hits that caused the Messerschmitt to dive. Hartley followed it down, firing, for about five thousand feet, then saw the pilot bail out. He continued to follow the enemy fighter down another five thousand feet, as it smoked and spun, until it hit the ground.

Above: An unidentified Luftwaffe pilot in the cockpit of his Me 109.

Right: A close-up view of a P-38 flying in formation over Italy.

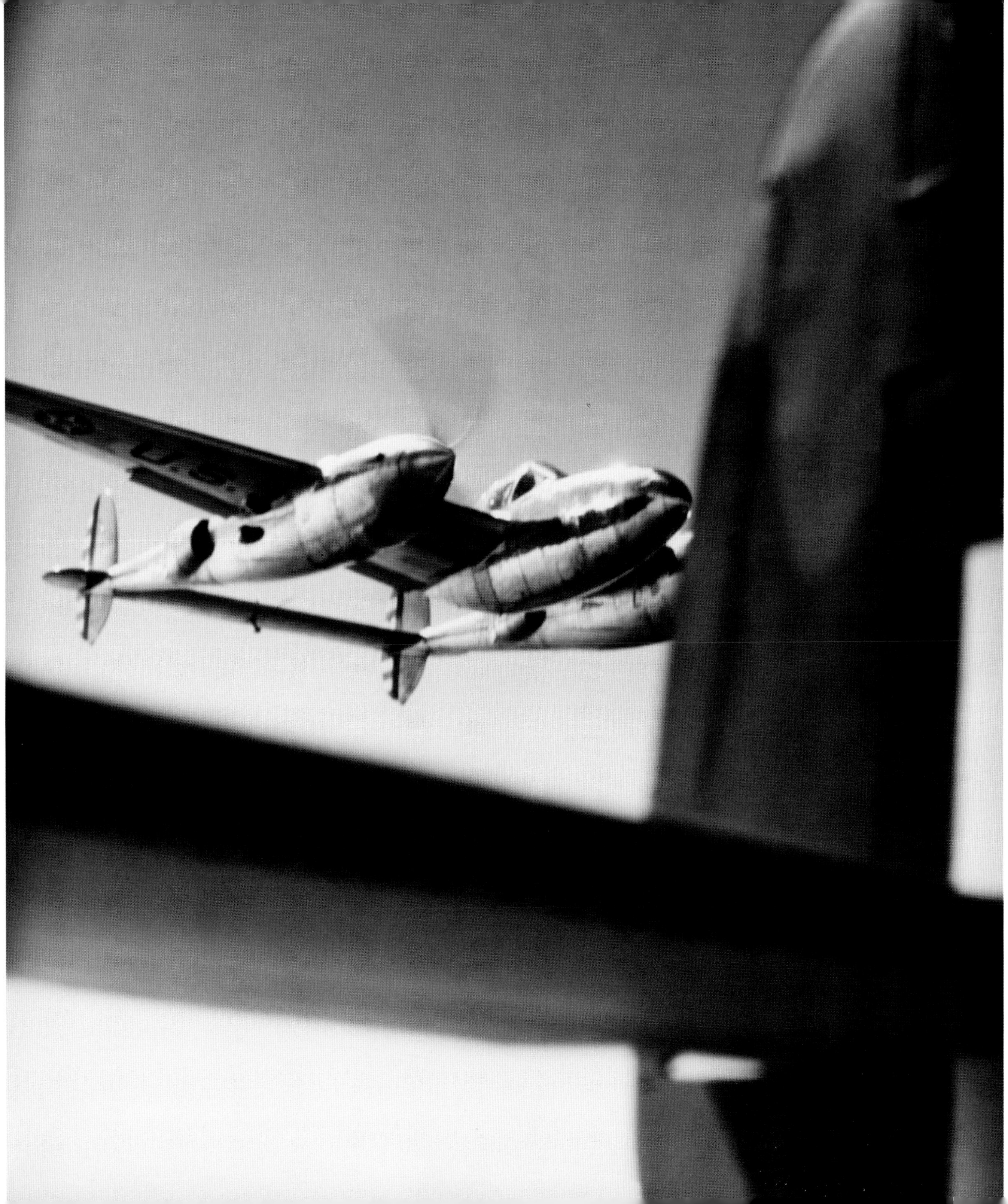

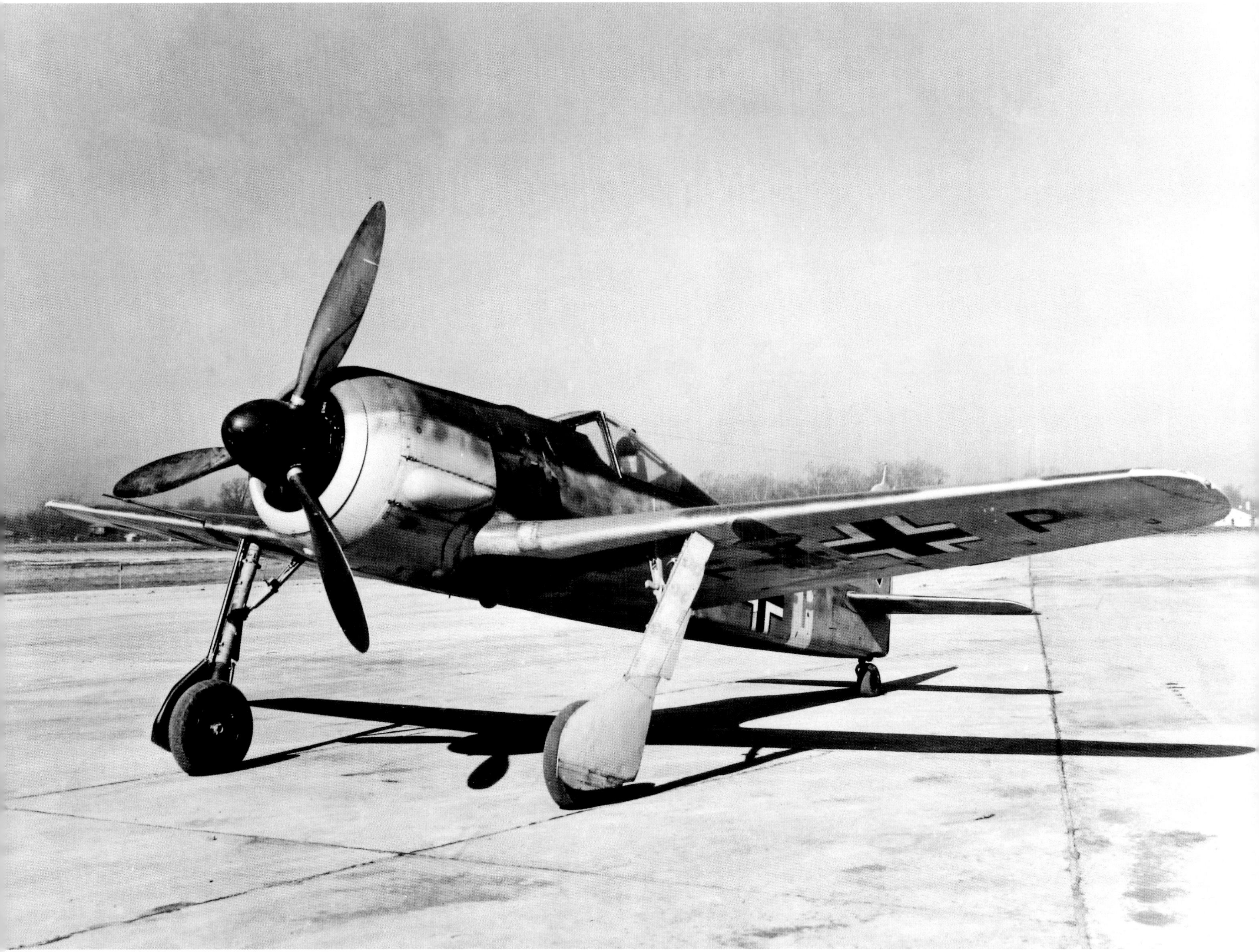

About ten minutes later, three more pilots scored victories. First Lieutenant James Strain saw an Me 109 lining up behind his flight leader, 1st Lt. Harry Parker, and tried to get in position to attack it head-on, but could not do so. Parker was unable to drop one of his wing tanks, and the Messerschmitt maneuvered into position, fired, and hit his Thunderbolt, forcing him to bail out. Fortunately, he survived to become a prisoner of war. Strain was then able to get on the tail of the Me 109, fired, and hit the cockpit. The German fighter made a diving turn, caught fire, and went down in flames.

At the same time, another 325th pilot, 1st Lt. Richard Malloy, encountered two more Me 109s flying across his front. He immediately got on their tails and fired at the right-hand enemy, hitting its fuselage. The enemy fighter immediately turned, allowing Malloy to hit it again. The 109 then did several split S maneuvers and was seen by another pilot to go down to the ground without pulling out.

While Malloy was busy, 2nd Lt. Benjamin Emmert damaged a third Messerschmitt. He went after the same pair of Messerschmitts as Malloy and made a good deflection shot at the left-hand aircraft, from about two hundred yards. The enemy fighter broke right, emitting white smoke from its engine, flew a split S, and dived out of sight. This was not the black smoke that 109s could emit when accelerating, but an obvious sign of damage to the engine. Although this fighter was not shot down, it was out of the fight.

Five minutes after these two victories, two more Messerschmitts went down before the guns of the Thunderbolts. Second Lieutenant Essel Paulk was flying above and behind the bombers, keeping an eye out for attackers. He saw a lone Me 109 flying parallel to the bombers,

Opposite page: The Focke-Wulf 190, one the major Luftwaffe antagonists to Fifteenth Air Force fighters.

Right: Luftwaffe ground crewmen prepare an Me 109 fighter for takeoff.

apparently looking them over before attacking. Paulk called out the enemy fighter over the radio, then set out to attack it. Making a diving turn, he got into position on the tail of the enemy fighter, which made a slight turn, providing a better target. Paulk fired a burst, scoring direct hits on the Messerschmitt, and it exploded in the air.

At the same time, 1st Lt. Richard Dunkin saw six Me 109s lining up to make an attack pass on several Liberators from the rear. He instantly dived on them and fired at one from above and directly behind it. The Messerschmitt flamed and began to disintegrate in midair.

The last victory of the day for the 325th went to 1st Lt. Gilbert Gerkin, about five minutes after the two shot down by Paulk and Dunkin. Leading his flight, Gerkin saw a single Me 109 flying about five thousand feet below him. With his wingman, he dived on it as the 109 made for the deck. The wingman fired but missed. Gerkin got on its tail, closed to less than three hundred yards, and fired a short burst that hit the fuselage. The rear of the Messerschmitt burst into flames and plummeted to the ground, observed by the wingman. All these six victories were later confirmed.[v]

Only a few days later, the 14th Fighter Group escorted Fifteenth Air Force bombers during the April 15 mission to Bucharest, Romania. Despite overcast that made a rendezvous with the bombers difficult, the group reached the target, where they encountered about twenty enemy fighters while answering a radio call for assistance from the bombers. They immediately engaged these Me 109s, and thirty more of the enemy soon joined the fracas. In the aerial melee that followed, the 14th destroyed five enemy aircraft. During the fight, Capt. Robert Zimmerman and his wingman, 2nd Lt. John Ingram, ran into trouble. Ingram reported that he had lost an engine and dived out of the fight. Unfortunately, his Lightning crashed and he was killed.

Zimmerman soon found himself attacked by eight to ten Me 109s and pushed his throttles to the limit to get away, but he was still hit by enemy fire. "I ducked down behind the armor plating and then discovered my right engine was on fire," he reported. Making himself as small as possible behind the armor plating in his seat for protection, Zimmerman watched as machine-gun and cannon fire hit his right engine, which immediately began to burn. Then his cockpit exploded and caught on fire. He released his canopy, and the slipstream pulled him partially out of the cockpit. Releasing his safety belt, he was sucked out and waited until he had fallen several thousand feet before pulling his ripcord to get away from the Me 109s, which were sometimes known to fire upon Allied pilots who bailed out.

Upon landing, he was soon captured by some Bulgarian policemen. "After their usual barrage of threats to shoot me, I was taken to a hospital and treated for burns and a dislocated shoulder," he reported. After a month of rudimentary treatment, he was transferred to a Bulgarian prison camp, where he remained until liberated by Soviet troops on September 8, when he was taken by train, with other Allied prisoners, to Turkey.[vi]

The next day, April 16, another fighter pilot had the unfortunate distinction of being shot down, not by the enemy, but by an American bomber. Soon after the 31st Fighter Group converted to P-51 Mustangs and began escorting Fifteenth bombers, the group escorted a raid on Turnu Severin in Romania. After rendezvousing with the bombers, the Mustangs began to weave back and forth over the bomber formation to stay with the bombers as their Mustangs flew almost one hundred miles per hour faster. During one weave, a Liberator fired on 1st Lt. Howard Baetjer, mistaking him for an Me 109. Mustangs were new to the Fifteenth Air Force, and their silhouette was not familiar to many gunners; to an uninformed eye constantly searching for enemy fighters, it could be mistaken for a Messerschmitt. As soon as the .50-caliber rounds hit the engine, it began to smoke and Baetjer had to bail out, but he was fortunate to land in a small town in Yugoslavia not occupied by German troops. Greeted by the people of the town, he was taken to a headquarters of the Chetniks, one of the two Partisan resistance groups fighting the Germans, where he remained for about ten days. During this time, the crew of a 301st Bomb Group Fortress, flown by the crew of 2nd Lt. Albert Romans, turned up. They had crash-landed in Yugoslavia after two engines had malfunctioned during the January 24 mission to Sofia, Bulgaria, and had only just arrived at the Chetnik headquarters after an arduous journey. Baetjer and Romans's crew first moved to the town of Mihailovic, then finally reached an Allied landing strip in Partisan-controlled territory at the end of May. A C-47 flew them to Italy on May 28, and Baetjer returned to combat flying.[vii]

Only three days after Baetjer returned to Italy, two squadrons of the 52nd Fighter Group went after a group of more than thirty enemy fighters, a mix of Me 109s, Romanian IAR 80s, and Italian-made fighters flown by Romanians, while escorting the 47th Bomb Wing to Ploesti on May 31. The 52nd shot down fifteen of the enemy, but lost two of their own.

A flight leader, 1st Lt. Stanley Rollag, spotted three Me 109s underneath him and took his flight, 2nd Lts. Charles Denham and John Schumacher, in to attack them. Three Romanian IAR 80s got on the tail of the flight, but the Mustangs outturned them and got into firing position as the enemy planes dived toward the ground. Rollag fired at one, hitting it, and the enemy fighter crashed and burned. This was his second aerial victory, the first scored only the day before. As he pulled up, he saw another IAR 80 going down, shot down by Lieutenant Denham, whose Mustang was also damaged and was spinning toward the ground. Fortunately, Denham managed to bail out to become a prisoner of war in Romania. Lieutenant Schumacher got the third IAR 80, which also crashed. As he was climbing for altitude, he encountered another Romanian fighter, fired, and damaged it, but yet another Romanian got on his tail. Schumacher turned near the bomber formation with the Romanian aircraft following, and the bomber formation fired at both aircraft. Schumacher and the IAR 80 turned away, and the latter disappeared.

While Rollag's flight was in action, the flight led by Capt. Edwin Fuller located three more IAR 80s. He went after them with 2nd Lt. John Karle following him. Fuller fired on one Romanian, hit it hard, and had the satisfaction of seeing it crash to the ground. As he pulled up from this victory, an Me 109 flew underneath him. He turned, pursued, and fired at it, blowing off part of a wing. The Messerschmitt immediately went into a death dive. Karle then chased after a Romanian Air Force Macchi C.200, following him in a dive for ten thousand feet. In his own words: "I gave him several bursts on the way down and saw hits on the fuselage, engine, and cockpit. He slowed up and was out of control as I pulled up." The C.200 went out of control, and another pilot in the group saw it dive straight toward the ground.

Karle tried to rejoin his flight, but he couldn't find it as his engine began to act up a bit, so he turned for home and climbed for altitude. When he reached Yugoslavia, he found that his fuel supply was very low. With his engine running roughly, he considered trying to land, but decided to jump as the territory below looked too rough for a landing. He radioed his predicament to his comrades, but found that he couldn't hear their answer. Karle later reported: "I throttled back to 130 mph, jettisoned my canopy without trouble, and bailed out," making a good landing on a hillside and met some Yugoslav peasants within a half hour who helped him reach Partisans, and eventually Italy, in late June.

The total score of victories for the 52nd was fifteen for the day, as the 2nd Fighter Squadron accounted for another nine enemy fighters.[viii]

Besides such escort missions, fighters also took part in all of the Fifteenth Air Force shuttle missions flown to Russia during the summer of 1944. The first such mission was an escort of bombers during Operation Frantic Joe in early June. The second and third, however, were exclusively fighter operations after forty-three Eighth Air Force Fortresses were destroyed by a surprise Luftwaffe raid on their shuttle base in Poltava, in the Ukraine, on June 22.

The second shuttle mission flew to Russia on July 22. Lightnings from the 82nd Fighter Group strafed enemy airfields at Buzau and Zeilestia, Romania, while Lightnings from the 14th and Mustangs from the 31st flew as top cover. During the mission, the 31st encountered an Me 109, an Me 410, and several Fw 190s. The Mustangs quickly shot four of them down. Then an aerial melee ensued when thirty Fw 190s suddenly dived out of the sun and the Lightnings turned to meet them. The 190s mostly attacked in pairs, with each fighter firing at American aircraft in turn. American pilots found their opponents to be both experienced and aggressive. The dogfight lasted forty minutes and ended with eleven enemy planes downed by the 14th and another five by the 82nd. Strafing destroyed or damaged forty-one enemy fighters on the fields.

Five Lightnings went down during the battle, however. An Fw 190 got on the tail of 1st Lt. John Griffin from the 82nd. His Lightning began to burn, then the right wing came off and he crashed into the ground. In retaliation, 1st Lt. Leroy Lette shot down the attacker just after he broke away from nailing Griffin. Flak hit 2nd Lt. Andie McPhee's Lightning while he strafed the field, and he was killed. Lieutenant Earl Freestone from the 82nd also went down, becoming a prisoner of war. An Fw 190 shot down 2nd Lt. George O'Connor from the 14th. As cannon rounds splintered his canopy and instrument, O'Connor bailed out, also to be taken prisoner, as did 2nd Lt. Donald West, also from the 14th. He and his wingman, 1st Lt. William Chusin, had gone after an Me 109 during the strafing until the enemy broke away. During the chase, another Me 109 got on West's tail and shot up his engine. It began to burn, so West rolled the Lightning over and bailed out, to reach the ground safely.

The remaining aircraft continued on to airfields in the Ukraine: the 82nd to Poltava, the 14th to Mirgorod, and the 31st to Piryatin as Russian Yak-9 fighters met some of the American fighters over the Ukraine to lead them to their temporary Russian airfields. These fields were of simple, steel-plank construction, and grass had grown through many planks, making the strips difficult for the American pilots to spot.

After two days of bad weather, the three groups flew another strafing mission to Mielec, in Poland, on July 25. Strafing destroyed some planes on the ground, but the 31st, flying top cover for strafing Lightnings, had a field day with the enemy aircraft they encountered in the air, destroying twenty-nine of them and earning a Distinguished Unit Citation. The Mustangs began their score with an He 111 and two Ju 52s that had blundered into the area. Then a thunderstorm split up the flights of the 31st, and one flight ran into a gaggle of Ju 87 dive-bombers flying a ground-support mission for German troops facing the Soviet Army. A slaughter followed, and more than twenty of the went down to Mustang machine-gun fire.

The next day, the three groups returned to Italy, strafing airfields in Romania again, destroying sixteen more enemy aircraft on the way home, but losing three Lightnings.

Right: Lieutenant John Voll, of the 31st Fighter Group, in the cockpit of his P-51 Mustang. He is credited with twenty-one aerial victories between June and October 1944.

Below: Lieutenant Walter Goehausen sits in the cockpit of his P-51B Mustang, June 1944. A member of the 31st Fighter Group, he was officially credited with ten enemy aircraft destroyed.

The last fighter shuttle mission flown by the Fifteenth Air Force a short time later on August 4, 1944, included the dramatic rescue of a fighter pilot. Lightnings and Mustangs again strafed Romanian airfields but lost ten aircraft. One of them was a P-38 flown by 1st Lt. Richard Willsie, a flight leader in the 82nd Fighter Group. Flak hit his Lightning before he reached the enemy airfield, and he lost an engine. He continued on the mission, however, and strafed the field with the other planes, but flak then hit his second engine and he announced over the radio that he was going to have to crash-land. A member of his flight, Flying Officer Richard Andrews, heard the message and told him he would pick him up if he managed to crash-land in a suitable field. Willsie picked out a wheat field about fifteen miles from the Romanian airfield at Foscani and landed safely, hitting his face on the padded gun sight, otherwise uninjured. He quickly jumped out of the Lightning and, using a small phosphorus charge, set his plane on fire. Romanian troops in the distance, who had seen him crash, began to fire at him. As he ran for some trees, he saw Andrews landing along the line of the furrows in the field and ran toward the Lightning. Andrews threw out his parachute to accommodate Willsie, and the latter jumped on the wing, then climbed into the cockpit and sat in front of Andrews on his lap. As he was in front, he would fly the Lightning. Andrews had to put his right leg over Willsie's shoulder so the control column was accessible during the flight home.

As this rescue was going on, several other Lightnings from the 82nd flew overhead to protect them from Romanian troops. A half-dozen Me 109s were also in the area. Having seen the crash and subsequent landing, they awaited their chance to strafe the two aircraft still on the ground. One foolishly tried to do so and was shot down by 1st Lt. Nathaniel Pape. Unfortunately, another of the P-38s, flown by 2nd Lt. James Hardin, was hit by flak and exploded in the air, killing Hardin.

When the pair in the P-38 was ready, Willsie began to take off. The nose wheel temporarily dug into the plowed field, but an application of trim tabs raised the nose, and the aircraft moved, then took off, just missing some trees at one end of the field. They flew to southern Russia, as briefed, hugging the ground to avoid German and Russian flak, as the latter could, and did, fire at American aircraft. They arrived safely at the American base at Poltava and surprised the maintenance crews when two pilots emerged from the Lightning. Immediately upon their return to Italy on August 6, Gen. Nathan Twining, commander of the Fifteenth Air Force, decorated Andrews with the Silver Star and promoted him to second lieutenant.[ix]

Beginning the next month, fighter attacks on Fifteenth Air Force formations became noticeably less numerous as the campaign to bomb German oil facilities began to severely limit the availability of fuel for the Luftwaffe. This factor, and the established supremacy of American escort fighters in the skies of Europe, led the Germans to forbid attacks on American bomber formations unless their fighters had overwhelming superiority. The Eighth Air Force bore the brunt of such attacks after August 1944 as the Luftwaffe concentrated their dwindling day fighter forces against them.

The Fifteenth still occasionally encountered enemy fighters, however, in the months to come. One of these engagements took place during the October 16 mission by the 5th Bomb Wing to bomb the oil refinery at Brux, Czechoslovakia. The 325th Fighter Group was one of the escorting fighter groups, and a flight of four of its Mustangs attacked a group of about fifty Me 109s and Fw 190s when they made an attack pass on the bomber formation.

Second Lieutenant Sheldon Anderson, a flight leader, spotted the enemy fighters and dived on them, with the sun behind him. The Germans were completely surprised, and they did not

Pilots from the 325th Fighter Group chat with a Soviet officer at a Russian base during the first Russian shuttle mission, flown by the Fifteenth Air Force in early June 1944.

release their drop tanks until the Mustangs were upon them. Half the enemy fighters fled, but the other half chose to stay and fight, and an air battle ensued between the four Mustangs and twenty to twenty-five Me 109s and Fw 190s that lasted about fifteen minutes, beginning at thirty-two thousand feet and ending very close to the ground.

At the start the action, Anderson closed to within fifty feet of an Fw 190, fired, and hit its fuselage. The enemy exploded before him, his first victory of the day. Immediately afterward,

he went after an Me 109, again flew within fifty feet of it, and fired at the engine and fuselage. It also exploded.

Another member of his flight, 1st Lt. Leonard Voss, got within one thousand feet of an Me 109 during the surprise onslaught. He fired, and although he didn't see any of his rounds strike the enemy fighter, its pilot immediately bailed out. He then turned on another Me 109 that was going after another Mustang. He came up on the enemy fighter dead astern and got within five hundred feet before he opened fire. He scored a number of hits on the engine wing, and the Messerschmitt caught fire. This enemy pilot also bailed out.

A third member of the flight, 2nd Lt. Vernon Kahl, also got two fighters in the melee. During the initial surprise assault, he went after an Fw 190 from the rear. When he fired at it, his .50-caliber slugs laced the inside wing, fuselage, and engine. The Focke-Wulf began to emit smoke, turned slightly, then suddenly exploded, diving in flames. Almost immediately, Kahl got onto the tail of another Me 109, fired, and hit the engine, wing roots, and fuselage. The Messerschmitt began to burn with its engine on fire and spiraled down to the ground.

About ten minutes later, Anderson spotted an Me 109 and got on its tail, firing several bursts and hitting the fuselage. This Messerschmitt went into a spin and, before it entered the clouds

Brigadier General Dean Strother, commander of the 305th Fighter Wing, and Carl Schoeniger, head of the Veterans of Foreign Wars, listen to Flying Officer Andrews describe his daring rescue of squadron mate Willsie on his return to Italy.

below, caught fire. Three minutes after this kill, Anderson spotted another Me 109 and got on its tail. This time, his .50-caliber bursts hit the cockpit and wings. The pilot was apparently hit, as the plane came out of a turn, then appeared to fall flat toward the ground, tail down. It entered low clouds, then emerged still headed for the ground. By this time, the four Mustangs involved were forced to break off the engagement when they ran out of ammunition.

Anderson received confirmation for the three of his claims, with the other a probable. Voss and Kahl also got confirmation of their two successes each.[x]

While losses of fighters in aerial combat declined, flak continued to claim fighters, as it did bombers. Flak damage led to loss of two of four Lightnings by the 14th Fighter Group while escorting Liberators of the 55th Bomb Wing on the December 17 mission to Blechhammer during the Oil Blitz, the two-week campaign to finish off most German oil refineries, that month. Flak hit one P-38, flown by 1st Lt. George Johnson, over Gyor, Hungary. His Lightning caught fire and spun in, crashing on the ground. Fortunately, he was able to bail out to become a prisoner of war. Another pilot, 2nd Lt. Lorenz Weiglein, also went down on the mission.

On the return flight, the supercharger on his right engine stopped functioning, and he was forced to increase power in the left engine. He cross-fed this engine from the fuel tanks in the right wing but reported that while switching tanks, "my right engine coughed once or twice and then caught fire. White, acrid smoke started to fill the cockpit." His flight leader radioed him that his engine was on fire. He changed the fuel mixture and this temporarily subdued the flames, but soon the fire increased again. He was told to feather the engine, which he did.

"The smoke was very dense in the cockpit now and I was choking. I was told to bail out. . . . I popped the canopy and rolled down the window. At this stage I was feeling very groggy. . . . [I] rolled into my dead engine and left the plane when I thought it was inverted." It was really in a shallow dive, however, right-side up.

Weiglein managed to get halfway out of the cockpit before the slipstream pinned him against the back. Using his hands and feet, he thrust himself out and fell about four thousand feet before he pulled his ripcord. He was over the Adriatic Sea, close to the coast of Yugoslavia, off the port of Split. He tried to sideslip his chute toward land but still landed in the water. He got out of his parachute harness, then swam under the canopy and surfaced clear of it. He inflated his "Mae West" life vest and then his dingy, but he was only in the water for about ten minutes when a Yugoslav steam ship, crewed by Partisans, turned up and rescued him, although the area was heavily mined. The Partisans took him first to Split, then to Vis the next day. After a visit to the American mission on the island, he traveled by steamship to Bari, Italy, where he arrived on December 20.[xi]

One of the last large engagements of Fifteenth Air Force fighters with German fighters took place on March 15, during a mission to bomb the marshalling yards in the town of Nove Zamky, in Czechoslovakia. During the flight home, the 325th Fighter Group had several encounters with German fighters, Fw 190s and Me 109s. The Focke-Wulfs were ground-support aircraft operating in the vicinity of the Soviet-German front line, then less than fifty miles from Nove Zamky, and their pilots were no match for the experienced dogfighters of the 325th. Much of the action took place at relatively low altitude for bomber escorts, eight thousand feet and below.

Captain Leonard Voss, whom we have met before (now promoted to captain), and 2nd Lt. Robert Burns scored the first victories, shortly after one o'clock in the afternoon. Voss went after an Me 109G that approached his flight from below. Both fighters circled each other until Voss got the chance to fire at the enemy fighter from a high deflection angle and managed to hit the engine and cockpit. The Gustav immediately caught fire and spiraled to the ground. Lieutenant Burns caught sight of an Fw 190 that immediately dived into clouds below. He followed and opened fire while closing to five hundred feet, scoring hits on its engine. The stricken fighter immediately turned over and dived into the ground.

About ten minutes later, 2nd Lt. Joseph Barton saw another Focke-Wulf at 8,000 feet and dived on it. He opened fire from 750 feet and hit the wing roots of the Focke-Wulf, which immediately went into a vertical dive, from only 2,000 feet. At the same time, Capt. Harry Parker, whom we also met earlier and who had also been promoted to captain, spotted another Focke-Wulf and dived on it as well. He began to fire when some distance from the enemy, continuing to do so until he was only 50 feet away. He plastered the 190, and pieces flew off it. It went into a spin, and the pilot bailed out, but his parachute did not open.

The action continued, as shortly thereafter 2nd Lt. Ernest Bradley and 1st Lt. John Henry each bagged a Focke-Wulf. Henry fired about 2,000 feet away from the enemy fighters, but his

Smoke rises through the smoke screen over the Xenia Oil Refinery in Ploesti, Romania as 49th Bomb Wing Liberators pass by on the way home after bombing the plant on August 10, 1944.

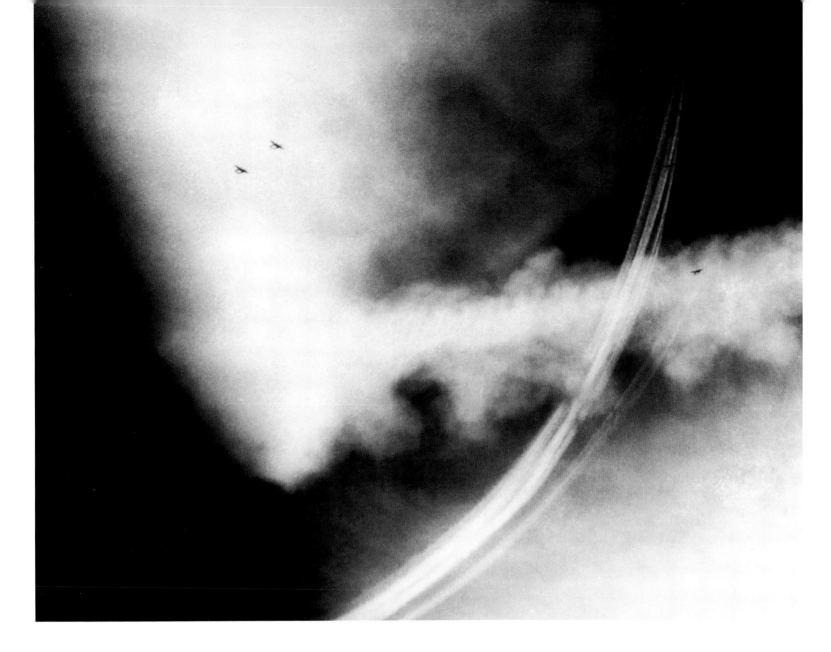

Fifteenth Air Force Lightnings leave contrails behind during a dogfight over Czechoslovakia in the late summer of 1944.

marksmanship immediately scored hits that caused the Luftwaffe pilot to jettison his canopy and bail out. Bradley's prey tried to dive away from him, and Bradley began fire while still 1,500 feet from the enemy. His .50-caliber machine-gun rounds were also right on target, hitting the enemy fighter's engine and cockpit. The Focke-Wulf immediately caught fire and headed for the ground.

Five minutes later, five 325th pilots each shot down a Focke-Wulf. First Lieutenant Walter Selenger scored hits on the wing root of one, at a range varying from 3,000 to 1,000 feet. His quarry rolled over, did a split S maneuver, and crashed into the ground. Second Lieutenant William Aron attacked another, scoring hits on the fuselage that caused it to immediately crash into the ground. Harry Parker took a crack at his second Focke-Wulf. He began firing at 4,500 feet from the enemy fighter and continued to fire bursts until only 50 feet away. He hit the wing root and fuselage, and the enemy fighter crashed into the ground. A fourth Focke-Wulf went down to the guns of 1st Lt. Joseph Pace, who began firing while still 3,000 feet away. His rounds hit the 190's wings, and the enemy began to smoke and soon crashed into the ground. Second Lieutenant Paul Murphy brought down the fifth enemy loss. He got on the tail of the enemy fighter and shot it down, but immediately headed for nearby Russian lines, as he was low on fuel. He managed to crash-land behind Russian lines and returned to the 325th in early April.

During this dogfight, 1st Lt. Gordon McDaniel accounted for five more of the enemy all by himself, high above the melee already described. He encountered four Focke-Wulfs at seventeen thousand feet. He fired at one from two hundred feet and hit the tail, fuselage, and wings; the target dived into overcast and exploded. He got another Focke-Wulf from much longer range as his machine-gun fire hit the wings and fuselage. Pieces flew off, and it began to burn. His wingman, Lieutenant Burns, saw it hit the ground. McDaniel spotted another Focke-Wulf directly behind him, turned, got on the enemy's tail, and fired, damaging it severely. The enemy pilot tried to escape by diving into undercast, but a wing came off, the Fw 190 caught fire, and it spun into the clouds below. A fourth enemy went down as McDaniel drew to within six hundred feet to finish it off. A wing came off this enemy fighter, too, and it crashed. The pilot of his fifth victim attempted to bail out after McDaniel's fire riddled his entire aircraft, but his chute failed to open.

Shortly after McDaniel's excellent work, Lieutenant Aron got his second victory of the day. He dived on a Focke-Wulf and riddled its tail and wings. The enemy aircraft headed down and crashed.

By two o'clock the action was almost over, but two more 325th pilots got in their licks, one shooting down three more of the enemy. First Lieutenants Thomas Bevan and James Chamberlin each got a Focke-Wulf at the same time, Bevan attacking one that dived into the undercast below to escape. He followed, firing and hitting its fuselage and wings as the enemy continued its dive, to crash into the ground. Chamberlin changed the victim class a bit by attacking an Me 109, one of a formation of six he encountered. He fired from about four hundred yards away and hit the cockpit. The Messerschmitt lowered its wheels, a sign of surrender, as it began to burn. The enemy pilot did not bail out, however, staying with the aircraft until it went into the ground.

Five minutes after these two combats, Bevan met up with another Focke-Wulf at only two thousand feet. He got on its tail and fired, hitting the fuselage. The 190 made a split S turn, then crashed into the ground. Just after dispatching this aircraft, Bevan made the final kill of the day for the 325th. Still at low altitude, he got on the tail of another 190, fired, and hit its fuselage. The enemy fighter immediately went into a dive, and his wingman saw it crash into the ground.

Of the twenty-one combats described here, the 325th eventually received confirmation for twenty, an unusually high tally for any fighter group in the Mediterranean Theater in the final months of the war.[xii]

*　*　*　*　*

As encounters with piston-engine fighters began to decline sharply for the fighters of the Fifteenth, they began to meet with a menace of the future: jet fighters. Although German jets initially went after photo reconnaissance flights, during the second half of 1944, as they developed tactics and pilots became familiar with their revolutionary aircraft, they began to appear when bombing missions penetrated Germany, at the end of the year. The Mustang escort during the December 9

Lieutenants Voss, Anderson, and Kahl after the aerial battle of October 16, 1944.

mission to bomb oil storage in the city of Regensburg was one of the first to encounter them, and several pilots from the 332nd Fighter Group, known as the Red Tails, reported their encounters with this elusive foe.

Near the target, Lt. Alvin Temple noticed an Me 262 ahead of the bomber formation. Suddenly it turned swiftly and approached his Mustang, flying ahead, well out of range. Temple dropped his wing fuel tanks in preparation for combat and tried to turn inside the jet, but the latter stayed out of range as it turned and headed toward a Lightning from the 1st Fighter Group that had joined the mission when weather prevented the group from their briefed mission to escort some Liberators. The Lightning dived out of danger, and the jet tried to turn inside it. Temple reported: "I was in trail but I attempted to turn inside in an effort to close the distance between my aircraft and that of the enemy aircraft. The jet-propelled aircraft made a 180 degree turn. . . ." During this turn, Temple "picked up a lead. Although the jet-propelled aircraft was out of range, I fired at it. No damage was observed." The jet then headed toward the bomber formation and flew alongside them, but did not attack.[xiii]

Another Red Tail, Lt. Edward Thomas, also had a crack at an Me 262 on the same mission. His flight went after one that turned in front of them. Thomas was in a position to make a deflection shot from less than five hundred yards. He later reported: "He passed through my sights so fast that it is unlikely I hit him."[xiv] His flight, and Mustangs from another group, attempted to follow the Messerschmitt without success as the jet dived swiftly away.[xv]

Such inconclusive engagements with bomber formations continued sporadically for the next few months, until March, when jets began to attack bombers in earnest. After several engagements with Eighth Air Force missions early in the month, jets attacked several Fifteenth Air Force missions in late March. During one of the longest missions flown by the Fifteenth, to Berlin on March 24, the 332nd Fighter Group tangled with jets and came out ahead. Not only were Me 262s involved, but also Me 163s, another German jet fighter.

Shortly after noon, as the bomber formation was approaching Berlin, the Mustangs of the 332nd, flying above them, engaged enemy fighters in a dogfight that continued for almost twenty minutes. Two Me 262s attacked 1st Lts. Robert Williams and Samuel Watts when they were flying one above the other. Williams rolled over, stalled, and succeeded in getting on the tail of one of the jets as the enemy went into a shallow turn. He later reported: "I picked up a 2 1/2 radii lead [in my gun sight] on the jet on the right and fired a long burst. I fired another burst and held it for about two seconds. I noticed hits on the aircraft and saw him fall out of formation and I believe he went down."[xvi]

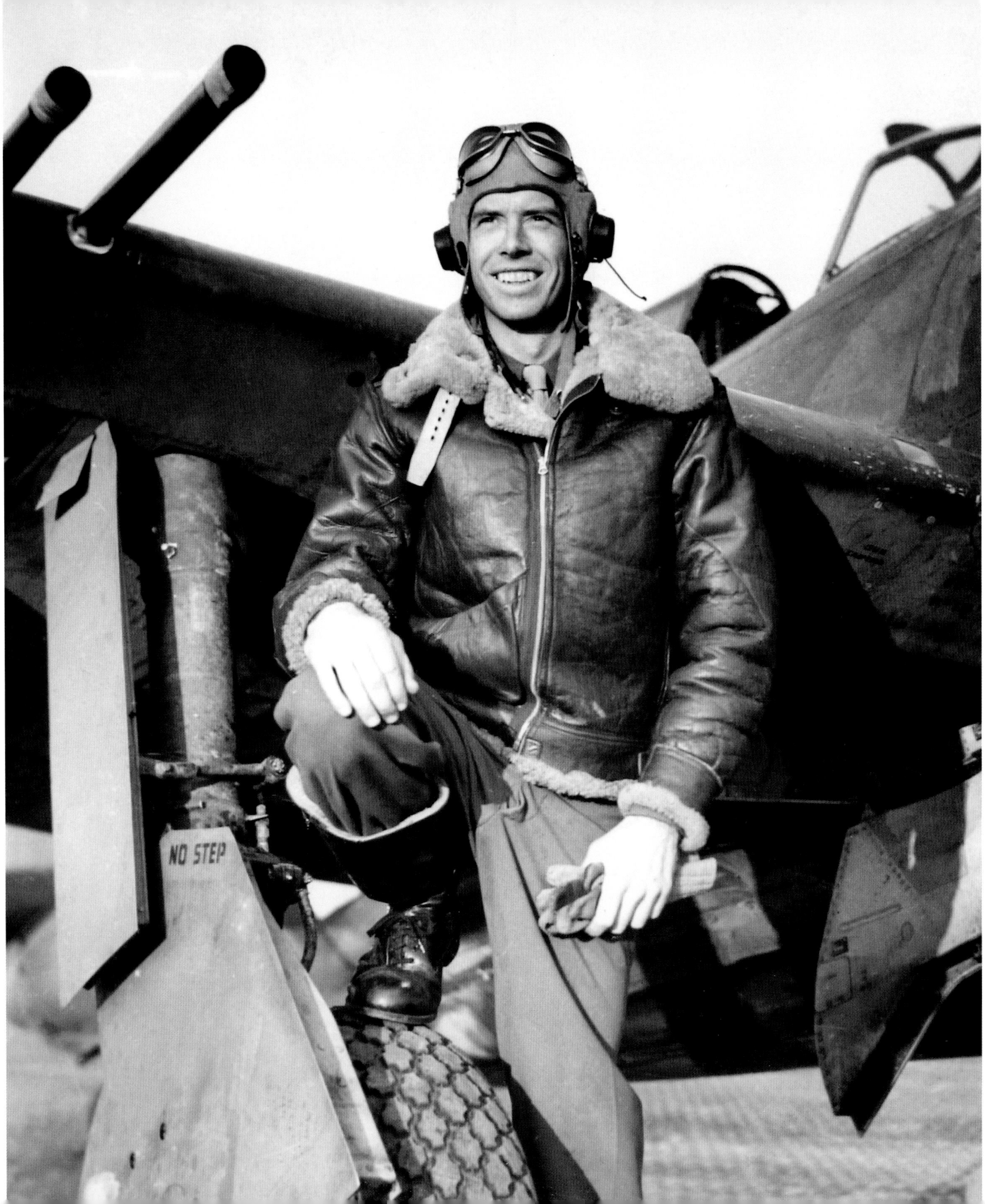
NO STEP

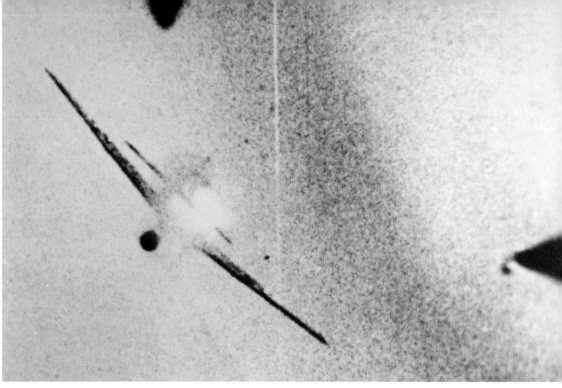

Above: Gun camera stills showing an Fw 190 being shot down by an American fighter, 1944.

Opposite page: Lieutenant Colonel Robert Baseler, commander of the 325th Fighter Group, standing before his P-47 Thunderbolt in early February 1944, just after the group destroyed thirty-seven German aircraft on the ground and in the air during an attack on the German airfield at Villorba, Italy. The 325th received a Distinguished Unit Citation, and Baseler the Silver Star Medal, for the successful mission.

At about the same time, Lt. Joseph Chineworth spotted the jets making an attack pass at the bombers and, dropping his wing tanks, dived after them. A jet passed in front of him and, joined by the number four in his flight, he went after it. Chineworth later said: "I made a ninety degree left turn and was on the tail of the jet about 1,500 feet away. I fired three long bursts and then my guns stopped. I saw hits and pieces flew off his plane. Black smoke came from the enemy aircraft as he started into what appeared to be an uncontrolled dive. . . . My attack lasted for about five minutes."[xvii]

Second Lieutenant Charles Brantley was flying with his wingman when two Me 262s passed them, not at full power. Brantley went after one: "I dropped my nose, being well within range, and made several bursts on the ship that was in front of me, from dead astern. My flight leader fired on the other. The jets broke in a slow turn in opposite directions, pulling us apart. I followed my target in a dive for a short while observing hits on the fuselage. I then broke off to join my flight leader. . . . As I broke away, the Me 262 steepened its rate of turn and dive. It was seen by my flight leader and other pilots to go down in flames."[xviii]

Lieutenant Reid Thompson saw three Me 262s making several attack passes on the Fortresses. He dived after them with his wing tanks still attached, but other Mustangs overtook him, so he pulled up, dropping his wing tanks. Thompson reported:

I saw an Me 163 in a turn to the left at two o'clock to me. I tightened my turn and fired two bursts . . . but I was out of range, at about 4,000 feet. The jet went into a dive . . . and I dived behind him, still out of range and looking for him to pull up and allow me a shot at him. We began to dive from 26,000 feet and on the way down, he did three barrel rolls . . . and I rolled with him. . . . I pulled out of the dive at 10,000 feet and leveled off. . . . [W]hen I last saw him he was still going down. I circled the area where I last saw him and located a puff of smoke and wreckage where I judged him to have gone in.[xix]

First Lieutenant Roscoe Brown saw three Me 262s making a head-on attack on the bomber formation from below. He dropped his tanks and intercepted them, firing at the right-most jet. He opened fire while 2,400 feet away and the jet dived for the ground with Brown in pursuit, but he soon had to pull out as the jet was going much too fast to overtake. He then spotted four more Me 262s going in the opposite direction, 3,000 feet below him. He turned around and gave chase, latching onto another jet that was climbing near him. He reported, "I saw a lone Me 262 at 24,000 feet, climbing at ninety degrees to me and 2,500 feet from me. I pulled up at him . . . and fired three long bursts at him from 2,000 feet . . . Almost immediately the pilot bailed out. . . ."[xx]

Edward Thomas, promoted to captain since the mission of December 9, and Lt. Vincent Mitchell also took part in the action. Thomas saw two Me 262s attacking the bombers, and the two dropped their wing tanks and set off in pursuit. Thomas reported: "The two Me 262s were in a loose string, so we attempted to catch the rear jet. Lieutenant Mitchell . . . closed with the ME to a range of about 450 yards and started firing from a forty-five degree deflection and we both observed hits on the jet. He apparently had not realized we were so close to him, for as soon as the hits were observed, he pulled up his nose, did a quarter roll to the right, and split 's'ed away from us."[xxi]

First Lieutenant Earl Lane had the last encounter in this fight. He saw three Me 262s pass underneath him, flying from left to right, preparing to attack the bombers. They were too far away to attack, but he soon spotted a lone Me 262 in a shallow dive attacking the bombers. He reported: "The Me 262 was in a thirty degree dive, coming across the bomber formation. He appeared as if he was peeling for an attack on the bombers, I came in for a thirty-degree deflection shot from 2,000 feet. He did not quite fully fill my gun sight. I fired

Above: A P-51C Mustang of the 332nd Fighter Group, piloted by Capt. Andrew Turner, taxies prior to takeoff. A ground crewman sits on the wing to direct the pilot.

Above right: Pilots from the 332nd Fighter Group attend a mission briefing.

Opposite page: Colonel Benjamin O. Davis, commander of the 332nd Fighter Group, stands beside a P-47 Thunderbolt in the spring of 1944. The 332nd completed the transition to P-51s Mustangs before their first combat mission with the Fifteenth in early June.

three short bursts and saw the plane emitting smoke. A piece of the plane, either the canopy or one of the jet orifices, flew off. I then pulled up and circled over the spot where he went down. I saw a crash and a puff of black smoke."[xxii]

In the final action of the day, Flying Officer Thurston Gaines spotted three Me 262s diving line astern on the rear of the bomber formation. Gaines dropped his wing tanks and went after one of the three after it had shot down a Flying Fortress. Finding that he could not keep up with the jet, he climbed away and spotted another Me 262 also in a turn, just off his nose. "I soon discovered that his rate of speed was too fast for me to close with him," reported Gaines. "Consequently, I started a climbing turn to the right at approximately 20,000 feet, when I observed an Me 262 in a steep right turn [at] about one o'clock, slightly high. I pulled the nose of my aircraft up and started firing from about 2,000 feet . . . and closed to approximately 800 feet . . . No strikes were observed nor did the enemy aircraft attempt to take evasive action."[xxiii]

Brantley, Lane, and Brown were later credited with confirmed kills.[xxiv]

* * * * *

Encounters with enemy fighters while escorting bombers were not the only opportunities for fighter pilots of Fifteenth to add to their score. Another mission type that often led to dogfights with enemy fighters was the fighter "sweep" of enemy airspace, a patrol intended to engage any enemy aircraft encountered. During one such sweep on January 21, 1944, the 325th Fighter Group took part in an aerial melee that netted four enemy fighters destroyed in the vicinity of Florence, Italy.

As the Thunderbolts flew at fifteen thousand feet, 1st Lt. William Elliott, one of the flight leaders, spotted enemy fighters and called out, "Boogies low at eleven o'clock!" The squadron leader

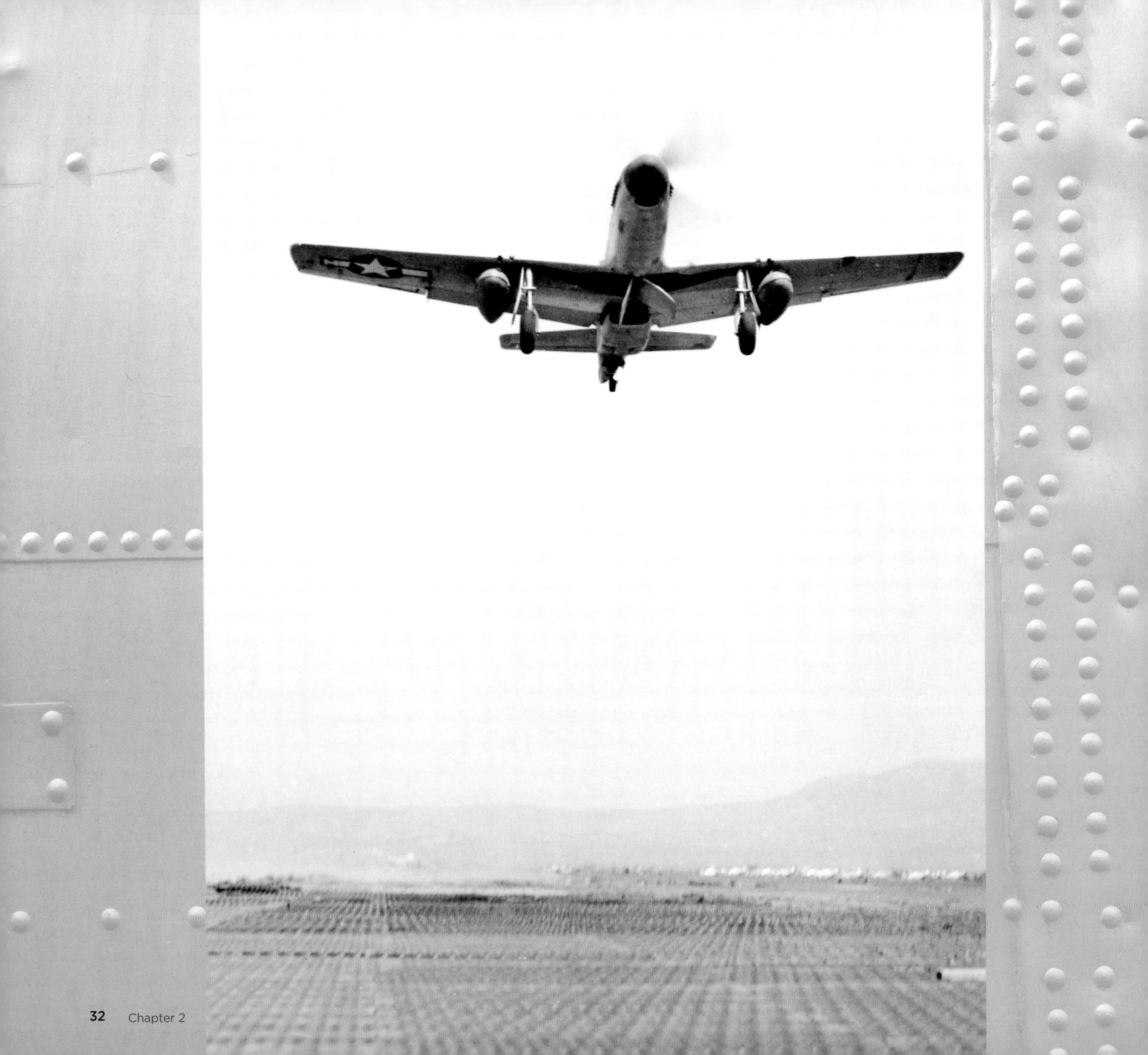

ordered him to intercept them, and Elliott divided his flight into two sections, the second led by then—1st Lt. Raymond Hartley. They dived on the enemy fighters, six Fw 190s that were climbing to engage the P-47s, in a line abreast. Elliott took the leftmost three and Hartley the right three.

Elliott was slightly ahead of Hartley and opened fire first, accompanied by his wingman, 2nd Lt. Fielder Smith. The Focke-Wulfs performed a split S, and Elliott aimed at the one farthest to the right, firing into its underside. Parts of the fighter flew off and it caught fire; the aircraft rolled on its back, and the pilot bailed out. Smith then took on the Focke-Wulf in the middle, leveling out from his dive and firing two bursts into its fuselage and wings. The 190 slowed, and Smith flew past it just as the pilot bailed out. The third Focke-Wulf then turned and began to pursue him. Elliott turned into it, but his gun sight had burned out. He aimed by eye and fired as he chased this enemy toward the ground, outturning him and finally pulling away as he dropped his wing tanks. Elliott and the German pilot made four passes at each other without either inflicting any damage before Elliott ran out of ammunition and decided to head for home. He applied emergency power and easily outran the Focke-Wulf.

Hartley was only seconds behind and chose one of the Fw 190s on the right, following it through a half roll and continuing to dive for two thousand feet, when he dropped his wings tanks and switched to his main tanks, causing a momentary drop in speed. Another P-47 pulled ahead of him, and they both chased the Focke-Wulf down to the deck. The interloper fired and scored a few hits on the 190's wing, then broke away to the left. Hartley continued his pursuit as the Focke-Wulf continued to weave, and eventually shortened the range.

Opposite page: A Fifteenth Air Force P-51 Mustang, possibly from the 332nd Fighter Group, takes off from an airfield in Italy. The steel Matson Matting was standard covering for air strips under primitive, field conditions such as those in Italy.

Below: The revolutionary German jet fighter, the Me 262.

"Closing to short range, I scored hits along the left wing and bottom of [the] fuselage. The FW started a hard, climbing turn to the right and I adjusted my lead and observed hits on the top of the fuselage. The FW then rolled easily onto its back . . . as a large sheet of flame came off his belly at the wing root [and then] he split s'ed into the ground from one hundred feet," he reported.

Another pilot, Flying Officer Harry Carroll, also claimed a Focke-Wulf in the melee. He went after two more of the six Fw 190s originally sighted until the enemy pair separated. He pursued one of them, dropped his wing tanks, and went to emergency power until he came within firing range after a five-minute chase. He opened fire, hit the Focke-Wulf hard, and watched it go into the ground from only fifty feet altitude.[xxv]

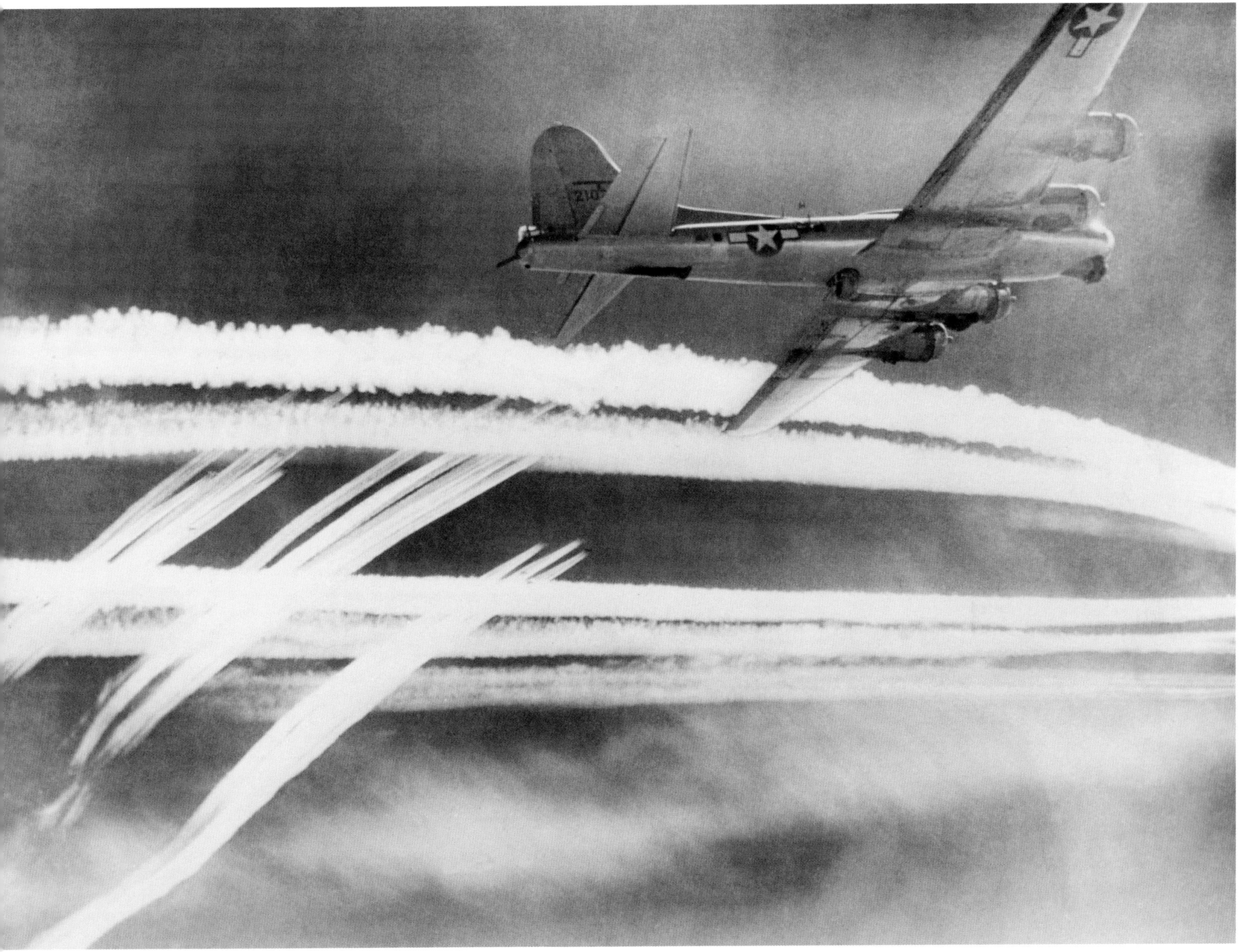

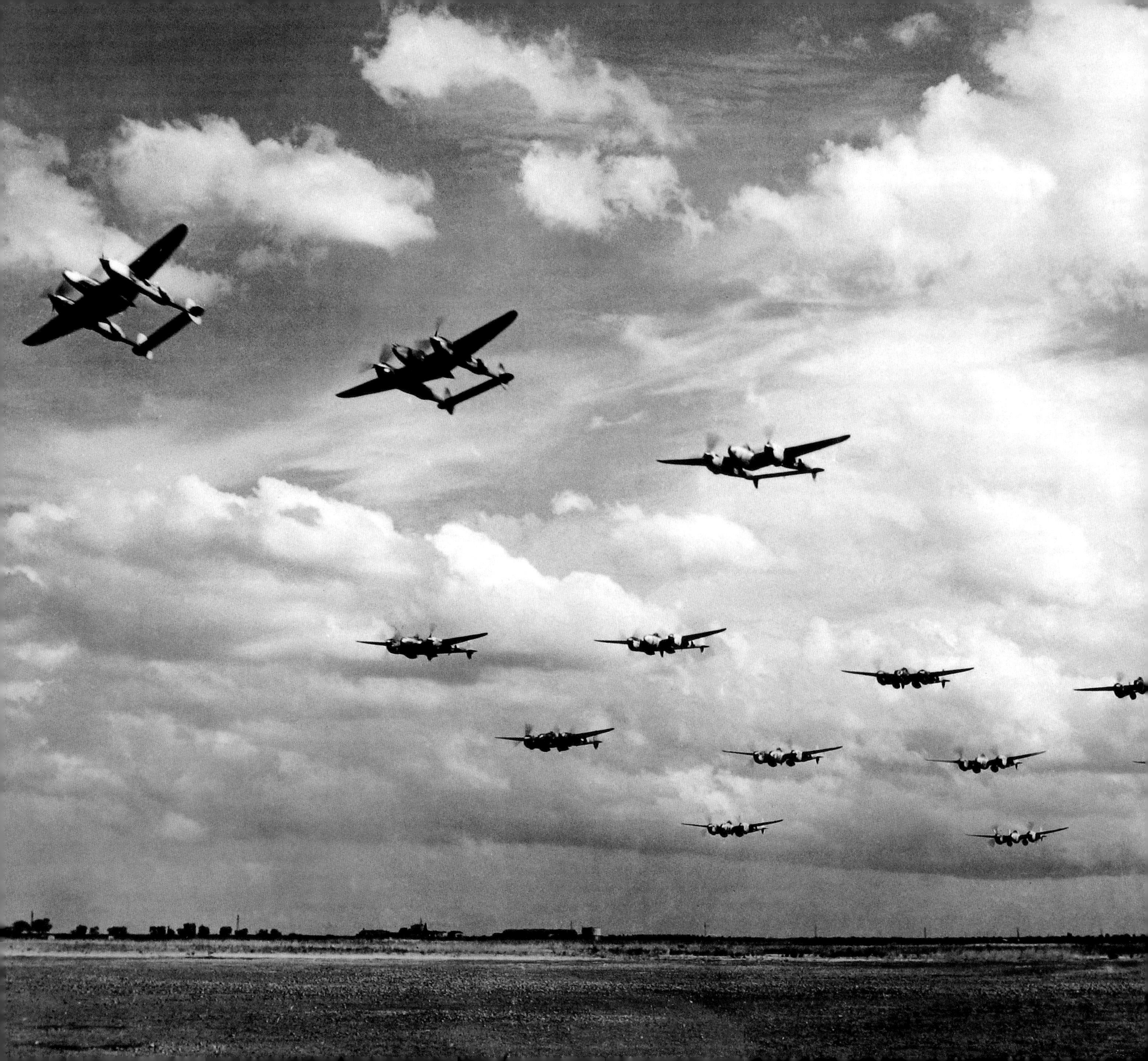

CHAPTER 3

STRAFING

As noted early in the last chapter, fighter pilots usually encountered their other major concern, flak, over a target—as missions were planned to avoid known concentrations of flak en route to their objectives—or during strafing missions.

While escorting bombers during the first Fifteenth Air Force mission to Greece on November 15, 1943, flak damaged a Lightning of the 1st Fighter Group piloted by 2nd Lt. James McClure. After the bombers hit their target, the airfield at Eleusis, near Athens, a flak burst hit his left wing between the cockpit and the left engine, damaging the engine. The P-38 immediately lost airspeed and began to trail the bombers. His comrades initially flew above him, providing cover from any German fighters that might be looking for an easy victory over a damaged fighter. McClure was unable to feather the propeller on the damaged engine, however, and continued to lose altitude as his speed dropped. After about twenty minutes, he had dropped so far behind the bombers and fighters that the latter could no longer cover him, and he disappeared from view. He radioed, "It looks like this is it." Further attempts to contact him were unsuccessful. His Lightning crashed near Thebes, Greece, close to Athens. His body was found near the plane. His remains were buried in the American cemetery at Nettuno, Italy, resting with many of those killed at Anzio.[xxvi]

Opposite page: P-38 Lightnings of the 1st Fighter Group return to their base in Italy after a bomber escort mission that included the strafing of ground targets in Austria.

While heavy flak led to McClure's loss, light flak and small-arms fire were often encountered by fighters strafing at low altitudes, making such missions particularly dangerous. If enemy fire damaged a fighter, there was little altitude, and hence little time, to handle the situation or bail out, and pilots often went straight in to crash or crash-land.

On January 22, 1944, Lightnings from the 82nd and 14th Fighter Groups flew close to the deck on a strafing mission near the town of Frosinone, east of Anzio, where Allied troops had landed the previous day. They damaged about twenty vehicles during their strafing runs. The crews of the vehicles were too busy taking cover to offer resistance, but flak emplacements in the area put up intense, light flak, mostly of the thirty-seven-millimeter variety. They failed to hit any of the American aircraft, however, and both groups began the return flight to base unhindered. On the return flight, the formation flew over a flak concentration in a valley. The 82nd, in the lead, got through unscathed, but as Lightnings of the 14th passed overhead, the German gunners were ready. Despite the P-38s taking evasive action, flak damaged several of them, including that flown by 2nd Lt. Paul Wingert.

The damage was slight, but Wingert's Lightning veered to the right, and he became separated from the others in this flight. He gained altitude to contact Big Fence, the Fifteenth Air Force beacon, which quickly gave him a heading for Allied lines. Flak had been following him during this climb, so he dived to avoid it, but as he later wrote: "On the way down and only a second or two after I started, I met a bundle of TNT coming up. My first sensation was big jar. . . . I knew from the way my ship jumped that I had been hit on the right side. The next thing I saw was big bump on top of my engine." Then he noticed smoke streaming from the engine. "At the bottom of the engine, I saw an even bigger hole. . . . My hands did a war dance all over the cockpit, getting everything to that engine shut off and the prop feathered. In those few seconds, I still hoped to save the ship."

Suddenly smoke began to enter the cockpit, and he decided to bail out: "I immediately pulled the emergency canopy release and started out; however I was going awfully fast . . ." The force of the slipstream moving past his plane meant he could make it only partway out of the cockpit as the slipstream pinned him against it. Wingert got back into the cockpit, calmly pulled the stick back to lower his speed, then stood on the seat to push himself out of the cockpit. "I remember just faintly that the fire came up in my face," he wrote, but his flight gear, goggles, and oxygen mask protected him, and his next recollection was "falling straight down head first."

Despite losing a large portion of the rudder of his Mustang to ground fire, Lt. Kenneth Steglein of the 325th Fighter Group managed to bring his aircraft home. Here, he examines the damage with members of his ground crew.

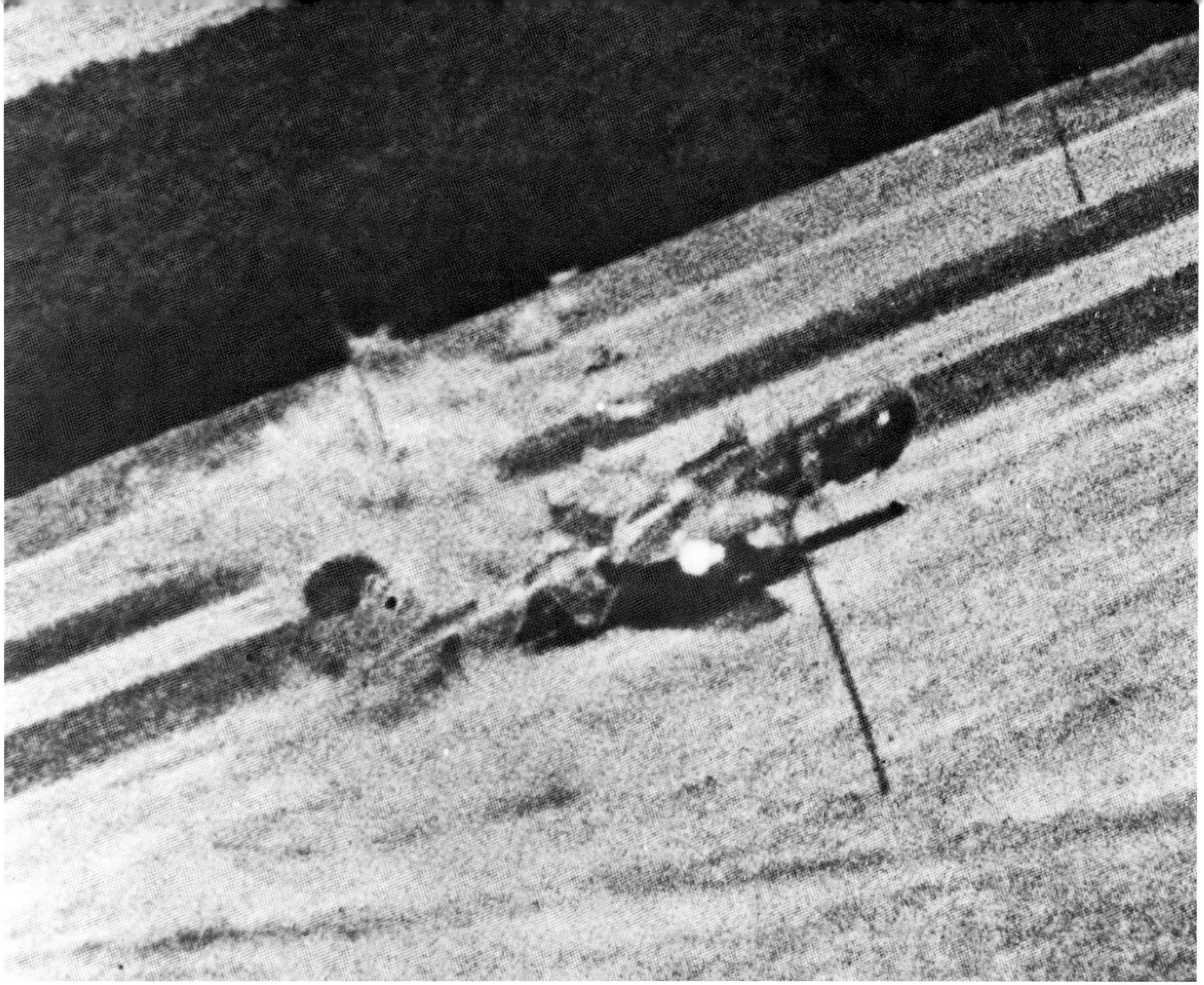

Machine-gun fire from a strafing American fighter destroys a Heinkel He 177 bomber, early in the winter of 1945.

Although the slipstream momentarily pinned his arms to his sides, he still managed to pull the ripcord, which promptly came away without opening the parachute. "I waited for what I thought ought to be long enough for the chute to open; then wondered if it was stuck," he reported. Feeling for the parachute, "I streamlined my hands along the sides and tried to pull [it] out." It began to come out of the pack, but "as the chute went out, somehow the shrouds got wrapped around my legs. At that time I thought it was the end . . . when I looked back over my shoulder there was just a streamer of white flapping back there. I was sure it was the end and then the thing opened."

He floated down toward a soldiers' bivouac, unsure whether it was Allied or German. Close to the ground, he "could identify one of [the] good old U.S. Army dark brown square tents" that confirmed that he was on the right side of the front line.

Pulling on his shroud lines to avoid trees, he landed in open ground, rolling as he landed. Standing up, he found himself surrounded by GIs and some Italian girls from a nearby village. It turned out he had almost landed in a chow line. He immediately gathered up his chute and joined the GIs in their meal. His Lightning had crashed nearby, and he later went to view the wreck, really only a hole in the ground. His legs were stiff from the landing, but he was otherwise unhurt and returned to the 14th the next day in a small liaison plane.[xxvii]

Left: Ground crewman salvage a Lightning of the 37th Fighter Squadron, 1st Fighter Group, that crash-landed on the island of Vis.

Opposite page top: P-38 Lightnings from the 94th Fighter Squadron, 1st Fighter Group, take off from their home field at Salsola, Italy.

Opposite page bottom: A droop-snoot P-38, a specially modified Lightning that carried a bombardier in the nose. These were used late in the war on P-38 bombing missions that supplemented the usual bomber escort and strafing missions.

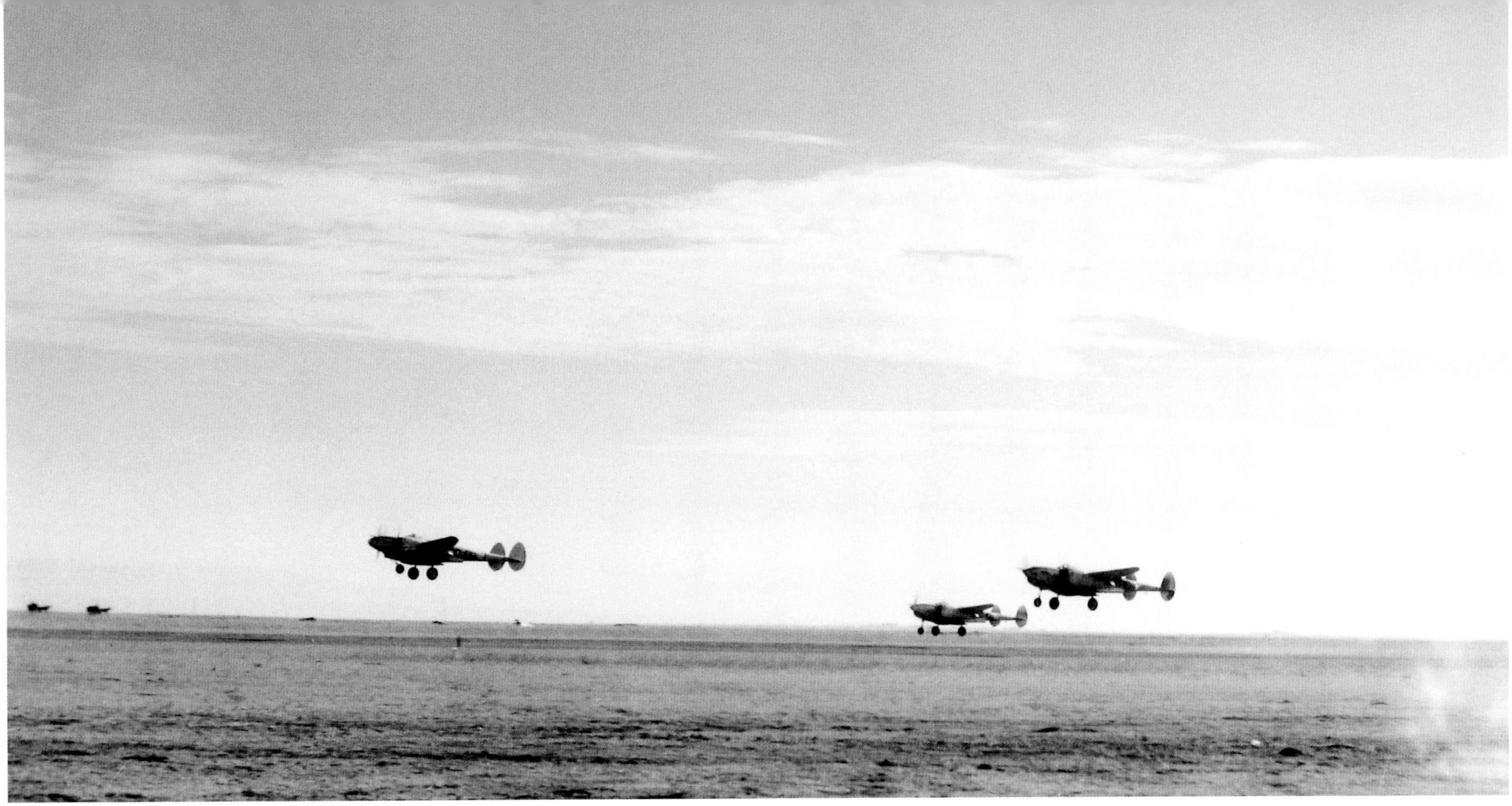

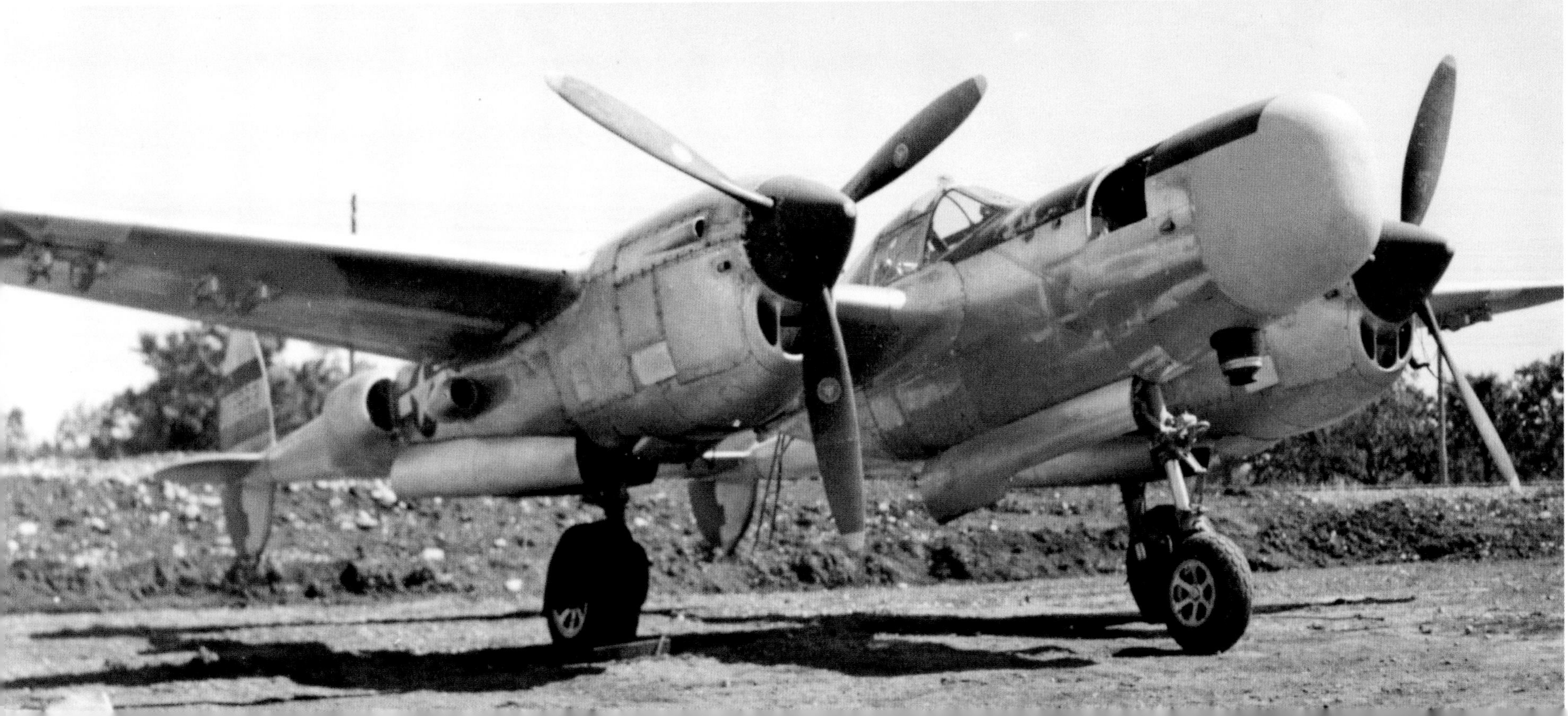

With the Luftwaffe fighter arm on the wane in the late summer of 1944, Fifteenth Air Force fighter groups turned to more ground attacks, strafing airfields, railroads, and highways deep behind enemy lines. Many of these missions were planned for strafing at the outset, rather than as an adjunct to the escort of bombers. The hazards of such missions soon became apparent, as the 52nd Fighter Group discovered on September 3. This mission culminated several days of strafing in Yugoslavia, with each squadron assigned a specific area to rough up. The 2nd Fighter Squadron strafed truck convoys with two flights as the third remained overhead to provide cover. Although they destroyed some trucks and injured or killed a number of German soldiers, the squadron lost two Mustangs on the mission. One, flown by 1st Lt. William Cowan, was flying too low while strafing and crashed into a truck, killing him instantly. Light flak hit another, piloted by Lt. Joseph Randerson, while he was strafing a locomotive. His engine stopped and he crash-landed, wheels up, but got out of the plane badly burned. Serbian farmers cared for him and passed him to Partisan control, and he eventually returned to Italy in November.

The mission also included attacks on several small marshalling yards. The Mustangs hit a number of railcars loaded with ammunition at one yard; they blew up, damaging one of the low-flying Mustangs. The 4th Fighter Squadron hit some locomotives and freight cars but didn't hang around, as light flak was evident, instead carrying on along a highway until they came upon a column of horse-drawn artillery. They fired at the head of column to stop it, killing some horses, but stopped the attack as they couldn't be sure the troops were German. They continued to roam, strafing more locomotives and trucks, but flak shot down two of their pilots and damaged several more. Flak hit Flying Officer Edward Cobbey's P-51, and he went directly into the ground and crashed. First Lieutenant Roy Frye, of the same squadron, hit some trees and also crashed. Both men were killed.

The Mustangs of the 5th Fighter Squadron strafed rail lines and locomotives, as well as trucks on highways and a radar station, while some stayed overhead to provide cover. They also lost two Mustangs. Second Lieutenant Lloyd Hargrave was hit while strafing a truck but was able to climb several hundred feet and then bail out. Although his parachute did not open completely before he hit the ground, he managed to land safely and reached some farmers in the area. The story of how he evaded is related in a subsequent chapter. Flak also hit the Mustang of Lt. Robert Fulk while he was strafing a locomotive very close to the ground, and he bellied his damaged Mustang into a cornfield. Fulk was injured in the crash-landing, but Chetnik Partisans rescued him and cared for him until he made his way to Belgrade in early November, meeting Randerson there. Both men flew back to Italy, with Fulk returning to the United States and Randerson to flying with the 52nd.

Although the price was high—three men killed and three shot down behind enemy lines—the 52nd claimed forty-five locomotives destroyed or badly damaged on this mission, along with almost forty-five railcars and more than sixty trucks.[xxviii]

The famous Red Tails, the 332nd Fighter Group, flew a similar strafing mission the next month, attacking Greek airfields on October 6 during the German withdrawal from Greece. One pilot, Lt. Lincoln Hudson, crashed soon after takeoff near their base at Rametelli, Italy. He survived but was later shot down and taken prisoner in March 1945. The other pilots continued on the mission and ran into the major hazard of ground attacks for fighters: light flak. One Red Tail, Lt. Carroll Woods, was shot down near an airfield he had strafed and was immediately taken prisoner. Another, Lt. Joe Lewis, was last seen by the group with his engine on fire over the Aegean, but he survived to become a prisoner of war. Flak shot down two more, but both pilots managed to evade capture and returned to Italy later in the month.

Lieutenant Freddie Hutchin's Mustang was hit in the engine while strafing ground targets at an altitude of only ten feet. His Mustang immediately crashed on a hillside. Several Greek farmers got him out the plane and took him to a farmhouse and later to a town where a resistance headquarters was located. A doctor checked him for injuries and then turned him over to an Allied mission, who placed him in the mayor's house in a town for a week. He eventually reached Athens, now under British control after the Germans had evacuated the city, by truck on October 19. He flew back to Italy a few days later.

Lieutenant Andrew Marshall was also shot down while strafing on October 6. Flak damaged the oil lines in his engine while he strafed an airfield, and he headed for the coast, intending to crash-land on a beach. He found the latter much too rocky and ended up crash-landing through some trees, then sliding down a hill on the island of Salamis. Marshall's Mustang caught fire as he quickly climbed out. He threw his Mae West and parachute into the fire and hightailed it from the wreck. He soon encountered some Greek civilians, who hid him in a field for two days before bringing him to a farmhouse, where he stayed until the Germans evacuated the island on October 13. Greeks then took him to a town in the midst of celebration of the German retreat. From here, he traveled by boat to the town of Megara, where he contacted British paratroopers who had recently occupied the town. American war correspondents were with the paratroopers, and Marshall spent the night with their party, then flew back to Italy the next day.[xxix]

Lieutenant Armour McDaniel of the 332nd Fighter Group points out flak damage on the wing of his Mustang to member of his ground crew.

Fifteenth fighter pilots also strafed ground targets as an extra-curricular activity during bomber escort missions, after the bombers had bombed their target and turned for home. As the German fighters disappeared from the scene in the fall of 1944, such missions became much more common, as did dedicated strafing missions. Strafing accounted for many of the Fifteenth Air Force fighters lost in the last six months of the war.

When the 31st Fighter Group flew a strafing mission to the German airfield at Kurilovec, Yugoslavia, on February 2, 1945, enemy resistance at the field was very heavy, with intense light flak shooting down six of the strafing Mustangs. The strafers did not encounter flak on the first pass, but when they returned again for a second, the Germans were ready. By the fourth and fifth attack passes, although the flak defenses were firing intensely, on target, the Mustangs succeeded in destroying eight enemy aircraft and damaging two more, as well as putting two flak positions out of action.

Above: The board recording lost and missing aircraft at Fifteenth Air Force headquarters, as it appeared on October 6, 1944. All 332nd Fighter Group pilots listed fortunately survived. *US Air Force*

Left: A German Ju 88 is riddled by the .50-caliber rounds from a strafing American fighter on a German airfield in the summer of 1944.

Below left: Lieutenant Andrew Marshall of the 332nd Fighter Group, after his return to Allied control in Greece following the crash of his Mustang on October 6, 1944.

Below right: Captain Wendell Pruitt, 302nd Fighter Squadron, 332nd Fighter Group, with his crew chief, Staff Sgt. Samuel Jacobs, standing before his P-51 Mustang, nicknamed *Alice-Jo*. Pruitt was officially credited with two enemy aircraft destroyed.

The 31st lost six Mustangs during these attacks. Flak hit the Mustang of Lt. Harry Carlton, but he managed to fly some distance, to Sisak, Yugoslavia, before crash-landing and walked away from the wreck. Lieutenant Alton Hall's Mustang suffered hits in its engine, but he also reached the vicinity of Sisak, where he also crash-landed. The only pilot to be killed on the mission was Lt. George Gibson. Flak hit his P-51 over the field, and it turned on its back, on fire, then righted itself before it crashed into the ground. Flak also damaged the engine of Lt. Luther Martin's Mustang. He pulled up to about 1,500 feet, jettisoned his canopy, and bailed out, reaching the ground safely a few miles from the enemy airdrome and successfully evading enemy troops. Major Frank Wagner, also hit in the engine, managed to climb to 6,000 feet and fly about ten miles until he had to bail out. He fractured his leg on landing and ended up in a Partisan-run hospital. Lieutenant Ralph Lockney was the last to be shot down and also managed to evade capture. All but Major Wagner returned to Italy with the assistance of Yugoslav Partisans by the end of the month.[xxx]

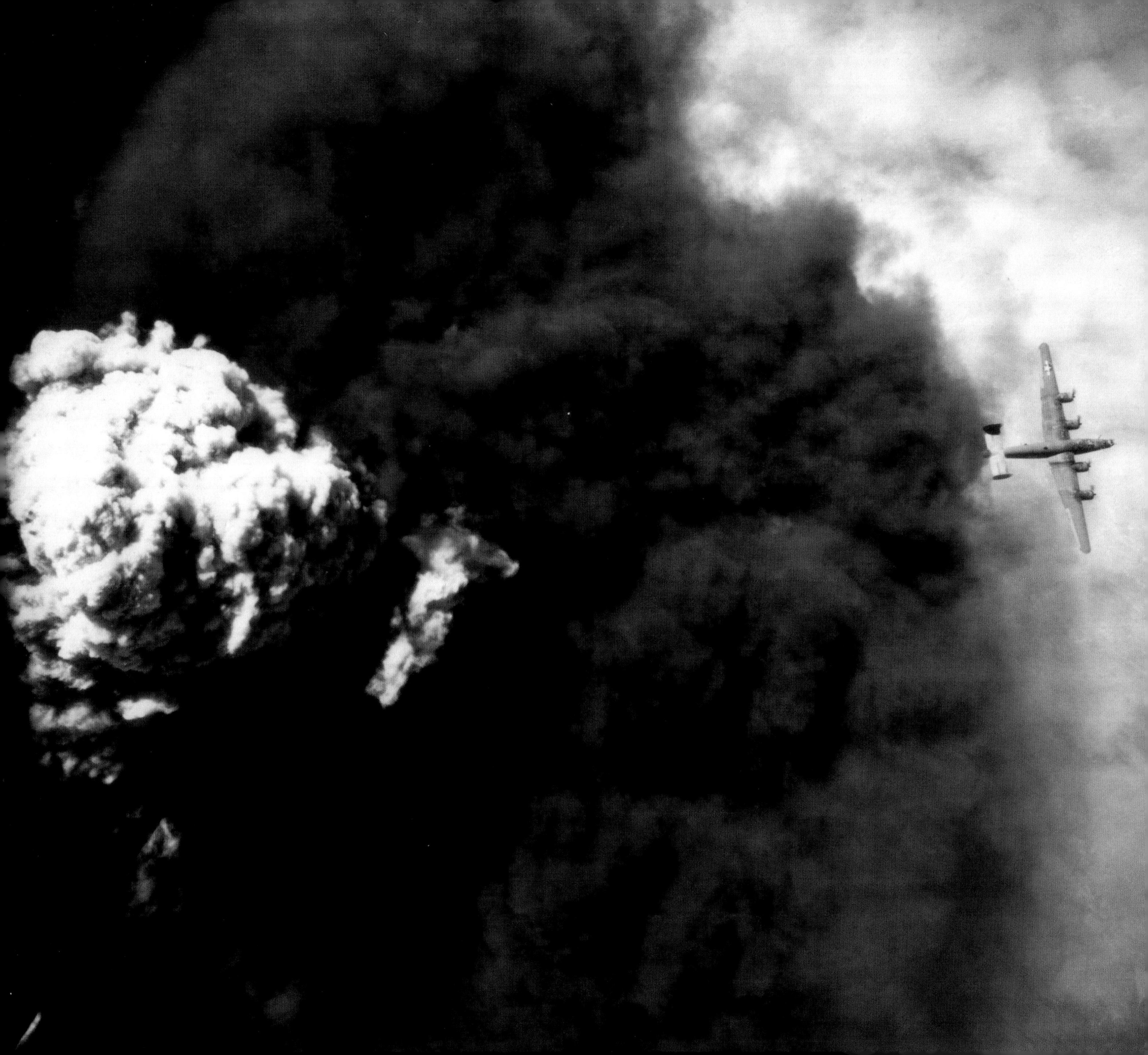

CHAPTER 4

BOMBERS AGAINST THE LUFTWAFFE

As a strategic air force, the bomber strength of the Fifteenth was the core of its operations. After its creation in November 1943, bomber strength quickly rose to twenty-one groups by the spring of 1944. Their major opponents throughout the campaign against the German war machine were, as for American fighters, the German fighter force and antiaircraft artillery. Both fighters and flak were formidable foes when the Fifteenth began operations, but the former accounted for more bombers lost until the German fighter arm dwindled in the summer of 1944.

Opposite page: A 451st Bomb Group B-24 flies over a smoke-covered Xenia Oil Refinery in Ploesti during the raid of August 10, 1944. The black smoke is from fires started by the bombing, not the German-generated smoke screen.

In late 1943, bombers flew many missions to targets in northern Italy and often encountered German fighters, as occurred on the mission to bomb the marshalling yards at Rimini, Italy, on November 27. Flying Fortress number 42-30705, of the 97th Bomb Group, led the group on this mission and lost an engine to a mechanical problem when approaching the target. The Fortress had to relinquish its lead position in the formation and salvo its bombs. After his return from captivity in June 1945, the copilot, Maj. Marvin Waldroup, recounted the experience.

A B-24 from the 513th Bomb Squadron, 376th Bomb Group, flies over the Alps on the way to bomb the Messerschmitt aircraft factory at Augsburg, Germany, on December 19, 1943.

An intelligence officer points out the current Bomb Line to members of the 450th Bomb Group during a mission briefing in December 1944. Bombers could not drop their bombs beyond the Bomb Line, to prevent hitting American, British, and Soviet troops. It was updated every day.

As the B-17 dropped behind the formation, Waldroup told the pilot, 1st Lt. Oscar Stedman, to increase power to catch up. They did so with some difficulty. Meeting overcast as they approached the target, the formation turned out to sea, flying in a large circle, to approach Rimini again, hoping to find a hole in the overcast so they could bomb the yards. Flak was conspicuously absent on the second approach to the target, a definite sign German fighters were in the vicinity.

On this approach, Waldroup told Stedman "to make a short cut across the circle, in order to catch up with the group. . . . As we approached land, slightly ahead of the more rapidly moving group . . . another B-17 with one engine feathered, was overtaking us from the rear . . ." As their bomber broke out of the overcast, the number three engine lost power as Waldroup saw:

> . . . about 25 Me 109s German fighter aircraft coming to attack us. I saw no friendly ships near us except . . . [the] other . . . B-17 which was [now] being relentlessly shot up by enemy fighters. . . . The first burst of fighter fire raked our B-17 . . . from the tail to the nose. . . . Soon the number two engine began to blaze and [then] the entire left wing. I told Stedman that we should try to get everyone out. . . . We were having difficulty keeping the ship level. . . . I dropped down between our seats and yelled to Lieutenants Parks [the navigator, Walter Parks] and Shube [the bombardier, George Shube] to jump. Lieutenant Parks seemed to be fastening on his chute. . . . I intended to be the last one to jump . . . as I was senior in rank. The cockpit . . . was all shot all to bits and how any of us escaped alive is a miracle to me. Just as I turned to get into my seat, everything went black . . . apparently . . . [from] the concussion of the ship exploding.

Armorers load bombs into the bomb bay of a B-17 before a mission to hit marshalling yards in northern Italy in the spring of 1944.

Although he was unconscious, the explosion blew open Waldroup's chute. He was still unconscious when he landed, injured, and Italian police swiftly captured him.

During the first attack pass by the German fighters, the only other survivor from the crew—the right waist gunner, Staff Sgt. Joseph Christie—heard the flight engineer, Tech. Sgt. Ray Shupe, shout "Fighters!" over the intercom. He recalled hearing "machine gun shells cracking through the ship" as Me 109s raked the fuselage of the Flying Fortress from tail to nose. The oxygen line to the ball turret caught fire, and the gunner, Staff Sgt. James Melton, got out of his turret. Christie and Shupe both fired at an Me 109 that closed to within a few hundred yards of the Fortress, from four o'clock high. Christie recalled: "It seemed to me as though Shupe had been doing the best shooting," but both scored hits on the enemy fighter. Immediately, "one of the Me 109s came streaking down from approximately two o'clock and passed my waist window with a terrible streak of smoke pouring from under his wing. I gave him a few bursts as he went by. He was headed for the ground when I last observed him."

The other waist gunner, Staff Sgt. James Sandford, then pointed out the burning number-two engine to Christie as the tail gunner ran past them, headed for the radio compartment, and closed the door behind him. Christie noted: "Pieces of shrapnel and fire scattered all through the plane." Sandford turned to the escape hatch in the floor of the fuselage. He had trouble moving the release latch, but eventually managed to open it, with Christie's assistance. Christie then returned to his machine gun and "kept firing at two Me 109s that were flying along with us." As Sandford opened the hatch, "machine gun and cannon fire pierced the ship. On this attack both of us were hit by either machine gun or cannon fire" that wounded Sanford badly in the stomach and Christie in the leg, as well as killing Sergeant Shupe. Christie again recalled:

I was also hit in the right leg and knocked to the left side of the ship. . . . I immediately got up and tried to fire at the two fighters that were coming in at approximately 6 o'clock high, but they were far to the right and my gun kept hitting the rear of the window. At this time, pieces of shrapnel and fire raked all through the ship. The ship seemed torn to pieces. It dawned on me that the ship was headed for the ground. . . . I then went back to see if I could do something for Sandford, but it seemed that there was no use. My right leg was bleeding terribly for the blood soaked through my pants, heated suit, and through my coveralls. It seemed as though I couldn't stand anymore and I remember it seemed as though everything was red to me. At this time, I was looking out of the hatch. The next thing I remembered I was falling with my feet down toward the earth. I had a difficult time pulling my rip cord, but somehow I managed to pull it out. I remember the flutter of the chute.

He noticed another chute on the way down: Major Waldroup.

After Christie reached the ground, he put a tourniquet on his leg. Some Italian farmers found him and carried him to a farmhouse, where he received some rudimentary first aid. Then an Italian soldier soon took him prisoner. While he was being carried down a mountain, an English-speaking Italian girl told Christie that another crewman was unconscious nearby. His party went to the location and found Waldroup unconscious.

The two were taken to an Italian civilian hospital and later a German military hospital, where Waldroup regained consciousness after five days. Both men were later transported to the Luftwaffe interrogation facility at Frankfurt am Main, then to different prisoner-of-war camps. Although the pilot of another Fortress had seen three chutes open just before the bomber exploded, they were the only two members of the crew to survive.[xxxi]

The effectiveness of fighter attacks such as those against Flying Fortress number 42-30705 began to diminish on missions over northern Italy following several Fifteenth Air Force attacks on airfields in northern Italy at the end of January 1944. These raids depleted the Luftwaffe fighter force opposing American bombers to the extent that many of the German fighters facing Fifteenth bomber formations from this point on came from bases in Austria and Germany. Although most of the Luftwaffe's fighter strength was based in Germany facing the American Eighth Air Force and the Royal Air Force's Bomber Command, Fifteenth Air Force raids to southern Germany and Austria could, and did, continue to draw fierce fighter opposition through the summer of 1944, as did raids against the heavily defended oil refineries at Ploesti, Romania.

Luftwaffe pilots flew most of the enemy aircraft encountered in the air battles of 1944, joined by pilots of Germany's Axis partners: Italy, Hungary, Romania, and Bulgaria. The Me 109 was the most common fighter encountered (some flown by Hungarian and Romanian pilots), followed by Fw 190s; twin-engine Me 110s, 210s, and 410s; and some Italian models. American pilots often mis-identified Romanian IAR 80s in the confusion of combat because of their similar appearance to the Fw 190. Besides cannon and machine guns, these fighters also used rockets against bomber formations, launched beyond the range of the defensive fire of bombers, as well as aerial bombs hung from cables.

German fighters concentrated on attacking the bombers until the spring of 1944, but just as long-range fighters joined the Fifteenth in April 1944, German fighter pilots were officially permitted to attack the fighter escort, as mentioned earlier. Attacks by waves of German fighters could extend the duration of attacks for a half hour or longer. But bombers straggling from group formations became their target of choice once American fighters gained air superiority in the spring of 1944.

A Flying Fortress hit by flak over Ploesti during the attack of July 9, 1944.

Although Luftwaffe fighter opposition to the Fifteenth waned at the end of the summer, for many months leading up to that time they presented a mortal threat to Fifteenth bomber crews. A month after the loss of Fortress number 42-30705, a Liberator crew from the 376th Bomb Group became another victim of German fighters. During the December 28 raid on Vincenza, Italy, Luftwaffe fighters shot down B-24 42-72088, piloted by 2nd Lt. Harlan Wenzinger, about forty miles from the target.

During the approach to the target, over the Adriatic Sea, the 376th formation of seventeen aircraft missed the rendezvous with the other group on the mission and the fighter escort. The other group, the 98th Bomb Group, with the fighter escort, had returned to base after weather reconnaissance reported that all potential targets were covered by clouds. The 376th missed the recall, however, and continued on to the briefed target. As the bombers approached it, a waist gunner, Staff Sgt. Donald Carlton, moved to the nose turret, and the flight engineer, Tech. Sgt. Bruce Dunkin, moved to man his waist gun, in expectation of an enemy fighter attack.

After the 376th crossed the coast, climbing to bombing altitude, more than one hundred German fighters attacked them from out of the sun. Sergeant Herbert Esaw, a gunner in another squadron

continued on page 56

Porto San Stefano, Italy, is smothered by bombs during the attack of May 12, 1944. A 450th Bomb Group B-24 is at the top of the photo.

Left: One of the two Liberators from the 450th Bomb Group lost during the mission to San Stefano, Italy, on May 12, 1944. As the group left the target after bombs away, flak blew off the rudder of the B-24 flown by Lieutenant Word, shown here. This Liberator then collided with another B-24, flown by Lieutenant Smith, and both aircraft plunged into the sea. There were no survivors from either crew.

Below: Lieutenant Word's Liberator as the crew lost control and it began to fall from the formation.

Above: Word's Liberator in its death dive toward the sea.

Right: The crew of the B-24D nicknamed *Chug-a-lug*, of the 345th Bomb Squadron, 98th Bomb Group, celebrate the 105th mission completed by the bomber. It returned to the United States for a war bond tour shortly afterward.

GERMANY
AUSTRIA
EGYPT
LIBYA
TUNISIA
SICILY
GREECE
CRETE
BU
RU

ITALY
YUGOSLAVIA
HUNGARY
DODECANESE
FRANCE

105

HUG-A-L

in the group, reported after the mission that "the first fighters attacked them [Wenzinger's squadron] from behind, out of the sun. Then they came in from every direction. The two wing men in B element were [the] first to go down. Then the leader . . . went down as they were making for our formation [for cover against the attackers], the other two [Liberators] each had two engines smoking and went down about 1,500 to 2,000 yards before they got to us. During this time I saw six fighters go down and chutes opening in every direction from the B-24s. . . . One B-24 blew up before it hit the ground and the others all went into spins."

The attack set Wenzinger's Liberator on fire above the bomb bay and the waist. Cannon shells also blew the tail turret out of the aircraft, killing the gunner. A crewman in an aircraft alongside saw the propeller from an engine fly off and landing gear fall out. The second fighter pass set the oxygen system on fire, destroyed the intercom, and started a fire in the waist of the Liberator. The radio operator, Tech. Sgt. Robert Hagen, later recalled that as the disabled aircraft left the formation, Lieutenant Wenzinger "gave the order to abandon ship as our controls were gone, one engine out, tail turret blown out of the ship, and we were afire from the bomb bay back [to the tail of the Liberator]."

Fighters wounded Technical Sergeant Dunkin on the first fighter pass, and he jumped from his window; the right waist gunner, Frederick Ehman, bailed out from the waist, too. Staff Sergeant Carlton was unable to get out of the nose turret as the aircraft began to plunge toward the ground. The copilot was last seen preparing to jump but never got out of the bomber and was killed in the crash. The pilot, bombardier, navigator, ball-turret gunner, and radio operator managed to bail out, but the navigator was strangled by his shroud lines during the descent. The Liberator descended in a slow spin until it crashed. Four crew members were killed in all: the copilot, navigator, tail gunner, and assistant radio operator. The remainder became prisoners of war. During the disastrous mission, ten bombers from the 376th were lost, including all that had been put up from the 512th Bomb Squadron.[xxxii]

German fighters continued the pressure on Fifteenth Air Force bombers into the new year, as bombing raids spread to Luftwaffe airfields in southern France to keep Luftwaffe bombers from attacking the Anzio beachhead. Immediately afterward, in late February, the Fifteenth returned to bombing German aircraft factories in southern Germany. As expected, German

The gunners of a 765th Bomb Squadron, 461st Bomb Group Liberator who claimed fourteen German fighters shot down or damaged during the attack on the Herman Goering Tank Factory in Linz, Austria, on July 25, 1944.

An Me 109 goes down in flames to gunners of a Liberator over Austria in July 1944.

fighters came out in strength to oppose the raids that took place during Big Week, the series of raids flown by the Fifteenth and the Eighth Air Forces and Royal Air Force Bomber Command from England. The raids were intended to destroy a large portion of German fighter production and force Luftwaffe fighters up to defend these factories, so they could be shot down.

The Fifteenth's first mission during Big Week was to bomb aircraft factories at Regensburg on February 22. On the run up to the target, about fifteen minutes before bombs away, flak and fighters assaulted the formation. Eight Me 110s attacked a Liberator named *Butch*, part of the 98th Bomb Group. Four attacked the left side of the aircraft, and the left waist gunner, Staff Sgt. John Goldbach, exclaimed over the intercom: "Let 'em have it!" These attacks damaged the ball turret, and the radio operator tried to raise the turret and open the door to allow the gunner inside, Staff Sgt. Harold Carter, to get out, but did not succeed. He returned to his radio room to hitch up his intercom and tell the pilot the situation when the aircraft suddenly exploded. Crewmen in other Liberators alongside saw the explosion, possibly caused by a rocket. *Butch* immediately fell out of the formation, nose down, in a steady dive with the engines on the right wing on fire and gasoline leaking from the bomb bay tanks. When the B-24 exploded, Technical Sergeant Foury, the radio operator, lost consciousness, coming to at five thousand feet with his parachute fortuitously blown open by the explosion. The remainder of the crew went down with the ship and were killed. Foury was taken prisoner, the only survivor of his doomed aircraft.

The next day, February 23, a reconnaissance F-5 Lightning of the 15th Photo Reconnaissance Squadron, flown by 1st Lt. John Brennan, took off to photograph the damage inflicted by the raid. As was typical of such reconnaissance missions, he flew a circuit of targets in southern Germany and Austria, including marshalling yards and airfields at Wessling and Munich, Germany, and Innsbruck, Austria. At some point on the mission, which was his twenty-eighth combat reconnaissance mission, Brennan was shot down, probably near Munich. Admitted to a German military hospital with serious injuries on the same day, he unfortunately died of his wounds on March 14. His Lightning and *Butch* were but two of forty-two lost by the Fifteenth Air Force on these two days.[xxxiii]

On the final mission of Big Week, on February 25, the 301st Bomb Group was one of the groups that bombed the Prufening Me 109 factory in Regensburg. Although the Eighth Air Force also bombed the plant, the German fighter controller picked out the Fifteenth's formation as the target for German fighters. Of the 200 involved in the attack, the 301st reported ttacks by up to 150 fighters, with groups of 20 attacking each squadron while the bombers were still over Austria. They closed to within one hundred yards of the bombers during the ferocious combat; some even dropped aerial bombs on the formation. An aircraft resembling a B-24 was thought to have fired a large-caliber cannon at the formation, too, but this was probably a rocket attack from a two-engine fighter fired from near one of the Liberators on the mission.

One of the fourteen Fortresses lost by the 301st on the mission was number 42-30095, piloted by 2nd Lt. Robert Snyder. After the crew had seen four other B-17s shot down in a matter of minutes, including two in their own formation, about fifty fighters attacked their Fortress, from around the clock, all firing at the same time. Snyder later reported: "Our number three engine ran away and we could not feather the propeller. . . . Then our oxygen system was knocked out. There seemed to be an explosion in the aircraft. It must have been a 20mm [round]. At the same time our number three engine caught on fire." The oxygen system was vital to the crew's survival at their altitude of more than twenty thousand feet, as well as the intercom, so Snyder put the Fortress into a dive to reach an altitude where oxygen was not needed. The fighters continued their

An Me 410 turns away from a Flying Fortress during a mission to Brux, Czechoslovakia, in June 1944.

A B-24 of the 449th Bomb Group leaves towering clouds of smoke behind it during a raid on the oil refineries at Ploesti, Romania, in the spring of 1944.

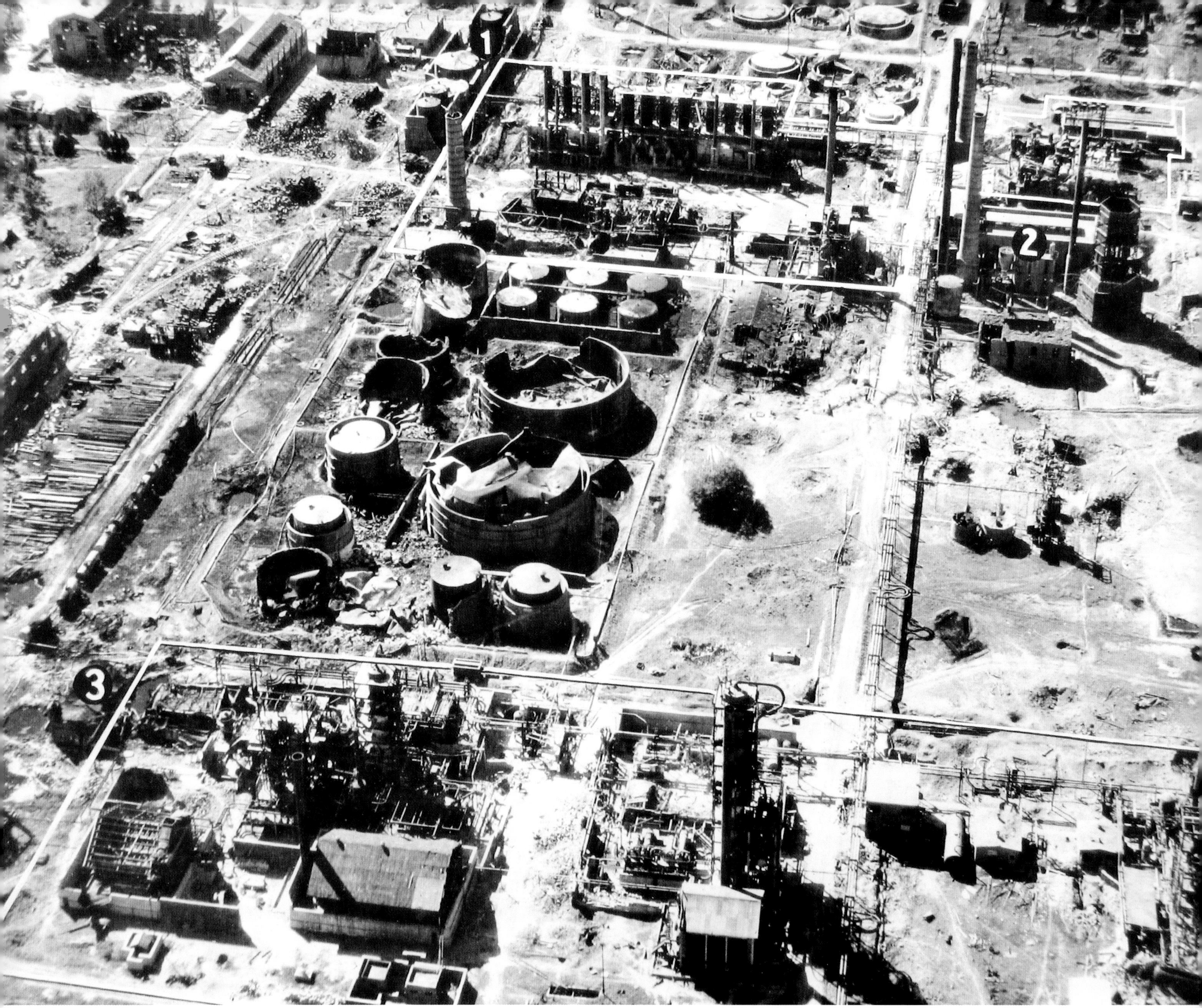
1
2
3

Opposite page: A view of the damage inflicted on the Romano Americano Oil Refinery by the Fifteenth Air Force during the raids from May through August 1944. The refinery was almost totally destroyed.

Right: With a rudder damaged by an enemy fighter attack, a 451st Bomb Group Liberator stays in formation during a mission to Vienna in the summer of 1944. The aircraft returned safely to base.

attack during the early part of the dive, but all but one turned away and climbed back into the fight above. This single fighter continued to follow the B-17 as it descended several more thousand feet, making one pass without firing. Evidently, the German pilot decided the bomber was doomed, as he too soon climbed away for more lucrative prey above.

Snyder continued: "The engineer said he saw the rest of the crew bailing out of the waist and the tail on the way down. . . . At about 15,000 feet, the bombardier bailed out. I tried to motion to him . . . but he left before I could make him understand the aircraft was still okay." Besides the bombardier, the radio operator and the ball-turret, waist, and tail gunners all bailed out as well, leaving only Snyder, the copilot, and the flight engineer to man the ship. The three managed to fly their badly damaged aircraft back to Italy, where they landed safely. We will meet several other crews who did the same in a later chapter. All the crewmen who bailed out were taken prisoner and liberated at the end of the war.[xxxiv]

Without fighter escorts, who lacked the range to protect them over Austrian and German targets at this time, the bombers of the Fifteenth returned to Italian targets in March, in part to conserve strength after the high losses in late February. On March 18, many Luftwaffe fighters attacked the bombers during raids on Luftwaffe airfields in northeast Italy, including the airfield at Villorba, after reconnaissance spotted a new buildup of enemy fighters.

A 5th Bomb Wing Flying Fortress drops its bombs over the refinery at Moosbierbaum, Austria, during the raid of August 28, 1944.

As the formation of Fortresses approached Villorba on the bomb run, one of the B-17s from the 99th Bomb Group was devastated during a fighter attack. The attacks, by Fw 190s and twin-engine Me 110s and Me 410s, lasted an hour. The Germans fired rockets from outside the range of the Fortresses' .50-caliber machine guns. The aim was good, as they hit four B-17s with rockets, downing all four. None of the American bombers initially fired at the fighters, as they were unsure of their identity, since the attack occurred at the time the Thunderbolt escort was to rendezvous with the bombers and the German aircraft had markings similar to some American fighters.

One of the bombers hit in the attack was number 41-22611 of the 99th, flown by the crew of 2nd Lt. Gerald Lombard. Four fighters attacked the ship from five o'clock, closing to within 150 yards before they fired their rockets. The rocket attack blew off the vertical and one horizontal stabilizer. The tail gunner was blown out of the Fortress by the explosion, passing over the wing of a plane flying behind the formation with his parachute streaming behind him. It did not open, and he was killed, most likely by the explosion that threw him from the plane. The waist gunner on 41-22611 reported to Lombard that the floor of fuselage up to the waist windows was destroyed. The tail began to smoke heavily, and after staying with the formation for a short time, the bomber turned away, losing altitude. A crewman on another plane reported the shootdown: "Four Me 109s . . . got within approximately 150 yards of [Lombard's Fortress]. . . . Still maintaining their formation, the first two Messerschmitts raised their noses slightly and fired. The other two fired a split second afterwards. The left horizontal stabilizer was shot off the B-17, which pulled up into a steep climb, rolled off on the left wing, and began to spin to the left. About halfway to the ground, the entire tail section separated and the ship's spin flattened out. . . . The Messerschmitts peeled off to the right, in formation, and disappeared in the haze."

As the aircraft flattened out, crewmen began to bail out through the bomb bay. As would be expected, Lombard was the last to leave, and all those who bailed out landed safely. All but one were captured—the waist gunner, Sgt. Raymond King, evaded capture and eventually reached Yugoslavia five months later.[xxxv]

Also over Yugoslavia, a 454th Bomb Group Liberator crew discovered that bombers that straggled from the protection of the combined firepower of their group formation became easy game for roaming German fighters.

Liberator number 41-29436, flown by 1st Lt. LeRoy Beck, lost some power in its engines on the approach to Bucharest on the May 7 mission but managed to stay with the group's formation and bomb the target. Then flak hit two engines, and the bomber began to straggle from the formation, losing altitude. The crew jettisoned equipment to lighten the ship, including the waist guns, flak suits, ammunition, and even the radio, but over Yugoslavia, on the way home, two Me 109s ambushed the bombers. The attack was devastating, wounding six of the crew and badly damaging the B-24.

The waist gunner and ball-turret gunner were either severely wounded or killed in the attack. The flight engineer, Tech. Sgt. Harry Boyer, and bombardier, 2nd Lt. Thomas Muirhead, both then behind the cockpit, were wounded. The tail gunner, Staff Sgt. Samuel Grieco, managed to return fire with the only machine gun still operating in the rear of the aircraft but was also wounded, as was the radio operator, Staff Sgt. William West.

With two crewmen dead or dying and four more wounded, the Liberator's bomb-bay fuel tanks began to burn. Beck gave the bailout order, and six of the crew managed to do so before the B-24 went into a spin and exploded. The nose-turret gunner, Sgt. John Warnock, last seen getting out of his turret, was found in the wreckage along with Lieutenant Beck, who had valiantly stayed to keep the doomed aircraft under control so the others could get out.

Of the six crewmen who did manage to bail out, the copilot was found dead with his hand on the ripcord handle; he had apparently jumped too late to open his chute. The parachute of Sergeant Boyer was riddled with bullet holes and only partially opened. He too was killed.

Sergeant West made it to the ground but was taken prisoner. Sergeant Grieco, Lieutenant Muirhead, and their navigator 2nd Lt. Thomas Kerrigan, parachuted safely, landing in Chetnik territory. The Chetniks treated Muirhead's and Grieco's injuries, but with the inadequate medical supplies available to them, Grieco's condition worsened. After several months, the Chetniks attempted to take him to a German hospital for treatment. Intercepted by Partisans, he was then taken to several Partisan hospitals but eventually died of his wounds. Kerrigan and Muirhead, separated from the Chetnik band, eventually reached Partisan-controlled territory and the main Partisan headquarters. From here they flew back to Italy in early July.[xxxvi]

*****

The German perspective is illustrated by the shootdown of a Fortress over Romania in June. The action was the first encounter of a German fighter pilot, Hauptmann Helmut Lipfert, with American aircraft after his *Gruppe* (group) transferred from the eastern front to Romania to bolster protection of the vital crude oil refineries in Ploesti. He met the 5th Bomb Wing as it returned from the first shuttle raid to Russia and bombed the airfield at Foscani, Romania, on June 11. The German fighter controllers easily vectored his flight of Messerschmitts to the American bomber column, where he could see the contrails of the escorts weaving overhead. The Germans climbed above the Fortress formation, past the escorting Mustangs, who apparently took no notice of them. At about twenty-one thousand feet Lipfert saw a straggling Fortress about a thousand feet below and dived on it with his wingman.

When he got within firing distance, he opened fire, initially hitting the fuselage, then concentrating on the outboard engine on the right wing. He hit it, and then the inboard engine on the same wing, and both engines caught fire. Suddenly, tracer fire passed over his canopy. His wingman was also firing on the B-17, aiming at and hitting the engines on the left wing. They both continued firing until the Fortress was completely engulfed in flames, after which it broke in two and headed for the ground. Fortunately, five crewmen managed to bail out.

As the Fortress plummeted earthward, the escorting Mustangs dived on the pair of Messerschmitts. The Germans headed for the deck with the P-51s in hot pursuit but managed to elude them by hugging the ground as they returned safely to their base at Zilistea.

A B-24 falls with a wing in flames after a German fighter attack over Austria in the summer of 1944. The victorious enemy fighter can be seen outlined against the clouds at the lower center of the photo.

The 463rd Bomb Group Flying Fortress nicknamed *The Biggest Bird* drops its bomb load on the Romano Americano Oil Refinery at Ploesti on June 23, 1944. This B-17 completed ninety-nine missions before it crash-landed in February 1945.

The Fortress Lipfert shot down was from the 97th Bomb Group. It had straggled from the formation and salvoed its bombs when he attacked it. The pilot, 2nd Lt. James Calloway, told the crew to bail out after the Fortress began to burn: "Get out, we're on fire." He stayed at the controls to allow the others to get out but was unable to get out himself and went down with the ship. The 97th Bomb Group photo officer, 1st Lt. Edward McKay, flying on the mission to record the historic shuttle mission and acting as a waist gunner, was killed by machine-gun fire while putting on his parachute. The rest of the crew was able to bail out, and all reached the ground safely, becoming prisoners of war.[xxxvii]

Romanian-based fighters had also accounted for one of the 449th Bomb Group Liberators lost during an early mission to the Ploesti refineries on May 5. Both German and Romanian fighters, Me 109s and IAR 80s, attacked the bombers over the target and during the first part of the flight home. They pressed home their attacks with great vigor, some closing to within twenty-five yards of the American bombers, firing rockets and dropping aerial bombs. The 449th lost five Liberators on the mission.

Eight fighters singled out Liberator number 42-50307, piloted by 2nd Lt. Bernard Armstrong, as he announced the attack over the intercom: "Fighter craft attacking us." During the attack, the nose gunner, Sgt. Carmen Gentile, called out, "Hit fighter craft going down," but communication between crew members soon ceased as the intercom was blown away. Cannon fire shattered the windshield in the cockpit and set the bomb bay ablaze, separating the crewmen in the nose and rear of the plane. An engine also began to burn, and the B-24 lost altitude until it reached about twelve thousand feet, where it leveled out as the crew prepared to leave their stricken craft.

Bombs dropped by the 376th Bomb Group bracket the railroad bridge at Nervesa, Italy, on June 22, 1944. The bridge was undamaged.

Lieutenant Armstrong told the copilot that the aircraft was on fire and they would have to bail out. Armstrong jumped with the navigator, who saw him preparing to jump as he exited the aircraft. A waist gunner, Sgt. Amarico Brioli, was wounded during the fighter attack. Dazed, he bailed out of the waist and came to while falling through the air. The ball-turret gunner was badly wounded or killed in the attack, as he didn't respond when the other waist gunner, Staff Sgt. George McKinley, attempted to get him out of his turret. McKinley then helped the tail gunner, who was badly wounded, to bail out of the rear escape hatch, then followed himself.

The bombardier, 2nd Lt. Solomon Abrams, helped Sergeant Gentile out of the nose turret. However, Gentile, who was near the nose escape hatch when Abrams jumped, was killed; Romanians later reported that his chute had not opened. Although last seen preparing to bail out, Armstrong was unable to do so before the ship exploded, carrying him and the ball-turret gunner to the ground. Their bodies were both found in the wreckage.

The seven crewmen who survived this ordeal became prisoners of war. Liberated after Romania surrendered, they returned to Italy as part of Operation Reunion, the rescue of Allied prisoners from Romania after that country's surrender, in September 1944.[xxxviii]

The pilot and ball-turret gunner from the 450th Bomb Group examine damage to the rudder of their Liberator made by cannon fire from a German fighter attack following the May 30, 1944, mission to bomb aircraft factories in Austria.

Such intense fighter attacks against Fifteenth Air Force formations began to decline in August, as the Luftwaffe fighter arm declined in strength and began to consolidate its force to combat American and British strategic bombing attacks from England. Air opposition to Fifteenth Air Force missions over Germany remained formidable, however, as the 465th Bomb Group discovered on the mission to bomb the aircraft factories in southwest Germany, at Friedrichshafen, on August 3.

After bombs away, flak damaged the lead aircraft in one of the group's combat boxes, and the bomber had trouble keeping up with the formation. The group leader slowed down to allow him to remain in formation, and the group slowly fell behind the rest of wing. This made protection by the escort much more difficult. Without the proximity of the rest of the bomber column, the group was too tempting a target for the thirty to forty Me 109s and Fw 109s that attacked them by climbing through clouds over Austria. The Germans made only one pass on the group, with flights of four fighters concentrating on one bomber each, and they shot down eight B-24s. The surviving bomber crews, however, claimed nine of the enemy fighters destroyed. The 325th Fighter Group broke up the attack of the second wave and turned away a third wave, as will be described later.

German fighters hit the Liberator flown by the crew of 1st Lt. Lawrence Crane from the rear and set the tail and rear of the fuselage on fire, so the crew prepared to bail out. When the tail gunner, Staff Sgt. Charles Sellars, who had been wounded, left his position, he discovered that his parachute had been burned and damaged. He joined several other crewmen in the bomb bay. A waist gunner, Sgt. Leeland Englehor, recalled: "While in the bomb bay section Sellars came out to me and motioned that his chute had been lost. I tried to get him to ride down pick-a-back, but he returned to the waist compartment which was badly burning." There were no spare chutes, and he was unable to jump, riding the aircraft down to his death when it crashed. The copilot, 2nd Lt. Robert Kurtz, reported on the fate of two more crewmen: "The nose gunner was ready to bail out from the nose immediately following him [the navigator] but evidently either the ship exploded before he jumped or he was killed in landing. . . ." The remaining crewmen were taken prisoner and survived the war.[xxxix]

The Liberator flown by 1st Lt. Lloyd Clarke caught fire during the fighter attack and left the formation with the rear of the fuselage riddled by cannon fire. Some of the gunners and the bombardier, who went to the tail after bombs away, were apparently wounded or killed and went down with the ship. Another gunner was killed on landing, after bailing out, but six crewmen, including Clarke, successfully reached the ground to become prisoners of war.

Smoke marks the grave of a Fifteenth Air Force damaged bomber that crashed in northern Italy in the fall of 1944 while returning from a mission to bomb rail targets on the Brenner Rail Line, a vital supply line for German troops fighting in northern Italy.

Fortresses on the way to bomb the large oil refinery at Brux, Czechoslovakia, leave contrails on the cold upper air.

A third B-24, piloted by Capt. Stanley Pace, caught fire in the bomb bay. The copilot, 2nd Lt. John Allen, caught his parachute on the floor of the cockpit, so Pace yanked him free and threw him into the burning bomb bay so he could jump, immediately following him. Both men, badly burned, were taken prisoner as they reached the ground. The other crewmen also bailed out, sustaining minor injuries. All eleven of the crew survived to become guests of the Reich until the war ended.

The crew of another Liberator lost, this one piloted by 1st Lt. Wilbert Elliott, also had good luck. Like Pace's crew, all of them survived from the stricken bomber. Luck did not, however, favor the crewmen on the bombers of Lts. Jack Favier and Howard Fiecoat, whose B-24s were also shot down in the attack; all were killed.

Another bomber lost, 2nd Lt. Myron Dodd's Liberator, exploded shortly after the enemy fighters hit the aircraft. The gunners were all killed, but the crewmen in the front of the aircraft—Dodd, his copilot, the bombardier, and the flight engineer—bailed out and were taken prisoner.

Second Lieutenant Theodore Poole flew the last Liberator lost. Two crewmen, Poole himself and tail gunner Tech. Sgt. Albert Hill, were both killed, Hill apparently crashing with the Liberator and Poole when his parachute failed to open. The other seven crewmen were taken prisoner. The 465th received a Distinguished Unit Citation for the mission.

The intervention of the 325th resulted in twelve enemy fighters shot down when they broke up the latter's attack. Following the mission, the 325th reported that the formation of the 465th was difficult to escort as it lagged behind the wing formation, preventing them from staving off the first wave of enemy fighters. When they arrived, however, they intercepted the second and third waves of attacking German fighters, undoubtedly saving additional Liberators from being shot down or badly damaged. Their dogfight with Luftwaffe fighters lasted almost half an hour.

The Mustangs shot down the first three enemy fighters at about the same time. Lt. Robert Brown went after an Me 109 in a steep climb, firing a high deflection shot from two hundred yards, then getting on its tail and closing to twenty feet before firing again, hitting the tail and wing. The enemy fighter did a split S and promptly crashed into a mountain.

Another Messerschmitt became the victim of 1st Lt. Harold Loftus. As it tried to dive for cover in some clouds, Loftus went after it. He came in from behind, fired a burst from three hundred

Extra Joker of the 725th Bomb Squadron, 451st Bomb Group, under attack by German Fw 190 fighters during the August 23, 1944, mission to bomb Markersdorf Airfield in Austria. Cannon fire has already made a hole in the trailing edge of the left wing and left vertical stabilizer.

Right: *Extra Joker* catches fire a few moments after the first photo was taken. The aircraft soon headed for the ground as enemy fighters circled, went into a spin, and exploded. All the crew were killed.

Below right: A 304th Bomb Wing Liberator goes down to enemy fighters during a mission to Campina, Romania.

yards, then closed to fifty yards behind its tail and fired again. The right wing and engine were hit by the burst, the engine began to smoke, and the pilot bailed out.

During this melee, a third German went down as 1st Lt. Edward Strauss dived after an Fw 190 that was tearing through the 465th Bomb Group formation. The German turned right after passing through the bombers, and Strauss came up on his tail and fired, hitting the engine, fuselage, and wings. The Focke-Wulf began to burn, and the pilot bailed out. Lieutenant John Reynolds also accounted for one of the attackers, the fourth to go down to the guns of the Mustangs.

About five minutes later, 1st Lt. John Simmons Jr. got a kill when he snuck up through clouds on an unsuspecting Me 109 that had made the cardinal error of flying straight and level during the dogfight. Attacking from six o'clock, he began firing at 500 yards and continued to fire bursts

During the June 16, 1944, mission to bomb Vienna, fighters hit the 460th Bomb Group Liberator flown by the crew of Lt. Frederick Smith, and it immediately caught fire. Other crews saw several crewmen leave the ship, but only three survived to become prisoners of war.

until he was only 50 yards from the enemy fighter. His .50-caliber rounds shattered the cockpit and left wing, and the fighter exploded. Minutes later, 1st Lt. Harry Parker, whom we met in chapter 2, scored the sixth victory of the day when he dove on three Me 109s and fired bursts until only 150 yards away from a Messerschmitt. He scored a number of hits on the wing and fuselage. As the Messerschmitt began to burn, the pilot bailed out. At the same time, Lt. Col. Ernest Beverley, a flight leader, observed twenty enemy fighters about to attack the 465th bomber formation. He attacked the entire enemy group by himself, got on the tail of an Fw 190, and fired several bursts of machine-gun fire that hit the cockpit and canopy. The enemy fighter spun earthward, and another pilot from the 325th saw it hit the ground. Lieutenant Jack Bond scored as well, at about the same time. He encountered an Fw 190 that appeared disinclined to engage him, heading into nearby clouds. Bond chased after him, firing bursts of machine-gun fire that hit the tail and wings of the Focke-Wulf. The pilot jettisoned the canopy and bailed out as his fighter caught fire and headed for the ground.

Five minutes later 1st Lt. Arthur Fitch went after another Me 109 that was diving away from the fight. He fired at it from three hundred yards, and although he did not see any hits, the German aircraft crashed into a mountain. He also bagged a second enemy fighter during the melee.

Lieutenant Colonel James Toner Jr. attacked an Fw 190 heading for the 465th formation. He got on its tail, firing from 300 to 150 yards as he rapidly overtook the enemy fighter. He was rewarded with hits on the tail, wings, and engine, and the enemy plane immediately caught fire and the pilot bailed out. Five minutes later, he scored the final victory of the day for the 325th when he got on the tail of another Focke-Wulf that began a series of turns in an attempt to shake him. This time he closed to 150 yards before opening fire, hitting the front of the cockpit and the engine. The enemy flipped over on his back and spiraled toward the ground, crashing into the side of hill.

Despite such occasional intense air battles, enemy fighter opposition was on the decline. They could still occasionally rough up the Fifteenth, however, as happened on the August 23, 1944, mission to the Markersdorf Airfield, Austria, when the 49th and 55th Bomb Wings came under fighter attack before they reached the target. The ensuing air battle lasted half an hour and the 451st Bomb Group lost nine Liberators, the 461st Bomb Group one. Second Lieutenant Gordon Rosencrans flew the latter with nine other crew members who had been in Italy for less than a month. During the run up to the target, under fighter attack, one of Rosencrans's engines began to run roughly, and the Liberator began to lose airspeed. It slowly dropped out the 461st formation as Rosencrans feathered the bad engine and the bombardier salvoed the bomb load. As the fighters continued to attack, they hit the left wing, which began to burn. The Liberator began to circle, losing altitude, then resumed course with the group, but several thousand feet lower and farther away. Soon it suddenly nosed down; several crewmen bailed out of the bomber, which turned over in a spin and went down. One of the waist gunners, Cpl. Jessie Whisenant, had his leg blown off by cannon fire during the fighter attack, but in the chaos there was no time to give him first aid. He was only partially conscious when the bail-out order was given, and several other crewmen helped him jump. The attack also wounded the tail-turret and ball-turret gunners, and another crewman had to help the tail gunner get his parachute on. Rosencrans and the flight engineer, Cpl. Roy Houck, were both wounded by German fighters during their descent, but all the crew reached the ground safely, landing in the same general area, and were taken prisoner. Unfortunately, Whisenant died soon after from loss of blood.

Besides the loss of Rosencrans's B-24, an unusual incident occurred during the mission. A mystery B-17, painted black with white trim on the tail—probably a captured aircraft utilized by the Germans—flew alongside the formation for about half an hour until fired upon. The attack caused it to depart.[xl]

Beginning in September, the decline of the Luftwaffe was evident, as concerted fighter attacks against Fifteenth Air Force bombers were few. In March of the following year, however, a new menace appeared in the form of jet fighters. Although jets attacked the Eighth Air Force bombers first, at the beginning of the month, the Fifteenth came in for their share at the end of March on several missions flown deep into Germany.

The first attacks by significant numbers of Me 262s against bombers of the Fifteenth took place during the long mission to the Ruhland refinery on March 22. Not only was flak heavy, as would be expected around one of Germany's vital refineries, but the bomber crews saw jets close up. A squadron commander in the 2nd Bomb Group, Maj. John Reardon, reported: "Looking out the window, I saw a big black something whiz by and as it banked to the left my heart skipped an odd beat or two for I saw it was a Jerry jet-propelled fighter."[xli] The bombers were, in fact, attacked by Me 410s and Me 109s as well as jets.

Just after bomb release, flak hit the nose and waist of Fortress number 42-107156, from the 483rd Bomb Group, flown by 2nd Lt. Con Robinson's crew on their first mission. Robinson later reported: "We . . . were separated from the

group when we were hit by 88mm flak behind the navigator's compartment. At the same time we received another hit in the waist. Jerry planes started coming into the formation and . . . we received a 20mm [shell] in the radio room. . . . Me 210s shot off the right horizontal stabilizer, the right aileron, and flaps. Several Me 109s made a frontal attack. . . . We pulled away from the formation with the oxygen supply shot out and the radio operator, [Corporal John] Chupa wounded so badly from machine gun fire that he died the next morning."

The ball-turret gunner, Cpl. Virgil Cochran, was the last man to leave his guns, and he broke up several Me 262 attacks, most of which were made from below a bomber formation so they could streak away from the bomber's formidable defensive firepower of massed .50-caliber machine guns. Robinson pulled out of the formation and headed east toward Russian lines. As the plane flew on, a waist gunner gave the radio operator his oxygen mask to use until he lost consciousness from loss of blood. Soon several Russian Yak fighters met the Fortress and, fortunately, recognized it as American.

While passing over the front line, near Breslau, they were fired upon again and some of the crew bailed out, using a static line to get the wounded radio operator out. Robinson, copilot Flying Officer Richard Craig, navigator 2nd Lt. James Kahide, and enlisted togglier Staff Sgt. Richard Andreola remained in the Fortress and crash-landed it soon afterward in the front line between German and Russian troops. Kahide reported: "They [the Germans] fired on us with machine guns and mortars. . . . [We ran] for a bunch of trees. There was a swamp on the other side of the trees and we dove into the water and they kept firing at us. We spotted a trench . . . and noticed some people there . . . [who] started waving to us to come on over to them. . . . They stuck up a red flag to show us that they were Russian. We crawled over and they [the Germans] started firing at us, so finally we decided to run for it. . . . About thirty feet from the lines . . . Craig received a bullet through the back which came through the stomach." The four continued to crawl to Russian lines, where Russian infantrymen helped drag him in. Craig was taken to a Russian hospital, but soon died. The remaining crewmen, reunited within several days, were taken to the American base at Poltava by the end of the month.[xlii]

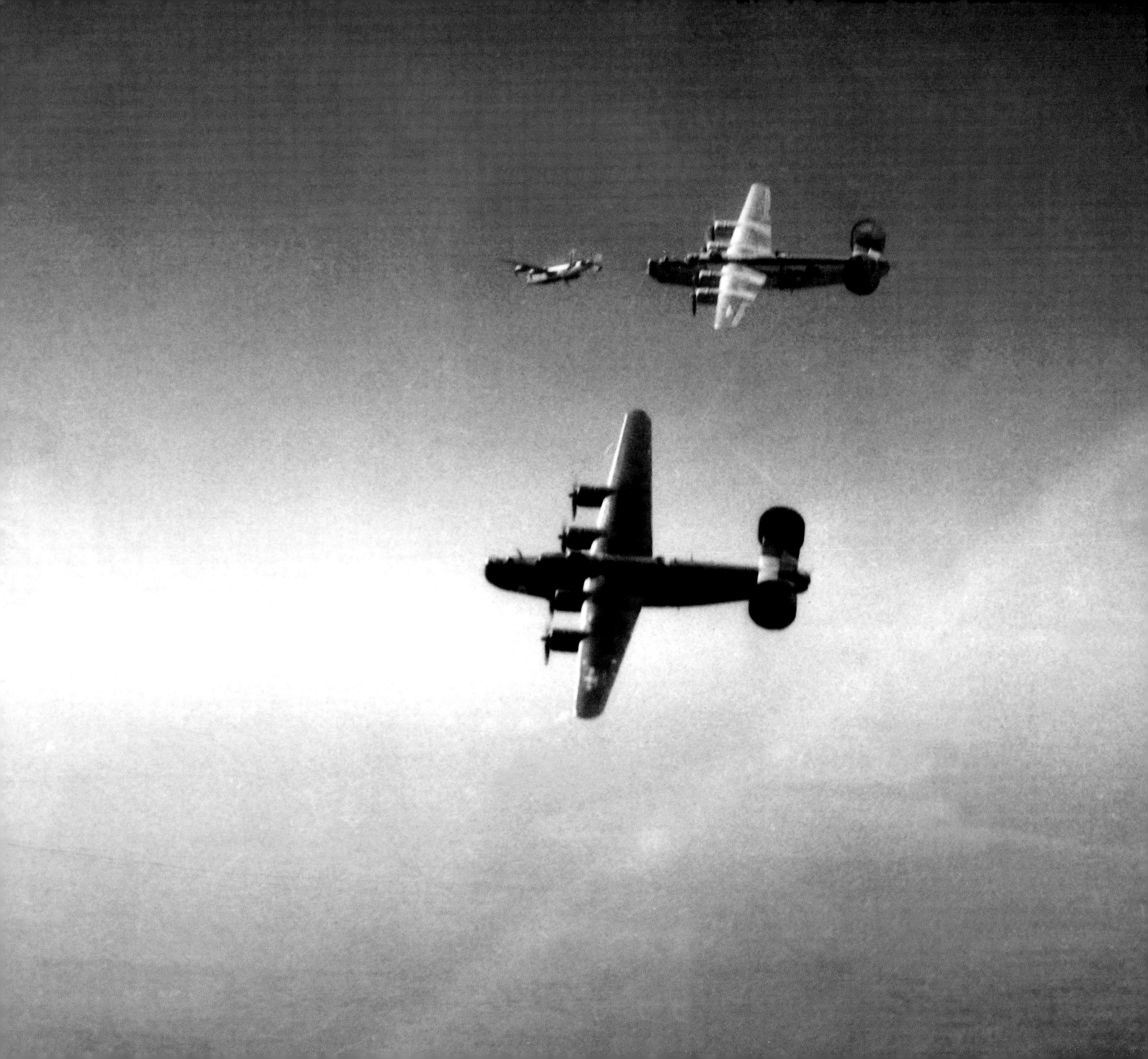

CHAPTER 5

FLAK

The other major hazard faced by bombers was the antiaircraft artillery that protected all important targets. It was always a primary defense, traditionally supporting the effort of Luftwaffe fighters to destroy enemy bombers. Heavy flak was the antagonist of the Fortresses and Liberators, while, as we have seen, light flak was the bane of fighters when dive-bombing or strafing ground targets. Flak guns were usually placed in fixed batteries or, during 1944 and 1945, in mobile batteries often mounted on trains. The latter were always a concern of American flyers as intelligence about their location was problematic, causing unpleasant surprises, and losses.[xliii]

Opposite page: Liberators from the 47th Bomb Wing turn away from their target after bombs away as flak bursts below them.

During the period of Fifteenth Air Force operations, the Germans increasingly used *Grossbatterien*—a concentration of three flak batteries with four guns in each battery—that had, by the summer of 1944, become the standard flak defense, especially around synthetic oil refineries. These batteries increased the density of flak rounds exploding in a bomber formation, making it even more deadly.[xliv]

Beginning in June 1944, flak shot down more Eighth and Fifteenth Air Force bombers than fighters and inflicted ten times more damage on bombers than fighters, a trend that continued through the end of the war. Aircraft losses to flak rose constantly during most of 1944, due, in part, to the increased number of flak guns employed by the Germans, many in *Grossbatterien*, as well as the use of gun-laying radar, much of it increasingly immune from Allied jamming.[xlv]

Despite increased accuracy and the employment of more guns, ammunition supplies suffered as a result of American attacks on the same oil refineries these guns often protected. Nitrogen, an important component in explosive manufacture, was produced by oil refineries. As American bombers damaged the refineries, they produced less nitrogen, reducing the production of ammunition needed by flak batteries.

Despite these problems, the Fifteenth continued to lose aircraft to flak for the remainder of the war. A major Fifteenth Air Force target, Vienna, Austria, was reputed to be the second most heavily defended city in the Reich.

It was flak that claimed a Liberator on the second mission flown by the Fifteenth Air Force, to the Messerschmitt factory at Wiener Neustadt, Austria, on November 2, 1943. The arduous round-trip flight from North Africa, with a stop in Italy on the outbound flight for those aircraft that bombed the target and returned, varied between ten and a half and thirteen hours in length, and opposition from flak and fighters was heavy.

One of the eleven bombers lost on the mission was B-24 number 42-728 of the 98th Bomb Group, flown by the crew of 2nd Lt. French Jeffries. The Liberator took two flak bursts in a wing and more in the bomb bay and vertical stabilizer. A crewman on another Liberator described what happened to Jeffries's aircraft next: "He stayed in formation the best he could until I saw flames burn through the top of the ship above the bomb bay. At the same time . . . one person was seen to jump out of the bomb bay. The ship soon got a little out of control as the flames appeared in the back windows. Four more [men jumped] out just before the ship broke in half. . . . The tail section broke apart and the front turned over on its back and went into a spin. The wing tips came

A German eighty-five-millimeter flak gun, the primary German antiaircraft weapon used against high-altitude, strategic bombing missions.

Believed to be one of the three Liberators lost by the 98th Bomb Group, possibly Lieutenant Price's B-24, during the first long-range mission flown by the Fifteenth Air Force, on November 2, 1943, to bomb the Messerschmitt fighter factory at Wiener Neustadt, Austria. The fuselage behind the wing has been badly damaged by flak.

off after it had made about a turn and a half. Other small parts [flew] off . . . as the ship went down. One chute was seen to open . . . ," followed shortly thereafter by four more from the rear of the aircraft. A German fighter strafed one of the crew in his chute, which caught fire. The front of the fuselage went into a spin, shedding its wings before hitting the ground shortly after 12:30 p.m., near Poettsching, Austria, about six miles east of Wiener Neustadt. The four crewmen in the nose of the ship who didn't bail out, and the gunner whose chute caught fire, were killed. The flight engineer, Tech. Sgt. Harold Fulwilar; the radio operator, Tech. Sgt. Gordon Rowe; the assistant engineer, Staff Sgt. Fred Bonnet; and the gunners, Staff Sgts. Charles Rickard and Lawrence Wolfe, were taken prisoner and liberated at the end of the war.

One Luftwaffe flak battery was officially credited with shooting down the Liberator—2nd Battery, 290th Heavy Flak Battalion, assisted by several other batteries from the 88th Flak Regiment. The German also gave an assist to a fighter, although the American flyers and some flak gunners did not report any fighter activity during the shootdown.

The weather was sunny, with high haze, so the flak guns sighted visually rather than with radar. A battery of four eighty-eight-millimeter flak guns fired eight rapid bursts, totaling thirty-two rounds in just one minute while the American formation, estimated to be forty to fifty bombers, flying at an altitude of about twenty-five thousand feet, was in range. The German gunners observed several hits on several aircraft and smoke trailing from several Liberators, including Jeffries's. The entire action, from the time the guns fired until Jeffries's Liberator crashed, took less than two minutes.[xlvi]

The crew members of another Liberator were also victims of Austrian flak, but they were able to fly to Yugoslavia and reach the Allied-controlled island of Vis, the location of an Allied fighter strip also used for emergency landings. A flak barrage hit the 450th Bomb Group Liberator flown by the crew of 1st Lt. Jack Morris on their seventeenth mission, to Ebreichsdorf, Austria, on May 30, 1944. It damaged the fuel tanks, and aviation gasoline began to leak from them. An engine also had to be feathered. The Liberator left the formation and began the return flight to Italy, just missing an attack on the 450th by a mixed bag of German aircraft after the escort had left the bombers.

The luck of Morris's crew, however, didn't last as the loss of an engine slowed the Liberator and increased fuel consumption. The leaks in the gas tanks became worse, and as the Liberator reached the coast of Yugoslavia, it became obvious that they did not have enough fuel to reach Italy. Approaching Vis, the crew contacted the field. They were told they should bail out over the Adriatic, near the island, rather than attempt a landing, and an air-sea rescue launch would be standing by to pick them up. Morris flew along the coast and ordered the crew to bail out. The gunners in the rear went out first, followed by the rest of the crew; then the Liberator crashed on the island. Six of them landed on Vis, one injured in the landing, while the four others landed in water. Morris later reported that the rescue launches made no attempt to pick up the men the water, who were rescued by Yugoslav fishing boats. Unfortunately, they couldn't find the radio operator, Staff Sgt. Frank Riley. Although his parachute had opened, he drowned after he hit the water. A boat from the island soon picked up the other three crewmen. The crew was reunited on the island and returned to Italy, by boat, to continue their combat tour with the Fifteenth.

The same 98th Bomb Group B-24 shown on the previous page, just before it dived into the ground.

Flak shot the Liberator carrying some of the same crew only a few weeks later, during a mission to Giurgiu, Romania, on July 3. Hit by flak, they once again had to leave the formation and headed for home on their own. Their pilot, 2nd Lt. William Cubbins, copilot on the May 30 mission, recalled: "Due to the intense damage we suffered, we were forced to leave the formation. All crew members were wounded." The navigator, 2nd Lt. Oliver King, and flight engineer, Tech. Sgt. Frank Lynch, both of whom survived their trial at Vis, tried to stem a fuel leak in the bomb bay tanks but were both overcome by the fumes and lack of oxygen. The copilot on this mission, 2nd Lt. William Kappeler, revived King, and both men put a parachute on the still-unconscious Lynch, fashioning a line to his ripcord, then dropped him through the open bomb bay. He landed safely on the ground. Morris, Green, and King then left the ship. All the crew were taken prisoner by the Romanians and became prisoners of war until they were repatriated as part of Operation Reunion.[xlvii]

It was not only flak at Romanian targets, such as Giurgiu and the refineries at Ploesti, that claimed American bombers. German missions were, along with Ploesti, the toughest for the Fifteenth during the summer of 1944, particularly oil refineries that were feeling the effect of Allied bombing since late in the spring. Besides the concentration of German fighter forces in the greater Reich, the number of flak guns protecting refineries steadily increased. Their barrages could have a devastating effect on American bombers, such as the damage they inflicted to Liberator number 41-2887 of the 455th Bomb Group on July 21.

This was a so-called Mickey ship—a bomber with H2X radar bombing gear, known as a Mickey set, on board—designated as deputy leader of the group on the mission. After arising at 3:30 a.m.

Above: This dramatic photo shows three crewman bailing out of a stricken Liberator over Germany. One was jumping from a waist window when the photo was taken; two others are already out of the aircraft but have not yet pulled their rip cords.

Right: During the attack on aircraft factories at Wels, Austria, on May 30, 1944, flak hit this B-24, and one crewman can be seen just after he bailed out. The aircraft exploded shortly afterward.

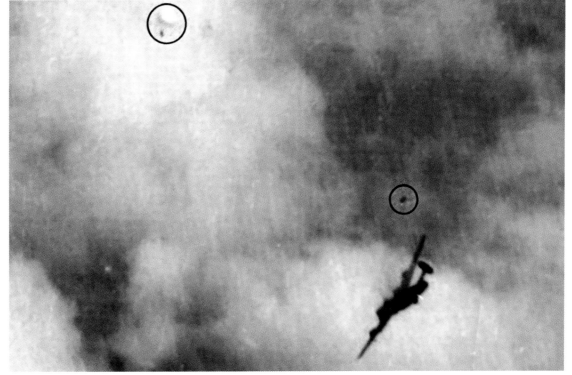

for the mission, the crew, with a squadron commander, Maj. Horace Landford, on board, took off at 7:00 a.m. and headed for the oil refinery at Brux, Czechoslovakia. Over the target on the bomb run, flak hit their Liberator several times. Despite damage to the right rudder and three engines, they dropped their bombs, then pulled out of the formation because they could no longer stay with the other bombers as the Liberator began to vibrate. With two engines that could not be feathered and the supercharger, vital to high-altitude flight, damaged on a third, problems now rapidly worsened as gas tanks in the right wing began to leak badly. Despite the damage, the B-24 stayed in the air and began the flight home. Losing altitude, the crew succeeded in crossing the Alps into northern Italy, heading for the Adriatic Sea. North of Udine, however, flak struck the bomber again with serious effect, hitting the only unaffected engine and damaging the left wing. A burst in the nose wounded the

Ground crewmen repair a B-24 that made an emergency landing on the island of Vis, off the Yugoslav coast. The island, under Allied control from spring 1944, provided safe haven for many stricken Fifteenth Air Force aircraft that otherwise would have been lost in Yugoslavia or the Adriatic Sea.

bombardier, cut the flying boot of the copilot, 2nd Lt. Lewis Nixon, and destroyed the remaining manual controls in the cockpit. Major Landford cleverly engaged the automatic pilot to keep the Liberator in the air. The pilots managed to turn the aircraft by adjusting the throttles and flew for about ten minutes more, until the autopilot cut out over the western-most part of Yugoslavia. As the plane began to pitch and roll, Landford gave the order to bail out. All of the crew bailed out just as the plane began to spiral to the ground. A wing came off, and it crashed. Five crew members became prisoners of war, but the other five, including Landford, evaded capture and eventually returned to Italy.

Copilot Nixon was knocked out as he hit some trees and awoke to find himself half submerged in a stream, suspended from his harness. He hid his chute and traveled down the stream for a bit, then headed farther into Yugoslavia, while the Germans searched for him. Fortunately, he soon met a Yugoslav farmer who hid him

Above: A B-24 just before it began its plunge to the ground over Ploesti, Romania, on May 5, 1944. The aircraft is believed to have been flown by the crew of Lt. Lawrence Peterson of the 745th Bomb Squadron, 456th Bomb Group. Unfortunately, none of the crew survived.

Right: After 5th Bomb Wing B-17s have dropped their bombs, towering columns of smoke rise from the refineries at Ploesti during the one of the early missions to the city in spring 1944. Black smoke from flak is visible in the background.

in a farmhouse. Later he encountered some Partisans, who hid him in a barn, then took him to their Partisan headquarters. With their assistance, he managed to reach an Allied landing field within a week and flew out of Yugoslavia. The radio operator, Sgt. Vincent Siemon, also succeeded in evading capture. After receiving slight injuries in landing, he walked for most of the day, drawing near to the town of Ljubljana in the evening. Following a path, he suddenly encountered a German patrol. They shot at him, and he took cover. In a few minutes, two Germans approached with a flashlight. Siemon shot both of them with his pistol and ran. Traveling throughout the night, he continued on the next day and finally met a Yugoslav farmer, who went to a nearby village and returned with a Partisan who spoke English. The pair took him into the hills, to a Partisan unit. Continuing on with a Partisan officer, he finally reached a British mission to the Partisans. Siemon then traveled by truck to the town of Nettick, where he was evacuated to Italy in a special operations plane on August 1.[xlviii]

Flak brings down a Fortress over Ploesti, Romania, on May 5, 1944, during one of the early raids on the oil refineries that ringed the city.

Right: A 47th Bomb Wing Liberator continues the mission after flak badly damaged a wing just after bombs away during an attack on the harbor facilities in Toulon, France, on August 6, 1944, just before the invasion of southern France.

Below: A crew from the 49th Bomb Squadron, 2nd Bomb Group, examines heavy flak damage to the wing of their Fortress in late 1944.

A 451st Bomb Group crew traveled to a prison camp, instead, when Viennese flak shot down their Liberator during the raid on the Florisdorf Oil Refinery near Vienna on October 13, 1944. B-24 number 42-51764, flown by the crew of 1st Lt. Robert Baker, was hit over the refinery, just after the bombs had been dropped. Three bursts of flak devastated the plane, part of a box barrage put up by a battery of flak guns. One burst near the nose, killing the nose gunner. The copilot, 2nd Lt. Garfield Andrews, described what happened: "Seconds after bombs were away . . . we received three simultaneous direct hits from 88mm flak. . . . The plane was hit in the nose, the forward part of the bomb bay, and between the engine on the right wing, and immediately [burst] into flames. . . . It was impossible for either the pilot or myself to go to any part of the plane. The interphone was shot out. . . . The pilot and I stayed as long as we could [with a fire raging behind them], keeping the plane straight and level [to give anyone surviving from the nine-man crew time to get out after they had rung] the alarm to bail out. We used every setting [on the intercom to reach the rest of the crew] but we never got a response from any of them."

As they held the plane in the air, it slid under the group formation, and those crewmen who could bailed out. Sergeant Clenon Earnest, the left waist gunner, was able to bail out of the rear door, the only man from that part of the plane to survive. Flak mortally wounded the right waist gunner and radio operator, as well as the ball-turret gunner. The tail gunner, Sgt. Sam Holquin, got out of his position and was last seen near a hatch, apparently ready to jump. He may have delayed bailing out to help the ball-turret gunner, a close friend, and could not bail out before the Liberator exploded in the air. The pilots, Baker and Andrews, bailed out last. Andrews continued: "I bailed out with the pilot right after me, and as soon as I opened my chute, I looked up just in time to see the plane blow up." The pair and the navigator, bombardier, and flight engineer were the only men to survive the ordeal, as prisoners of war.[xlix]

The other important oil targets for the Fifteenth in the summer and fall of 1944 were the synthetic oil refineries in Silesia. Like any German refinery their flak defenses were formidable, making attacks on them a dangerous enterprise. Liberator number 41-28853 of the 465th Bomb Group, with group commander Col. Clarence Lokker aboard, was a victim of this flak on November 20, an event captured in the dramatic photo shown.

At the start of the bomb run the top turret gunner, Sgt. Jack Rabkin, remarked, "It really looks rough up there," referring to their target, the southern refinery at Blechhammer. A few minutes later, just seconds before bombs away, a burst of heavy flak hit the Liberator through the open bomb bay, and several bombs tumbled out. The ship then exploded. Amazingly six of the crew bailed out, but unfortunately several more were not wearing their parachutes—not unusual, as it was difficult to fit inside turrets wearing one. Sergeant Rabkin and one of the two bombardiers usually carried in a lead ship couldn't extricate themselves before the plane turned onto its back and went into a spin. Flak had wounded the Mickey operator, and he was not able to bail out either.

The explosion blew a gunner, Sgt. James Bourne, and the flight engineer, Tech. Sgt. Lee Billings, out of the aircraft, but as they had their chutes on, they reached the ground safely. The navigator, Capt. Joseph Kutger, grabbed his chute just before the explosion but hadn't yet buckled it onto his harness when he was also blown from the plane by the explosion. He somehow managed to clip the parachute to his harness as he fell through the air and opened it. The radio operator had been throwing chaff, small strips of metal designed to confuse enemy radar, out of the waist and was last seen near an escape hatch, but went down with the ship. The tail gunner was enveloped in flames by the explosion and didn't get out of the stricken bomber either.

German flak claims a Liberator, possibly from the 465th Bomb Group, over Munich in November 1944

Lokker, copilot Capt. Milton Duckworth, and second bombardier (included with a lead crew) 1st Lt. Robert Hockman all bailed out as the plane was spinning its way to the ground. All six survivors were immediately captured. Lokker and Duckworth were held in a farmhouse, but both soon tried to escape. Lokker was last seen pursued by the Germans shooting at him and was later reported killed by his pursuers.[1]

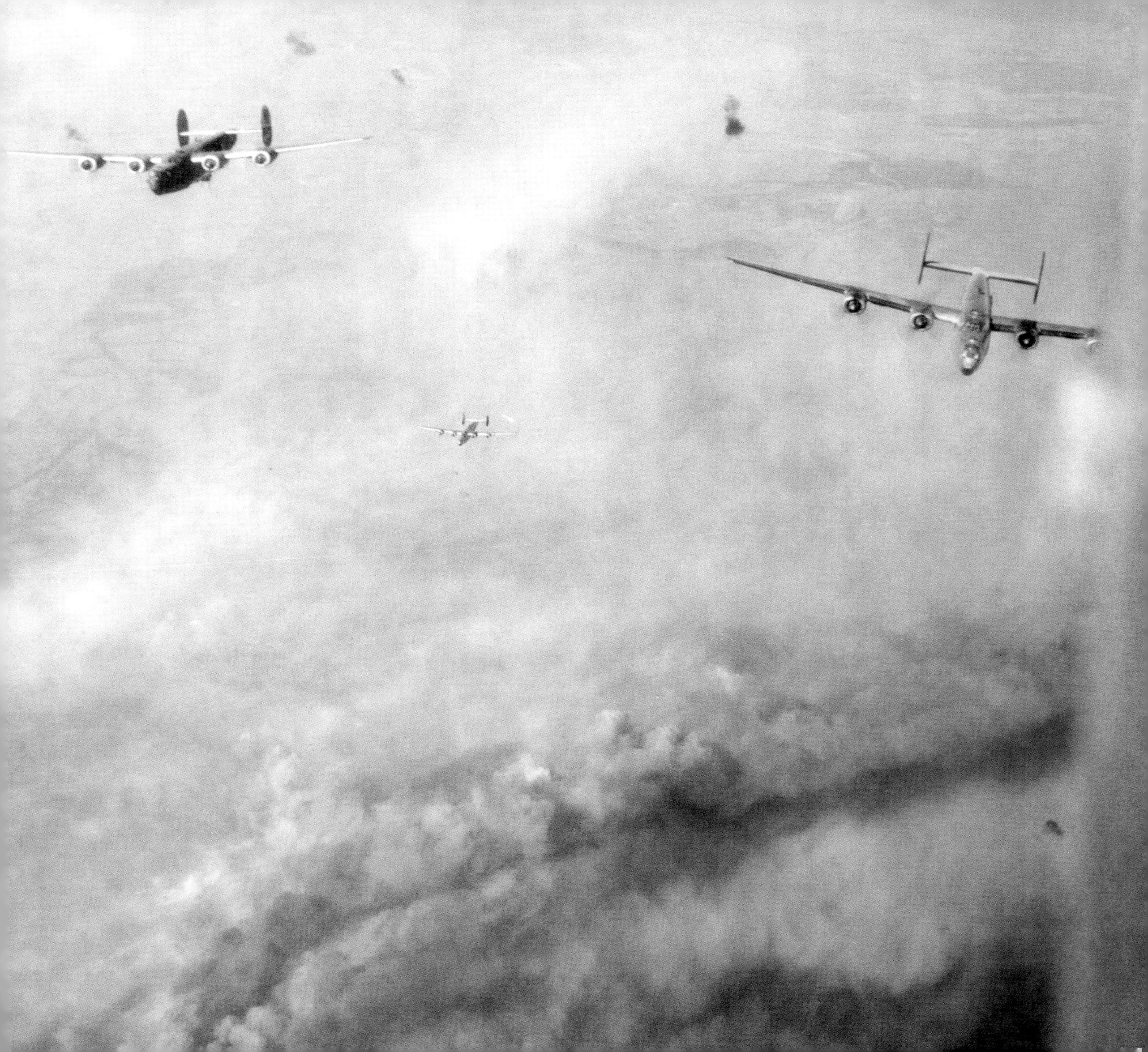

Right: A crewman from a Fortress badly damaged by flak during the mission to bomb the aircraft factories at Wiener Neustadt on May 10, 1944, bails out, and his partially open chute can be seen behind the stricken bomber. A few moments after this photo was taken, the B-17 exploded.

Below: A B-24 falls in pieces after a direct hit by flak in the open bomb bay during the bomb run blew the aircraft in two. The aircraft was lost on the July 26, 1944, mission to bomb targets in Vienna.

Opposite page: Liberators, possibly from the 465th Bomb Group, fly through flak over the smoke-covered synthetic oil refinery at Blechhammer, Germany, in late 1944. The Germans generated the smoke to obscure the refinery from Fifteenth Air Force bombardiers.

Above: Colonel Lokker's Liberator as it exploded over Blechhammer on November 20, 1944.

Right: A B-24 damaged by flak falls from a group formation during a bombing mission.

Opposite page: The same Liberator shown on page 90 explodes. Liberators were prone to exploding in the air when hit by flak.

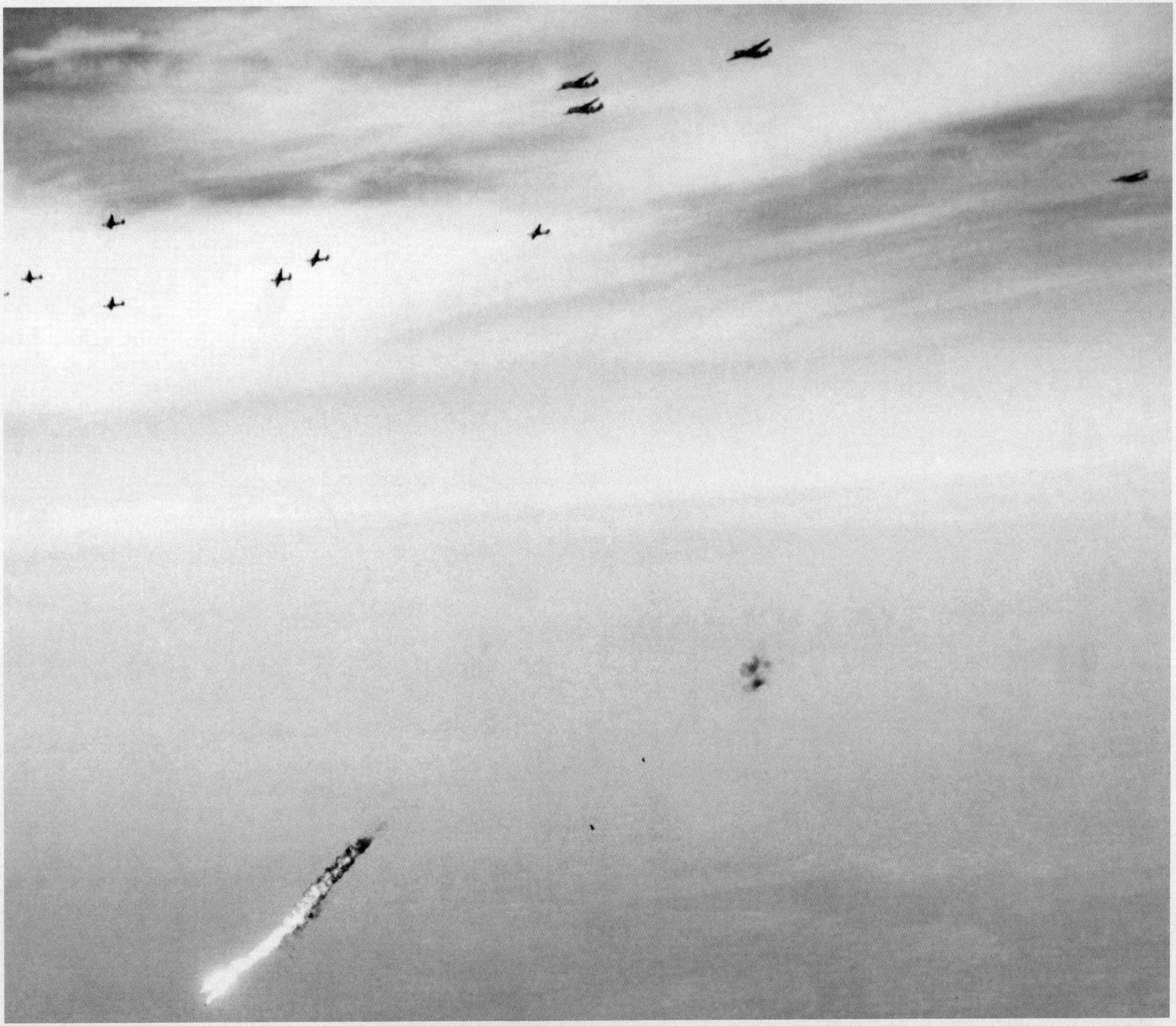

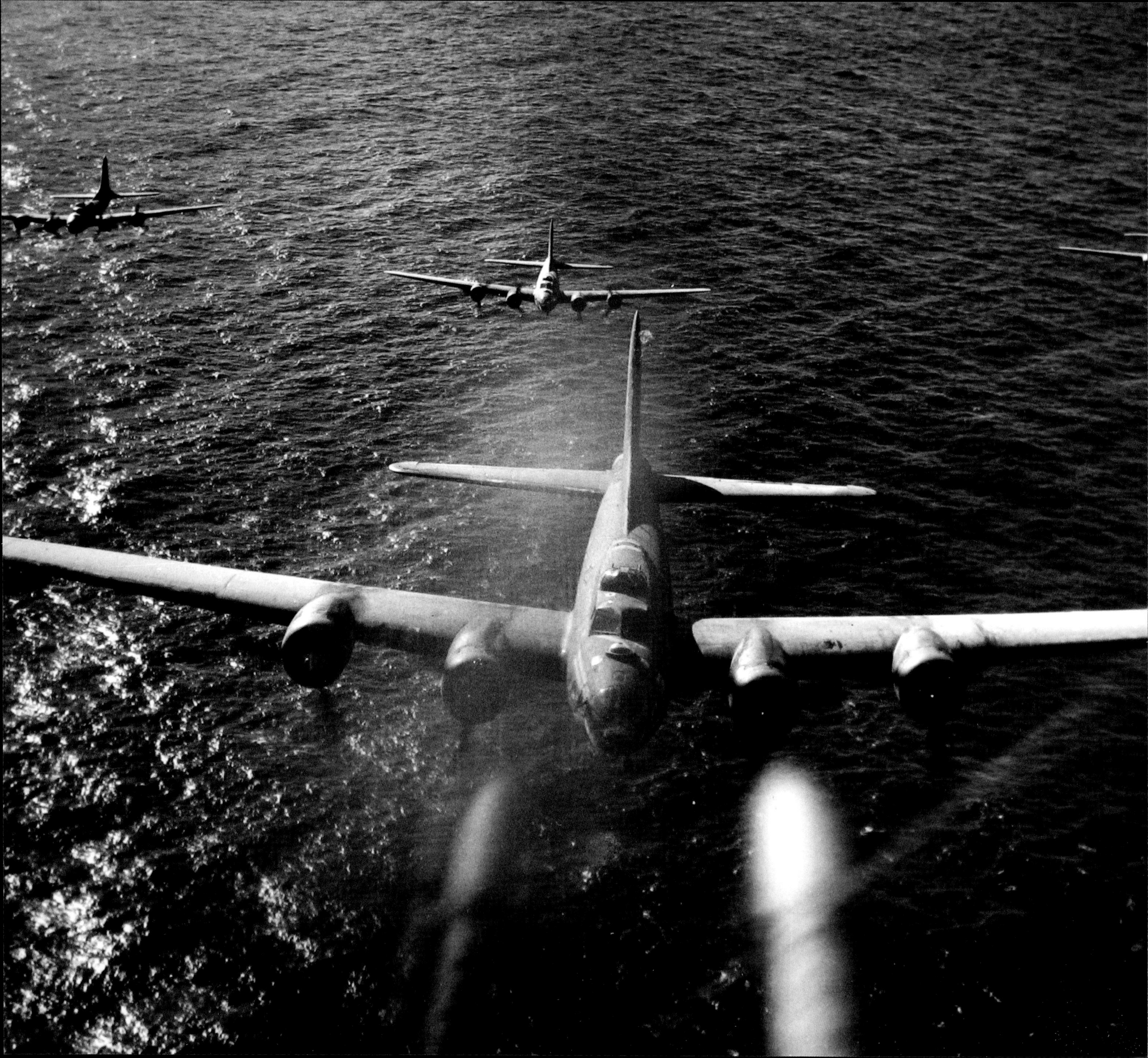

CHAPTER 6

IN THE DRINK

The most dangerous hazard facing Fifteenth Air Force crews whose damaged aircraft managed to reach the Mediterranean or Adriatic Seas was bailing out of their stricken aircraft over the Mediterranean or Adriatic, with ditching in the sea a close second. The chances for survival after bailing out in these conditions were extremely low, while landing an aircraft in the water was almost as perilous. Many crews did not survive either.

Opposite page: An interesting view of 5th Bomb Wing B-17s, taken from the tail turret of another Fortress, flying over the Mediterranean on a mission to bomb Luftwaffe airfields in southern France to support Allied troops at Anzio during the later winter of 1944.

The type of aircraft was an important factor in crew survival in any ditching. The Flying Fortress was universally considered to have better ditching characteristics than the Liberator: the B-24's fuselage took the initial shock and often broke apart as it hit the water, as the wings were located high on the fuselage. The Fortress's wing, on the other hand, was positioned on the bottom of the fuselage and helped distribute the shock of a water landing, improving the crew's chances of survival. Many B-17s still crashed, however, while attempting to ditch, as we will see.

99th Bomb Group Flying Fortresses fly over a Roman aqueduct on their way to bomb a target in northern Italy in early 1944.

B-17s bomb the naval base at Toulon, France, during the raid flown on April 29, 1944.

None of the aircraft from the 97th Bomb Group on the February 14, 1944, mission to northern Italy dropped their bombs, but they ran into the same opposition as those other groups that did. While on the abortive bomb run, fighters attacked the 97th, making a pass on the formation. One Flying Fortress, flown by 2nd Lt. Frank Chaplick on the edge of the formation, was forced outside the formation during a turn on the bomb run. Fighters badly damaged it as the pilot struggled to get underneath the group formation to gain some semblance of cover from its massed .50-caliber machine guns. As the bomber straggled, several fighters attacked and damaged it yet again. The tail gunner, Staff Sgt. Tony Duca, had called out the first attack from six o'clock, but his turret was soon put out of out of action, as was the top turret. Duca announced over the intercom that he was dying. He was, indeed, killed. One waist gunner and the radio operator were also killed, the other waist gunner badly wounded, as was Chaplick. The oxygen system to the nose was knocked out, as was the radio, but the bombardier, 2nd Lt. Armand Sedgley, managed to salvo the bombs.

During the last attack, a lone Me 109 initially flew alongside the badly damaged bomber, then turned to attack the nose. The navigator, 2nd Lt. Thomas Cowell, and Sedgeley, who operated the remotely controlled chin turret, both fired at the fighter, and Sedgeley had the satisfaction of seeing it explode just below the nose of the Fortress. Three Thunderbolts of the escort came to the aid of the wounded Fortress, and the enemy fighters fled. The P-47s stayed with the damaged bomber for several minutes to ensure that no more attacks occurred.

With one engine feathered, another overheating, and the throttle of a third damaged, the Fortress began to head for Corsica. Chaplick later reported: "I asked the navigator for the closest route to Corsica. Had quite a time keeping the ship on course as the fighter attack shot out the trim controls. Reached Calvi Airdrome that had a very short runway and high mountains on both sides. Number one engine was smoking very badly . . . number two engine was leaking oil from 20mm holes . . . [and] number three [had] the supercharger shot out." Chaplick decided to ditch the Fortress in a bay nearby. "[The] aircraft did not break up on ditching and stayed afloat for two minutes. Crew had ample time to get out, but could not remove the bodies of the three dead men."

Lieutenant Cowell described the sensation of ditching: "When the plane hit [the water], it was a very hard jolt, and everyone was thrown around the [radio] room. The water came in and half filled the ship immediately. I climbed out on the fuselage and seeing the left dingy [was] not inflating, pulled the release valve and jumped into the water beside it. The pilot and I were paddling with our feet to get away from the fast-sinking airplane."[li] The crew then got into life rafts, and a Royal Air Force Air Sea Rescue launch fortunately picked them up within ten minutes.[lii]

Late the previous year, on the mission to bomb the submarine pens at Toulon on November 24, 1943, a Fortress from the 99th Bomb Group had the worst luck near Corsica. They had to bail out over the Mediterranean, with dire results. On the return flight to Tunisia, the pilot, 2nd Lt. Silas Adams, reported he had a runaway propeller, which may have been caused by the heavy flak

Technical Sergeant Brian La Course and 1st Lt. Robert Gettens, of the 718th Bomb Squadron, 449th Bomb Group, swim toward an Air Sea Rescue Catalina amphibious aircraft after bailing out of the stricken Liberator *Peepy*, over the Adriatic Sea, near the island of Vis on October 13, 1944. Seven of the ten-man crew fortunately survived the ordeal; many crewmen who bailed out over the Adriatic did not.

encountered at the target. Other crews heard him alert air-sea rescue on Corsica, indicating that the crew might have to bail out. The Fortress was at the rear of the 99th formation and eventually lost altitude, dropping toward the ocean with two engines smoking, one of them feathered. Six parachutes opened before the B-17 penetrated the clouds below as several other Fortresses in the formation followed them down. When the other aircraft had cleared the clouds, they spotted an oil slick containing debris from the crash of the Fortress, including an oxygen bottle and a life preserver.

Second Lieutenant Howard Blum, in one of the circling bombers, described the scene: "After we descended through the overcast and got down to the deck, we saw an oil slick, but could only find three men in the water. . . . [T]hey were either in their chutes or . . . [holding on] to them. . . . The chutes were billowing [in a stiff breeze] and dragging the men in the general direction of Corsica. One man seemed to be dead or unconscious as he appeared to be lying . . . face down in the water.

Sergeants Willis Morlan and James Latta, also crewmen from *Peepy*, climb aboard the Catalina.

Two of the circling Fortresses dropped life rafts. One landed only one hundred feet from some of the men. A water survival kit landed quite near them, too, and one crewman waved at the bombers above. One of the B-17s continued to circle the area for about twenty minutes, attempting to reach the air-sea rescue unit at Alghero, Sardinia, now occupied by the Allies, but was unsuccessful. Turning for Tunisia, they soon diverted to another Allied base at Decimannu, also on Sardinia, landed, and reported the incident. Unfortunately, none of Adams's crew was ever found.[liii]

Bad luck also plagued the crew of the Fortress nicknamed *Alamo II* of the 483rd Bomb Group when the B-17 attempted to ditch while returning from the July 15 mission to Ploesti. Flak was heavy, as always at Ploesti, and *Alamo II* lost its number two engine over the target but kept up with the formation. It lost altitude, but continued on course, then became separated from the group formation when the latter crossed the coast of Yugoslavia. Flying low over the Adriatic, *Alamo II* hit the sea twice about forty miles from the coast of Italy, then disappeared. A 483rd Fortress turned back and circled the area, calling air-sea rescue, but could not see any wreckage or crewmen in the water. Unfortunately, the entire crew was lost.[liv]

Another crew did not have the option of ditching, being forced to bail out of their stricken aircraft over the Adriatic. Some, however, had better luck than the crew of *Alamo II* and survived this perilous ordeal. They were on one of the aircraft lost on the second raid to the synthetic oil and rubber refinery located next to the infamous concentration camp complex at Oswiecim, or Auschwitz, Poland, on September 13, 1944. Their Liberator, from the 460th Bomb Group, went down over the Adriatic on the return flight home. There was no report that the ship had been hit by flak, but as it cleared the coast of Yugoslavia, the pilot, 2nd Lt. Robert Reed, told the crew to put on their parachutes and to check that their Mae West flotation gear was well fitted. Fuel was low, and it was questionable if they would reach the Italian mainland, less than one hundred miles away. As they neared the Italian coast, Reed ordered them all to bail out, and all crew members did so. Another Liberator dropped a life raft to the survivors.

Three of the crew drowned. The nose gunner, Staff Sgt. James Mund, described the ordeal of bailing out over water: "When I released my parachute after hitting the water and [had] inflated my Mae West, I noticed that it had not inflated properly. I started to swim toward a life raft which had been dropped by another B-24 when I heard Staff Sergeant [Robert] Kerns [another crewman] shouting to me. He said he had no Mae West and that I shouldn't leave him. I swam to him and he clung to me while I tried to swim. The water was very rough and we were pulled down. We tried it a second time, but again, the waves forced us down. When I finally came up again, I looked for Kerns and told him to try to swim to the raft. The rough water separated us and when next I looked toward him, he had disappeared."[lv]

Mund managed to reach the raft but was too weak from his exertions to climb in. He hung on to the sides until some Italian fishermen picked him up. He was the last to be rescued, as the other surviving crew members were already on the fishing boat. Two more crewmen drowned.

The original crew of *Alamo II*. Back row of photo, left to right: the maintenance crew chief, Master Sgt. Joseph Sinnet (not a member of the aircrew); Lt. Victor Vlahovich, pilot—KIA; Lt. Michael Bellonio, copilot—KIA; Lt. Edward Gusicora, navigator—KIA; Lt. Arthur Ryan, bombardier—KIA; and Sgt. William Sloan, also a ground mechanic. Bottom row of photo: Staff Sgt. Steven Barton, tail gunner—KIA; Tech. Sgt. Bernard Fletcher, radio operator—KIA; Tech. Sgt. Charles Navarro, flight engineer—KIA; Staff Sgt. Alfred Van Deren, waist gunner—KIA; Staff Sgt. Jack Tuckman, waist gunner (not on the last flight); and Staff Sergeant Szteligo, ball-turret gunner (also not on the last flight).

A/C OUTSTANDING OR IN DISTRESS

INIT	TYPE	A/C NO	PILOT CREW	STATUS OF A/C CREW	POSITION OR BEARING	DATE TIME	REMARKS
231	WELL		BLYTH	LOST	CRASHED NEAR VOSTO		
231	WELL		SMITH	LOST	CRASHED NEAR PESCA		
2	B-17	490	STUCKEY	MISSING			
463		106	WATSON	LOST	CRASHED		10 CHUTES
		861	RHOADES	LOST	BLEW UP		
91		354	TONKOVICH	LOST	BLEW UP?		
		166	KNOBLOCK	LOST			
		648	WATERS	LOST			
		265	REARDON	LOST	MAY HAVE DITCHED		
		274	SHELTON	LOST			
483		412	ROBSON	MISSING			
		349	CONDRISKI	MISSING			
450	B-24	748	PATTERSON	MISSING			
		293	CHUBB	MISSING			
460		363	REE	LOST	DITCHED		8 SAFE
		487	CEQUIENOR	MISSING			
465		408	WEEGONER	MISSING	HEADED FOR RUSSIA		
		543	Col. CLARK	MISSING			
		123	AGNES	MISSING	HEADED FOR VIS		
		320	COCKRAN	MISSING			
		977	FISHBACK	MISSING	LAST SEEN TGT AREA		

SEE OTHER PHOTO

13 SEPT

The operations chalkboard maintained at Fifteenth Air Force headquarters to track lost and missing aircraft for September 13, 1944. Lieutenant Reed's aircraft is listed, with his name misspelled and the notation that eight of the crew survived. *US Air Force*

One was found dead in the water; the other was never found.

Seven of the surviving crewmen continued their combat tour and were shot down on November 18, during a mission to Udine, Italy. Flak hit their Liberator, *Yellow C for Charlie*, over the target, damaging two engines, and gas began streaming from a wing. The bombs in the bomb bay became stuck and would not drop. The Liberator temporarily left the formation but returned as the group crossed the coast and flew over the Adriatic. Within minutes, however, it turned east toward Yugoslavia, sparing the crew the perils of the sea a second time. The crew all bailed out over that country, near Lubiana. Four survivors of the September ordeal were taken prisoner, along with two replacement crew members. The pilot, copilot, navigator, and two gunners evaded capture and within a few days had reached a British mission to the Partisans. They traveled to Zara, on the coast, by early December and returned by ship to Italy early in the month.[lvi]

A similar mixed fate awaited the crew of the 97th Bomb Group Fortress flown by 2nd Lt. Eugene Sabelmann only a few weeks before the war ended. Flak hit the aircraft over an Italian bridge on April 6, 1945, and they lost an engine. The crew continued on the bomb run and dropped their bombs, but after bombs away, more flak bursts hit the Fortress, knocking out two more engines and leaving a large hole in the wing. The stricken aircraft now had only one engine. They flew on with this single engine for two hours, slowly losing altitude and dodging occasional flak, yet another example of the sturdiness and reliability of the B-17. As they passed near Venice, a flak barrage greeted them but fortunately did no more damage to the aircraft. The crew then headed for an emergency field near the town of Rimini on the east coast of Italy. They could not reach it with only one engine, however, and eventually had to ditch in the sea about twenty-five miles from Rimini. Despite extremely heavy seas, with waves towering up to forty feet high, Sabelmann made an excellent ditching, landing in a trough between waves. As the Fortress hit the water, the fuselage broke in two where the ball turret was located, forcing the nose into the water. All on board were severely stunned, and water quickly filled the cockpit. Sablemann climbed out the cockpit window by grasping the barrels of the guns on the top turret and moved down the fuselage. He released the two life rafts, but one that popped out on the right side of the aircraft was damaged by flak. The other, however, was seaworthy, but without the usual line tethering it to the Flying Fortress. Sabelman yelled to the crew, through the open radio room hatch, to get on the left wing, rather than the right wing as they had been trained, so they could use the only serviceable raft. He then got on the wing and jumped in the water and swam to it. He saw the rest of the crew exit the plane, but two crewmen, flight engineer Staff Sergeant Shockey and radio operator Sgt. Elmer Greene, went out on the right wing, as they had been trained, and were swept into the water as the wing submerged. The remaining crewmen joined Sabelmann in the raft, and they paddled in the direction of the two missing crewmen. The immense seas and strong wind took the two men away from the raft and they eventually drowned, their bodies later picked up by a British air sea rescue launch.

Soon two RAF Spitfires flew overhead and spotted the raft. About forty-five minutes later a PBY flying boat appeared and, following the prompting of the men in the raft, dropped another raft several miles away, where the two lost crewmen had drifted. The weather prevented the flying boat from landing, but an air sea rescue launch eventually picked them up about twelve hours later. Given dry clothes, they later arrived at Ancona, where they found the bodies of their drowned comrades, already recovered. After a few days in a hospital, all but one, injured in the ditching, returned to their group.[lvii]

Opposite page: Two 465th B-24s over the city of Ferrara during a mission to bomb the marshalling yards in the city on June 5, 1944.

Below: The Fifteenth Air Force headquarters chalkboard for April 6, 1945, listing Lieutenant Sableman's ditched Fortress as lost. The crew was fortunate that eight of them survived, as noted on the board. *US Air Force*

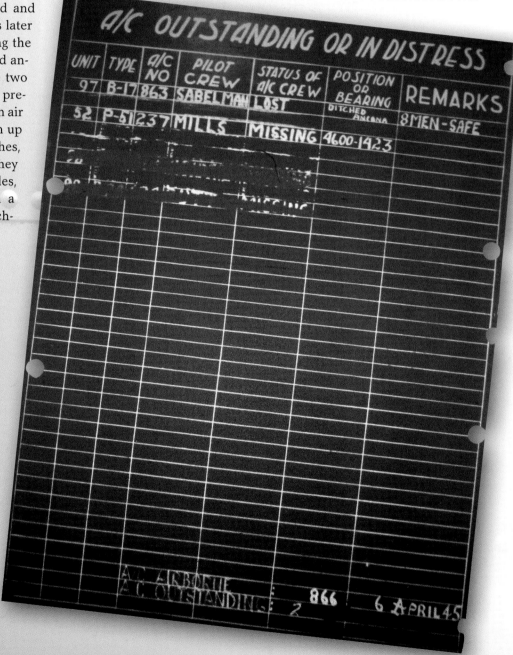

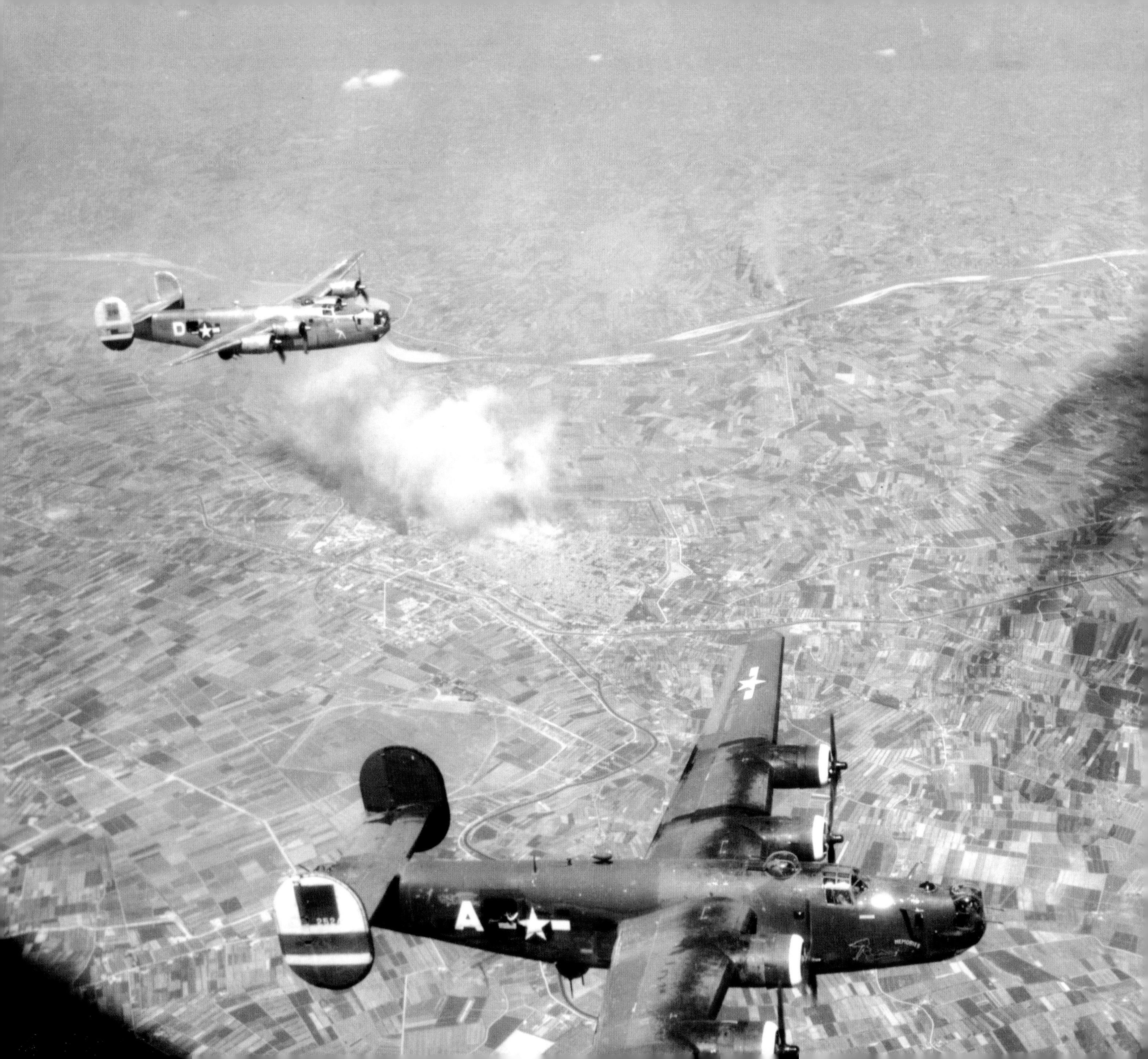
D
A

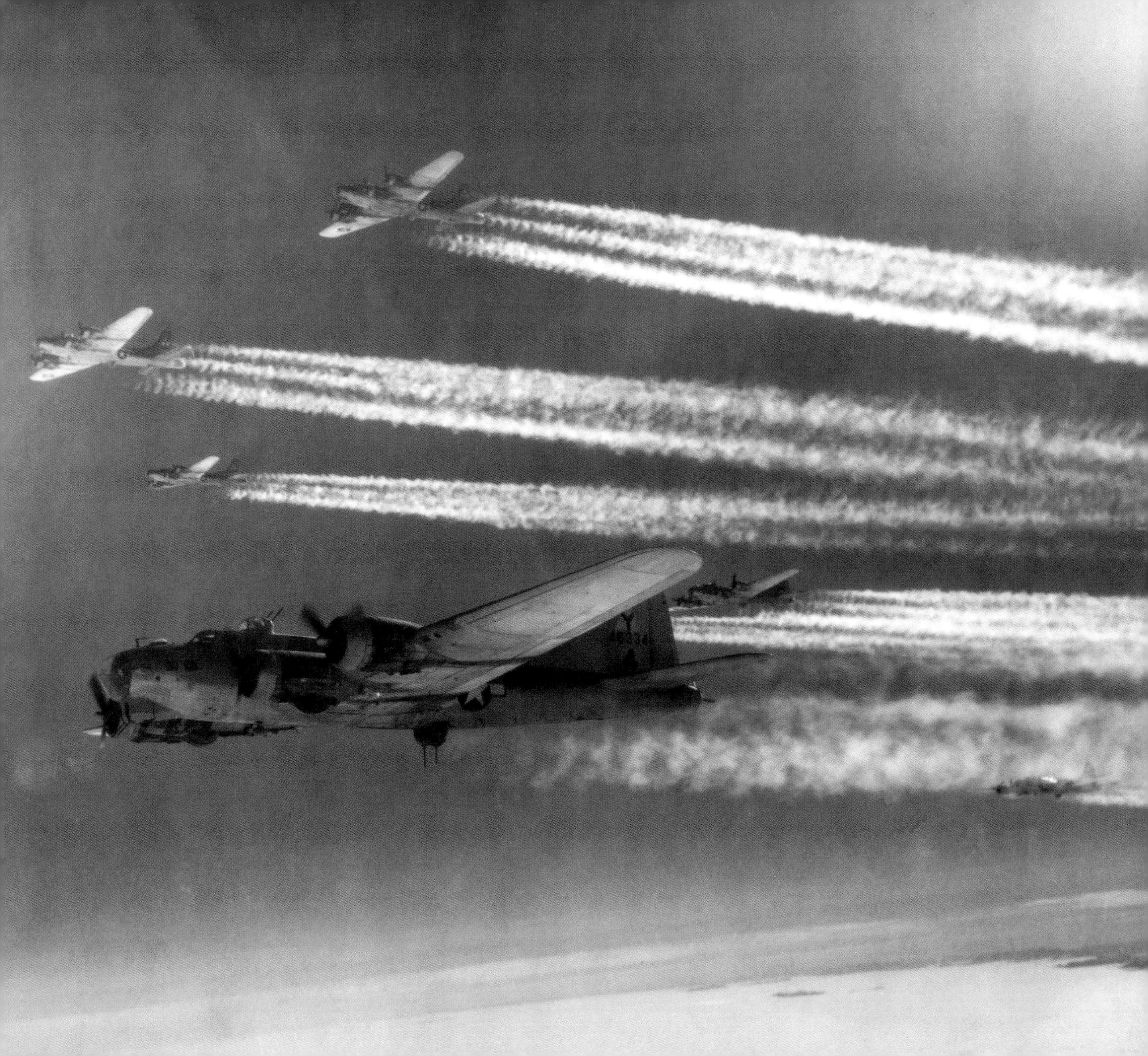

CHAPTER 7

BEHIND RUSSIAN LINES

As we have already seen in chapter 3, beginning in the fall of 1944, some crews of flak-damaged bombers had the option of evading capture by flying to Russian lines. Soviet forces had captured Romania and Bulgaria in the summer, liberated Belgrade with Yugoslav Partisan forces in October, and reached the gates of Budapest, Hungary, by November. Further north, the Soviet Army had retaken half of Poland and portions of Slovakia. This gave the crews of damaged bombers a new alternative to imprisonment by the Germans.

Opposite page: Fortresses of the 414th Bomb Squadron, 97th Bomb Group, leave contrails behind on the way to bomb marshalling yards in Vienna, Austria, on January 15, 1945.

During the mission to bomb the synthetic refineries at Odertal, Germany, on October 14, 1944, one of the three Liberators that failed to return to base from the 455th Bomb Group managed to reach Russian lines instead. Over the target, flak hit Liberator 42-78359, flown by 2nd Lt. John Polando, in the number four engine. The damaged prevented him from feathering the engine, and the resultant drag on the plane's performance caused it to lose altitude and veer from the group formation. At lower altitude, Polando was reluctant to return to the group because of the possibility of being hit by falling bombs from aircraft overhead. He continued to move out of the formation until they had left the flak barrage, only to find that they had lost too much altitude and lacked the speed to regain their position with the group. Polando decided to head for Russian lines, whose location was reported to crews at the briefing for each mission. They headed east and, after catching some flak as they passed over the front line, began to look for a place to land while continuing to lose altitude. Spotting a Russian-held fighter airfield about fifteen miles northeast of the Polish city of Krakow, they flew over the field with wheels extended, to identify themselves to the Russian troops below. The latter responded by shooting a flare, and the aircraft made a safe landing. They were immediately surrounded by Russian soldiers and then held at the base for about two weeks, under guard, although they were all allowed to keep their pistols. The Russians kept them away from the local people, and they slept in the headquarters. After two weeks at this base, a Russian C-47 landed and flew them to Lvov, then on to the American base at Poltava. Five days later, half the crew returned to Italy in an American aircraft while the others, including the pilots, remained in Poltava to fly another Liberator home. Another crew ended up flying this ship to Italy, so Polando returned to the fighter strip and retrieved his own aircraft, repaired in the meantime, and flew it to Poltava on November 21. After undergoing a complete overhaul by the American ground crews at the base, it was ready to return to Italy, but Polando needed a Russian navigator and radio operator, as his own had returned to Italy in early November. These arrived by mid-December, and the B-24 was flown to Teheran, Iran, where the two Russians were replaced by Americans and the plane continued on to Cairo; Benghazi, Libya; and finally San Giovanni on December 20, from which they had set on out their odyssey on October 14.[lviii]

A Fortress of the 2nd Bomb Group was not as lucky after it ran into trouble at the initial point during the attack on the southern oil refinery at Blechhammer on December 26, 1944. Flak hit it badly, just before the bombs dropped, so badly that the crews of other aircraft said the B-17 appeared to stop momentarily, in midair. Another bomber almost collided with it. One burst slightly wounded the copilot, 1st Lt. James McHood, while a second hit him much more seriously, shattering his leg. The flak also knocked out one engine, shot out the automatic pilot, and shattered the Plexiglas in the nose, damaging the bomb sight only seconds before bombs away. The number one engine also began running badly. The bombardier, Capt. William Underhill, waited about twenty seconds until he thought they were at the bomb release point and salvoed the bombs over the refinery. He then went to the cockpit and, with the flight engineer, moved McHood to the catwalk in the bomb bay, whose doors he had already closed. Underhill then returned to the cockpit as they entered another flak-box barrage, but although nearby blasts rocked the plane, it was fortunately not hit again. When they had passed through the second barrage, the pilot, Maj. George Redden, was able to feather the damaged engines, and the Fortress maintained an altitude of about eighteen thousand feet. The tail gunner, 2nd Lt. Sol Azur, an observer on the mission, came up to the cockpit to take over the copilot's seat, while Underhill returned to aid the copilot.

Opposite page: The synthetic oil refinery at Odertal under attack on October 14, 1944, during the mission on which Lieutenant Polando's Liberator landed in Poland. The white smoke streams are from German smoke generators used to cover the refinery during bombing raids.

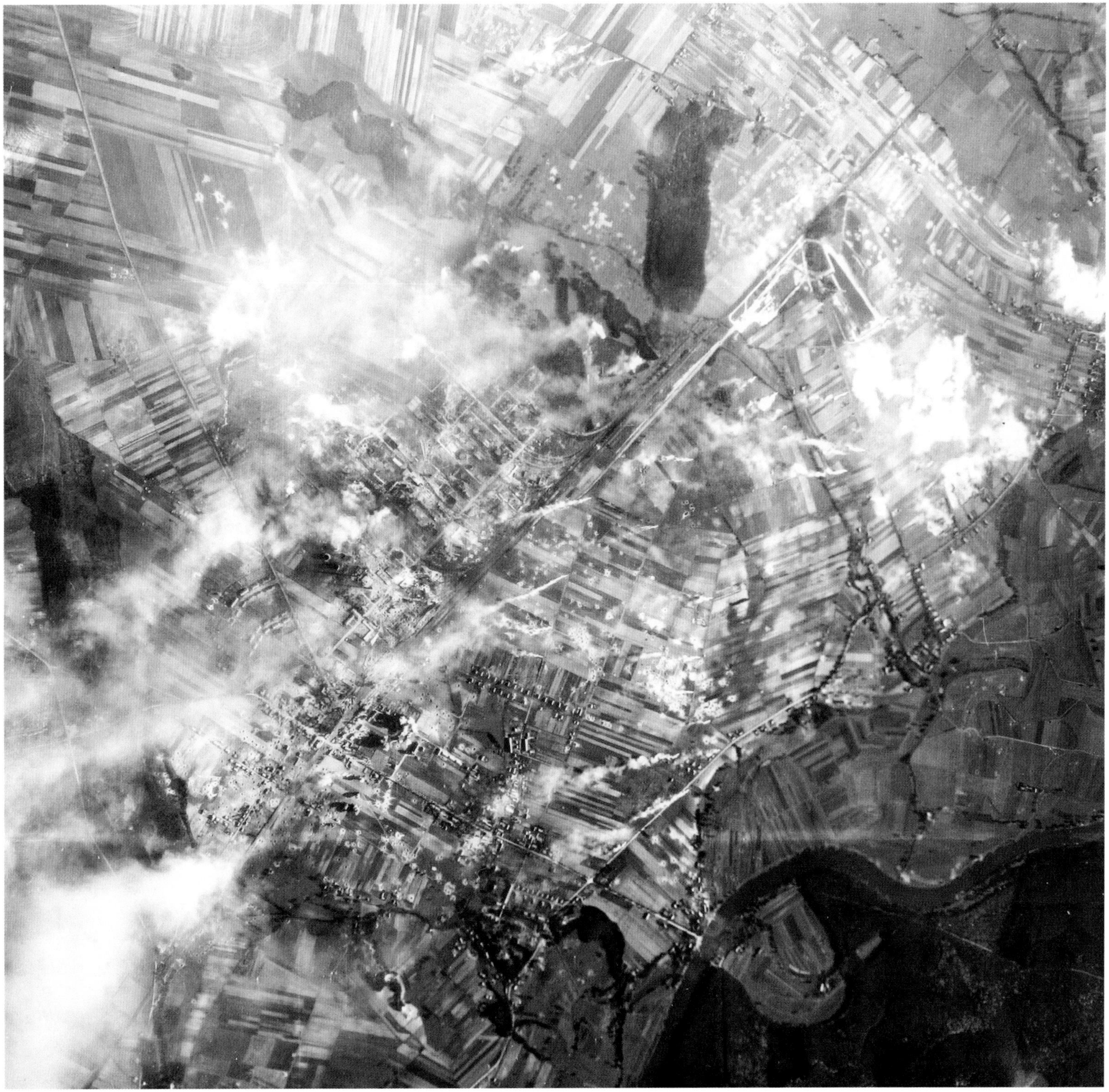

The Fortress headed east toward Russian lines and eventually flew over the town of Zesco and landed on a Russian airstrip, firing red flares to signal a wounded man on board. In their report of the flight, the crew reported: "We made a beautiful crash landing that was comparatively smooth. . . . We climbed out the plane and were at once surrounded by Polish and Russian soldiers. We then chopped the nose of the plane off and removed Lieutenant McHood, whom the Russians immediately rushed to a field hospital. . . . We were given supper."

At the hospital, McHood's shattered leg was amputated. The Russians quartered the other crewmen in houses in the town. After checking on McHood at the hospital, they were driven on December 28 to a small airfield, where they lived in a dugout with the crew of a B-24 that had also landed in the area until December 30, when a C-47 arrived. The wounded and about half the crewmen flew to Poltava, while the others waited until January 5, when they too reached Poltava. Flying to Teheran the next day, they returned to Italy through Cairo, arriving back in Italy on January 11.[lix]

Two crewmen from a 465th Bomb Group Liberator that crash-landed at Poltava, Russia, in early January 1945 stand by the aircraft.

Another 2nd Bomb Group Fortress, nicknamed *Old Bird,* that failed to return from a mission the month before Major Redden's B-17 crash-landed in Poland.

The crew of another 2nd Bomb Group B-17 was even less fortunate, when flak damage forced them to bail out of their stricken aircraft between German and Russian lines. Flak hit Fortress number 44-6689 from the 2nd Bomb Group, flown by 1st Lt. Eugene Bull, on mission to Vienna on February 21. After bombs away, a flak burst made a large hole in the wing, behind an engine, and cut the fuel lines to two engines. More flak damaged an aileron and blew away part of the

The 483rd Bomb Group Flying Fortress nicknamed *My Rose* goes down in flames from flak damage during the March 22, 1945, raid on the oil refinery at Ruhland, Germany. All crew members perished.

rudder and tail, wounding the tail gunner. The radio was also shot out. Pieces of the wing broke off as Bull flew the Fortress east, attempting to reach the Russian airfield at Kecskemet, Hungary. As they neared the front line, the crew noticed four fighters and, believing them to be Russian, fired flares and lowered their wheels to signal them. Unfortunately, the four fighters were Me 109s that patrolled the area, looking for damaged American bombers trying to reach Russian lines. They immediately attacked, hitting the flight deck and badly damaging it and the rear of the plane, wounding the waist gunners. Seeing that the Fortress couldn't remain in the air with such damage, Lieutenant Bull told the flight engineer to go to the rear of the aircraft and tell the crewmen there to bail out. They did so, jumping before those in the front of the Fortress, and landed behind German lines. The enemy fighters strafed these crewmen as they were descending; the tail gunner was shot again and later died in a German hospital.

Bull, copilot 2nd Lt. Harold Frazer, bombardier 2nd Lt. Robert C. Krejsa, and navigator 2nd Lt. John Specker jumped a few minutes later, and this delay made all the difference, as they landed quite near the Russian front line. Enemy fighters and German troops on the ground also shot at them in their chutes during their descent. Frazier recalled:

> I jumped . . . with my boots in hand . . . and I delayed opening my chute for about 2,500 feet, not wishing to have the fighters continue to fire on me. As I pulled the rip cord, I realized I did not have the leg straps harnessed. I hung on the lines with my hands to keep from slipping through. Looking up, I saw the four fighters were still firing at our plane. Bullets were whistling around my head, though looking down I could see no one firing at me. Evidently they were hiding; there were about fifteen holes in my chute and shroud lines.

As the ground came closer, some Stormoviks [sic] [Russian light bombers] whizzed by going after the Messerschmitts. When I was [at] about 1,500 feet, I saw our plane circling about a small wooded area, and finally crash.

Landing, I got out of my chute okay and started east . . . after twenty minutes a Russian horseman came across a field firing a pistol at me. I hollered "Americanski" and he stopped, dismounted, and came to about fifty feet from me. "Amerikanski" he quizzed. "Amerikanski," I affirmed. Looking over to the left, I saw a group of young fellows crowded around a machine gun. The Russian asked me for my pistol, so unzipping my pocket, I pointed to it. He took the pistol but did not search me.

Lieutenant Bull had an even more exciting landing:

> Due to the swiftness of my descent, I landed stiff as a board. Partly paralyzed, I rolled out of my chute. There were two Germans coming at me, so I pulled out my .45 [pistol]. They then ducked and I took off on a run toward the east. Hiding in corn shock, I saw a woods, and was undecided whether to head for it or remain in the corn shock. Suddenly, I saw a group of men who I thought were farmers. Looking closer, I saw they were armed and appeared to be drawing a bead on me. I dropped to the ground and hollered "Amerikanski." They waved me away from them and pointed to the north. After a while, I realized they were covering me from the Germans. A few yards further on, I came upon some Russians who haled me and stripped me of my watch and gun.

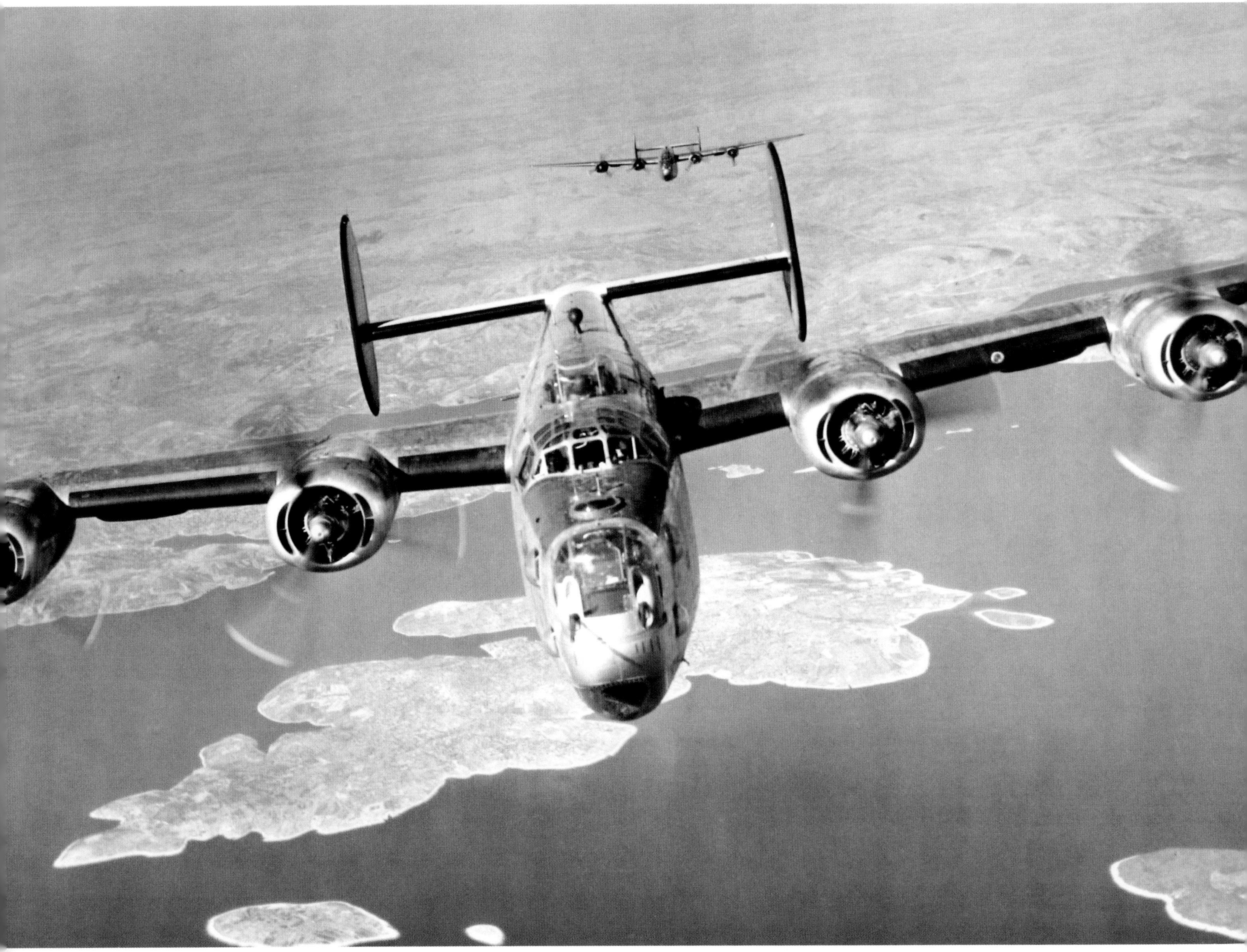

The pistol was returned at a local command post where Lieutenant Frazier soon joined Bull.

Lieutenant Specker had to pull his chute out of the pack after he jumped:

> I pulled the rip cord and the chute did not open. So I tore it open and pulled the silk out . . . then the chute opened. After the chute opened, I looked up and saw Kresja above me. At the same time, the Mes [Messerschmitts] started strafing us in the chutes. One hit me in the upper thigh and [it] went all the way through. The troops on the ground were also shooting at us. When I landed, I was very near the German lines. [As] I couldn't walk . . . I laid there near some bushes for an hour or two while bullets whizzed over my head. [Then] a Russian patrol picked me up and took me to a farmhouse where a field doctor gave me hypodermic injections and bandaged the leg.

After this rudimentary first aid, he ended up with the other crewmen at the Russian command post.

Lieutenant Krejsa was the last to bail out of the nose. An Me 109 also strafed him during his descent but fortunately only hit his parachute canopy. "After the 109s stopped shooting at me, the Germans from the ground kept shooting away at me. I hit the ground pretty hard and I laid in the mud for about fifteen minutes before I started walking toward the east. After walking about three-quarters of a mile, I was met by a Russian patrol. . . . I had to identify myself, which I did by calling out 'Amerikanski.' The Russians took my identification card. From here I walked about four miles" to the Russian command post, where he was reunited with the three other crewmen at the headquarters.

Over the next two and a half weeks, the crew stayed in several Hungarian towns until they finally reached the American mission at Debrecen, and in mid-March they flew to Italy. The four crewmen who became prisoners survived and were liberated that spring.[lx]

Opposite page: B-24 Liberators leave the marshalling yards at Mühldorf, Austria, after a bombing mission on March 19, 1945.

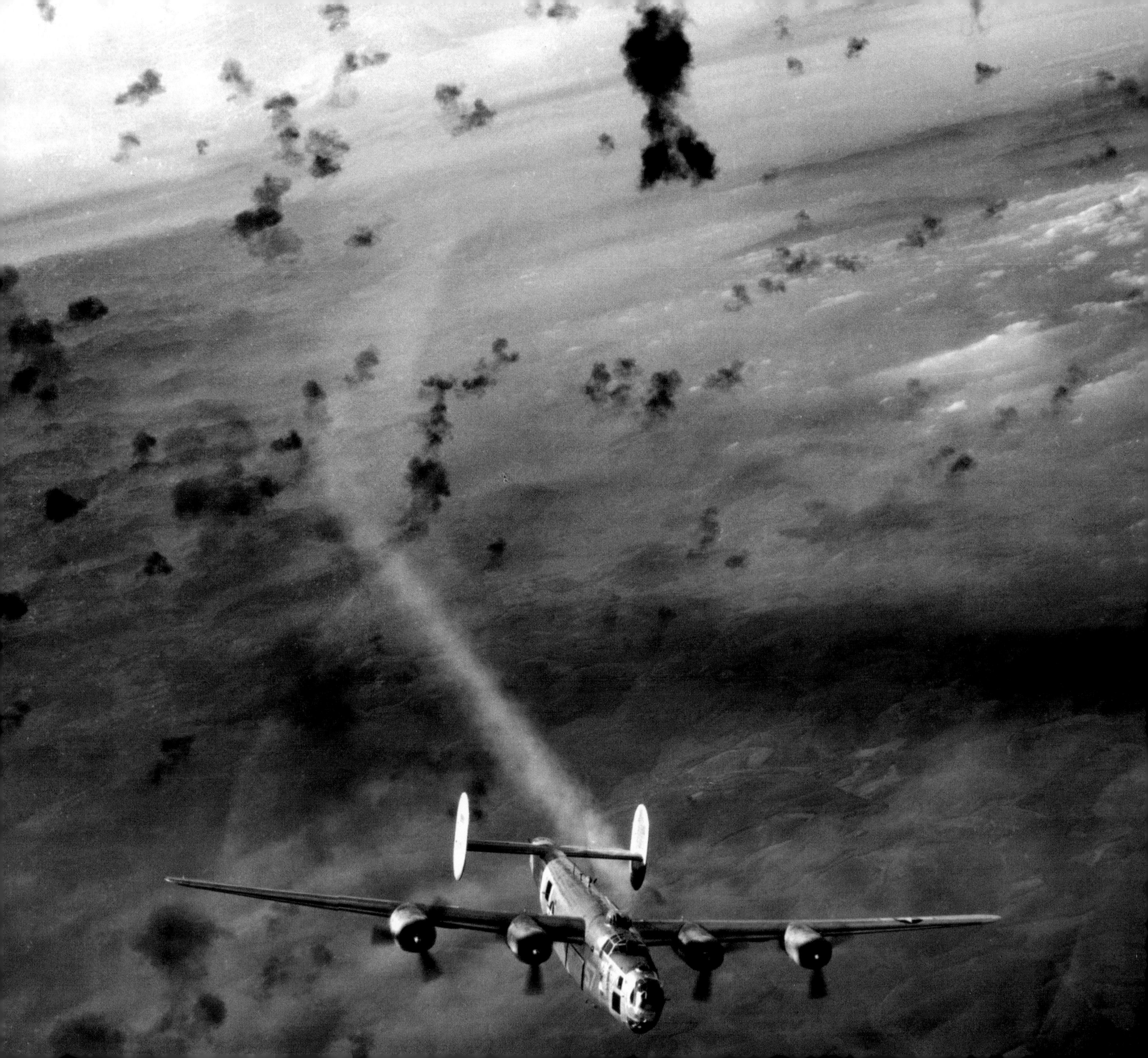

CHAPTER 8
SAFE AT BASE

Not all severely damaged aircraft were lost behind enemy lines. Some managed, through the perseverance of the crews, to return home. One such crew flew a 459th Bomb Group Liberator to base after they ran into trouble during the raid on the marshalling yards at Bucharest on April 4, 1944. During the first fighter pass by almost twenty German fighters, as the group neared the initial point, cannon fire hit one engine of the B-24 flown by Lt. Thomas Kennedy and the bomber immediately lost airspeed. It began to straggle from the group's formation just as two fighters attacked from the rear. Their combined cannon and machine-gun fire damaged the tail, including the turret and control surfaces. The tail gunner, Sgt. William Lewis, claimed one of the Me 109s as destroyed, but cannon fire from the second blew him out of his turret, all the way up to the waist gun positions farther down the fuselage, unconscious. One of the waist gunners was slightly wounded during the attack in which the nose turret gunner destroyed a fighter.

Opposite page: The 451st Bomb Group B-24 nicknamed *Betty Coed* flies over Vienna with an engine damaged by flak during the October 13, 1944, raid on the city. The aircraft returned safely to base.

The damage inflicted on *Sweet Pea* of the 2nd Bomb Group when flak bracketed the bomber during a raid on the Hungarian city of Debrecen on September 21, 1944. The blast from an eighty-eight-millimeter round nearly blew the plane in half, killing two crew members, wounding more, and trapping the ball-turret gunner in his turret. With wounded men aboard, the pilot, Lt. Guy Miller, decided to attempt to return to base, although most controls were shot away. The aircraft held together until he successfully landed at base, then sagged to the tarmac during the landing.

Enemy fire also damaged the nose and top turrets, one round penetrating the latter just where the gunner's head would normally be in action. Fortunately for the flight engineer who manned the gun, Sgt. George Lawson, he was in the cockpit at the time, handing the pilot a screwdriver for adjustment of the turbocharger control to increase speed. This slug continued on through the instrument panel into the nose, hitting the back of the flak jacket of the bombardier, Lt. Peter Rebich, who, fortunately uninjured, dropped the bombs.

With the bombs gone, the straggling Liberator turned for home with only the waist guns still in action. An Me 110 followed this apparently easy kill and attempted to finish them off. The waist gunner, Sgt. Everett Ruhl, however, kept him at bay, preventing him from turning in to attack and eventually hitting what may have been a rocket under his wing, as the fighter's right wing blew off and it spun to the ground.

Kennedy radioed for fighter escort, but three Liberators from another group suddenly appeared and escorted them until they had almost reached Yugoslavia. With increased drag from the damaged engine slowing them down and increasing gas consumption, Kennedy gradually lost altitude to stretch out their flight time and save fuel. Once over the Adriatic, the crew threw everything possible out of the Liberator, including the guns and their flak suits, to lighten the

A B-24D over the city of Bucharest, Romania, during the bombing raid of April 4, 1944, during which Lieutenant Kennedy's crew, from the 459th Bomb Group, barely managed to make it home.

plane and save fuel. They could not contact the field at Bari by radio and were forced to make a landing nonetheless. Forcing a C-47 out of its landing slot on their approach, they couldn't get their wheels down or the flaps to work as the hydraulic system that operated both had been shot out, so the bomber crash-landed on the strip. Kennedy feathered the three working engines just as they hit the ground, and the propeller from the damaged engine flew off. The crew scrambled out when the plane came to a halt. Ground crews later counted 389 holes in the Liberator, which was a total loss.[lxi]

The trio from Lieutenant Snyder's crew, mentioned in chapter 3, was certainly not the only bomber crew to return safely to Italy after severe damage led others to abandon their aircraft over enemy territory. The men who jumped had good reason to do so in such circumstances, as any delay could cost them their lives. In some cases, however, some crewmen found the aircraft flyable before they jumped and managed to fly back to base or Allied lines.

Another bomber literally lost an engine to flak, yet it still managed to return to base after radar-directed flak holed the aircraft during a mission to Vienna on July 16, 1944. During the mission, cloud cover forced some aircraft, including a 97th Bomb Group Fortress flown by 1st Lt. Kenneth Gallagher, to bomb marshalling yards instead of the assigned target, the Winterhaven Oil Depot. Just after bombs away, his aircraft ran into a radar-directed flak barrage that lasted almost ten minutes.

The oil pressure, required to feather the propeller, dropped too quickly for feathering to be possible, and the resultant "windmilling" of the propellers dropped the airspeed of the Fortress. After a few minutes, the left outboard engine ran out of control when the governor stopped working. It also began to windmill in the slipstream, further slowing the aircraft.

After applying more throttle to the inner two engines, Gallagher told his crewmates to lighten the plane by jettisoning equipment. Among the items discarded were their flak suits and, later, the machine guns. The radio operator, Staff Sgt. Victor DeMonte, later remarked, "I hope one of

Opposite page top: The bombardier of a damaged Flying Fortress took this photo of a damaged engine with a feathered propeller, June 1944.

Opposite page bottom: A 451st Bomb Group Liberator, *Tings is Tuff* makes a crash-landing at base after damage during one of the final missions to Ploesti on August 17, 1944.

Right: A 460th Bomb Group B-24 flying over the Adriatic with a smoking engine after flak damaged it over Bucharest, Romania, on April 25, 1944.

Below right: A flak-damaged 98th Bomb Group Liberator on the mission of April 24, 1944, to Ploesti managed to make it back to Italy, but crash-landed and buried its nose in the ground.

dio operator, Staff Sgt. Victor DeMonte, later remarked, "I hope one of them hit some Kraut on the head." To make matters worse, the cowling of the right outboard came apart and parts flew off the engine, causing the airplane to vibrate badly. Within seconds, however, the propeller sheared off the engine and flew into space, and the vibration stopped.

The Fortress had dropped to eleven thousand feet by this time as it continued to lose altitude, and the prospect of flying over the fifteen-thousand-foot-high Alps appeared daunting. The navigator, 2nd Lt. William Young, plotted a course down a mountain valley, and they eventually reached the Adriatic Sea, where their bomber continued to lose altitude. The crew dropped the ball turret from the plane over the sea, so the slipstream drew oil leaking from the engines into the rear of the fuselage. Despite these trials, the crew soon arrived at their base at Amendola, and Gallagher made a good landing.[lxii]

Another bomber, very badly hit by flak, had managed to return to base only a few days earlier. Flak hit the 483rd Bomb Group Fortress, flown by 1st Lt. Robert Goesling, as the bombardier, Lt. Robert Johnston, was about to drop their bombs during the raid on the shell oil refinery in Budapest on July 14. Flak hit the bomb bay and shot one door away, so two of the bombs wouldn't drop from the bay. To make matters worse, part of the controls were shot away. The navigator, radio operator, and right waist gunner were wounded, and the copilot, 2nd Lt. Homer Abbott, flew the plane while Goesling administered first aid to the navigator. The wounded radio operator had to be pulled from a hole in the floor of the radio compartment made by the explosion. Technical Sergeant George Freitag, the flight engineer, and Staff Sgt. Leo Dane, a waist gunner, both went to the bomb bay where a fire was raging. Using extinguishers, they managed to put it out.

Lieutenant Johnston tried to salvo the remaining bombs, but they wouldn't budge. With the fire in the bomb bay out, he entered it and spent forty-five minutes, with the assistance of ball-turret gunner Staff Sgt. Richard Warner, removing the fuses of the remaining bombs. When this task was completed, he used a screwdriver on the manual bomb release and managed to dislodge the bombs.

As the Fortress reached the Adriatic Sea, one engine failed as it ran out gas. Flak had also shot away the fuel-transfer system, so fuel from tanks for other engines could not be transferred to

Left: The 483rd Bomb Group Fortress *Mizpah* after a direct flak hit blew off the nose of the aircraft over Budapest on July 14, 1944, killing the navigator and bombardier. Incredibly, eight of the crew managed to bail out and become prisoners of war.

Opposite page top: Ground crewmen repair an engine damaged by flak. They worked completely outdoors, in the blistering heat of Italian summers and bitter cold of the winters to keep Fifteenth Air Force planes in the air. The Fifteenth's air campaign could not have taken place without them.

Opposite page bottom: A 99th Bomb Group B-17, nicknamed *Hammerhead*, makes an emergency landing at base in the early fall of 1944, after flak damaged the aircraft's brakes, instrument panel, and electrical system. The crew deployed a parachute from the tail gunner's turret to slow the plane during landing. This aircraft was shot down in November 1944, but fortunately the entire crew survived to become prisoners of war.

loose equipment to lighten the ship. This succeeded, and they were able to maintain altitude and reach a field in Italy.

Preparing to land, they discovered the flaps inoperable and the rear tire flat. As the controls were only partially operable, a successful landing was problematic. To slow the aircraft, the crew clipped parachutes to the waist-gun positions and pulled the ripcords when the plane landed. One of them opened, but the second had to be deployed by hand. Goesling still made a safe landing. Ground crewmen counted more than thirty thousand holes of various sizes in the Fortress, and all the crew members received well-deserved Silver Stars.[lxiii]

The crew of a third Fortress also returned home after flak damage made the prospects of doing so bleak, so much so that the pilot initially told the crew to bail out. A damaged intercom prevented crewmen in the rear from getting the word, however, and events transpired that allowed the pilot to stay with the aircraft to bring it, and them, home. On the 5th Bomb Wing mission to bomb the marshalling yards at St. Etiennne, France, on May 26, 1944, several flak rounds hit a 2nd Bomb Group Fortress, damaged the oxygen system, and started a fire that soon spread to the cockpit. The B-17 turned for home, flying at lower altitude so the crew could survive without the oxygen system. The ammunition in the top turret began to explode, and the fire became so intense that the copilot, 2nd Lt. Earl Rodenburg, asked the pilot, 2nd Lt.

B-17s of the 99th Bomb Group head for home after their bomb run on the oil refinery at Sète, France, on June 25, 1944.

Bombs fall in front of a 483rd Bomb Group B-17 as they plummet toward the smoke screen covering the oil refineries at Ploesti, Romania, on July 15, 1944.

Frederick Tompkins, if they should bail out. After attempts to put out the fire were unsuccessful, Tompkins told them to do so, and Rodenburg, the bombardier, navigator 2nd Lt. Fred Letz, and flight engineer Staff Sgt. Harold Bolick all bailed out. Tompkins headed the plane for Corsica, but with the intercom burned out by the fire, he couldn't contact the remaining crewman—the gunners and radioman in the rear. He put the Fortress on autopilot, opened the cockpit windows, and threw out anything that could still burn. The smoke was so thick that he disconnected his oxygen mask and put the hose out the cockpit window so he could breathe. Soot covered the windows from exploding ammunition, and Tompkins could only see outside the B-17 by putting his head out the window. Over the Mediterranean, he attempted to radio Corsica and found that he could contact the radio operator, Staff Sgt. Elmer Cutsinger. He learned that the men in the rear had stayed with the airplane. The tail gunner, Sgt. Joseph Jordan, had seen parachutes open as the other crewmen had jumped and, although he had no idea what had happened, stayed in his turret.

He then came forward and, using a fire extinguisher and canteen, put out some of the fire, joining Tompkins in the cockpit. Cutsinger also fashioned an intercom using the radio transmitter that allowed Tompkins to contact all the remaining crewmen.

The fire burned itself out when they were only minutes away from Corsica. Tompkins came in for an emergency landing, without brakes as the hydraulic system was burned out. To stop the plane from hitting a ditch, he had to ground-loop the Fortress, but all the men still in the craft got out safely.

Of the crewmen who bailed out, the bombardier was killed in the jump; the pilot chute of his parachute may have caught on the escape hatch door and the chute not opened properly. The other three landed safely, just inside the Italian border. Lieutenant Rodenburg was taken prisoner soon after landing, while Italian civilians aided Letz and Bolick. Both remained with Partisan units for several months, eventually joining a British special-operations unit that parachuted into the area to work with the Partisans after the invasion of southern France. Letz and Bolick became separated when German units moved into their area to eliminate the Partisans, and Letz was subsequently captured, remaining a prisoner of war until liberated

in May 1945. Bolick fought with Italian Partisans until late April 1945, when he contacted American forces as they took the city of Genoa.[lxiv]

Another Liberator that did not succumb to flak damage and returned to base a few months later also had a difficult time doing so. On what should have been a relatively safe mission, in comparison to missions to targets in Germany and Austria, flak hit Liberator 42-51888 of the 376th Bomb Group after it had released its bombs on the marshalling yards at Nis, Yugoslavia, on September 8, 1944. The plane began to dive, and the number three engine began to run wild and was feathered, but the pilot, 1st Lt. Franklin Christianson, managed to pull out of the dive. Flak hits had started a fire on the flight deck, and the flight engineer, Tech. Sgt. John Greene, put the fire out with his hands after a fire extinguisher proved ineffective. He then bailed out of the damaged Liberator.

At the same time, the ball-turret gunner, Staff Sgt. George Cabral, put out a fire in an ammunition box in his turret, then came up to the cockpit to report to the pilot that everything was under control in the rear of the Fortress. He next went down into the nose of the aircraft to check on three crewmen stationed there: the bombardier, navigator, and nose gunner. He found the nose empty as all had bailed out, too. Returning to the cockpit, he saw another fire had started there and put it out as well, then put out yet another fire in a flare box. At the same time, he also dressed wounds of the pilot.

Gasoline was leaking from a bomb-bay gas tank, so the bay doors were left open for much of the return flight. They had lost altitude but could still climb above the mountains of Yugoslavia by flying with the automatic pilot as the crew jettisoned equipment. The copilot, 1st Lt. John Griffin, used the navigator's maps to plot a course home. Flak bursts had knocked out the radio, so they couldn't tell their base their plight—nor, because of the gas leaks, could they signal with flares that they had wounded aboard.

As they neared their home field at San Pancrazio, Christianson later recalled, "the radio was out and we did not dare shoot flares because of the danger of fire. The copilot and I changed seats because of my leg. I didn't think I could handle the brakes. . . . [W]hen we were circling the field to land, we made a long approach. . . . The auxiliary hydraulic pump was used to get the main landing gears down. Upon landing, the copilot . . . [hit] the brakes and I hit the crash bar. . . . Landing was successful."[lxv]

All the crew were wounded, none seriously, and were taken to the hospital. An inspection of number 42-51888 after it landed revealed that the rudder controls had been shot away, the bomb bay fuel tanks were leaking gasoline, the number three engine and the oxygen system were shot out, and all the ammunition in the ball turret had exploded.

The nose gunner, Staff Sgt. William Trezise, and Technical Sergeant Greene were able evade capture, returning to Italy about a month later. The navigator and bombardier were taken prisoner and held until liberated in the spring of 1945. Partisans mistakenly reported one of them as killed in his chute.[lxvi]

Earlier in the year, none of 2nd Lt. Leo Fletcher's crew had to walk back to Allied lines after flak got them on the March 7, 1944, attack of the marshalling yards at Viterbo, but their Liberator never flew again. As their 459th Bomb Group Liberator arrived at the initial point to begin the bomb run, heavy flak damaged the rear of the fuselage of the bomber. They continued on, dropping their bombs, and began to turn away from the target when they were hit again, this time on the tail, with parts of both the left horizontal and vertical stabilizers blown away. Then to add to their problems, fighters attacked the 459th formation from the rear several minutes later, some closing to

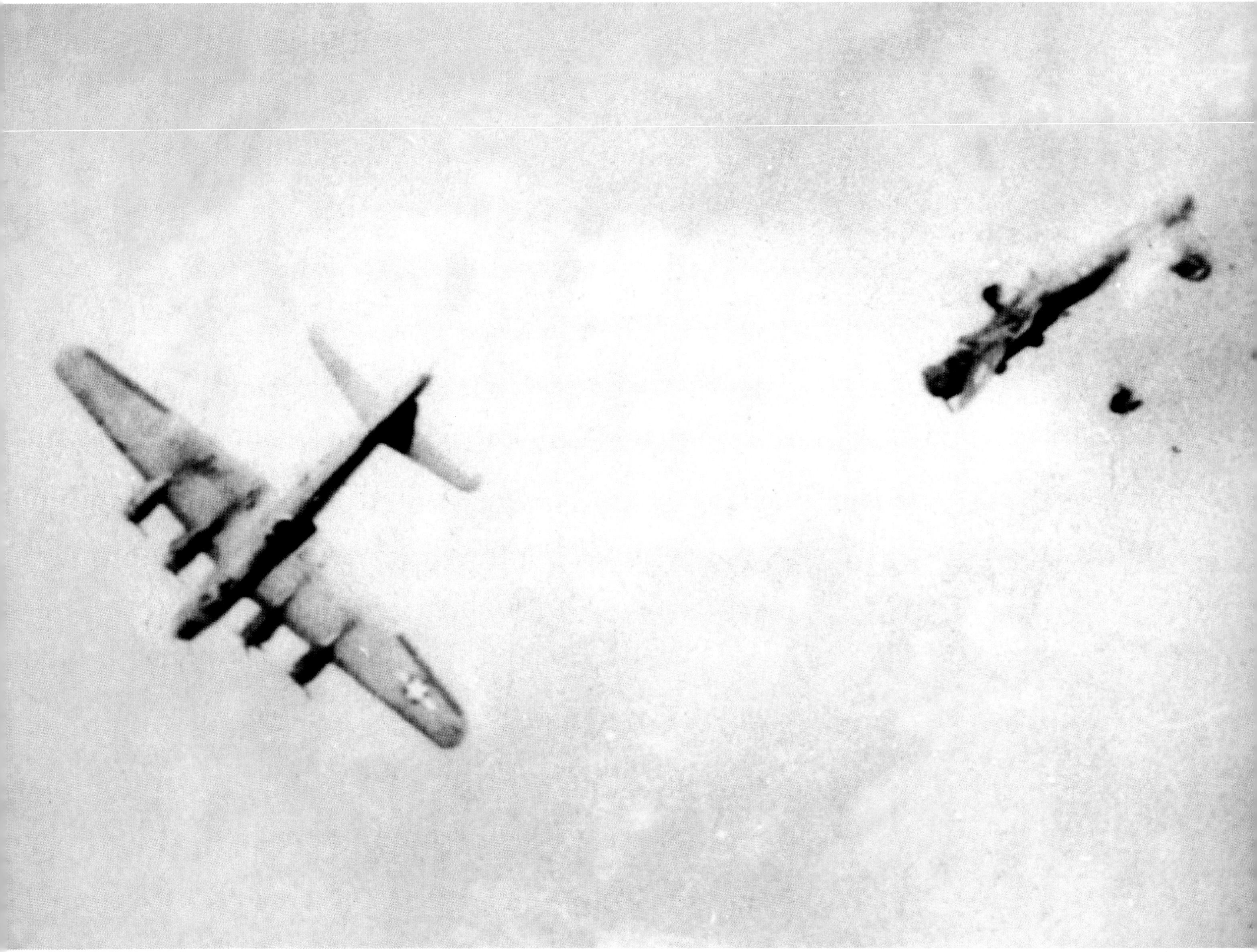

Above: This photo is believed to show a 483rd Bomb Group Flying Fortress with a feathered engine on the way to bomb Zwollfaxing, Austria.

Opposite page: A 463rd Bomb Group B-17, at right, goes down over Vienna after bombs from another aircraft hit the fuselage on the February 15, 1945, attack on a freight depot in Vienna. Three crewmen managed to bail out, but the others were killed.

within one hundred yards of the Liberators. Two Me 109s attacked Fletcher's ship, hitting the tail turret, disabling it, and blowing the gunner out of the turret. The ball turret was also hit in this attack. Flak blew off the door to the turret and threw the stunned gunner partially out of his turret, into the air. The attack also disabled one engine.

Another fighter attack, from the rear, hit the waist area, killing one waist gunner and badly wounding the other. The third fighter attack, made from several directions at the same time, included one by an Fw 190 that calmly lined up the Liberator's tail, since there were no gunners in the rear to return fire, and laced the aircraft with cannon and machine-gun fire from nose to tail.

At this point, the Liberator began to straggle from the formation, but by applying more throttle, Fletcher was able to regain the comparative safety of the group where he remained until the fighter attacks had ended. The aircraft was now leaking gasoline from wing tanks, the damaged engine, and the bomb bay tanks. The flight engineer endeavored to stop the leaks, while the bombardier tended to the wounded.

Returning to Italy, they approached a field near Naples. As Fletcher let the aircraft down for landing, he discovered that the hydraulic system that controlled the landing gear had been shot up, so the crew cranked down the gear manually. With flaps shot away, he landed on the field, but the aircraft began to drift left as the left tire had been shot out. With little control available, the Liberator veered off the runway, and the left landing gear dug into the ground. The left wing then hit the ground, causing the B-24 to turn around completely, or ground loop, coming to an abrupt stop. The propeller from one engine had come loose during the landing and penetrated the fuselage just behind the cockpit, but fortunately did not injure any of the crew. The unwounded crew members were able to walk away, and the injured were taken to a hospital. The Liberator never flew again, consigned for salvage. Fletcher received the Silver Star for his fine performance.[lxvii]

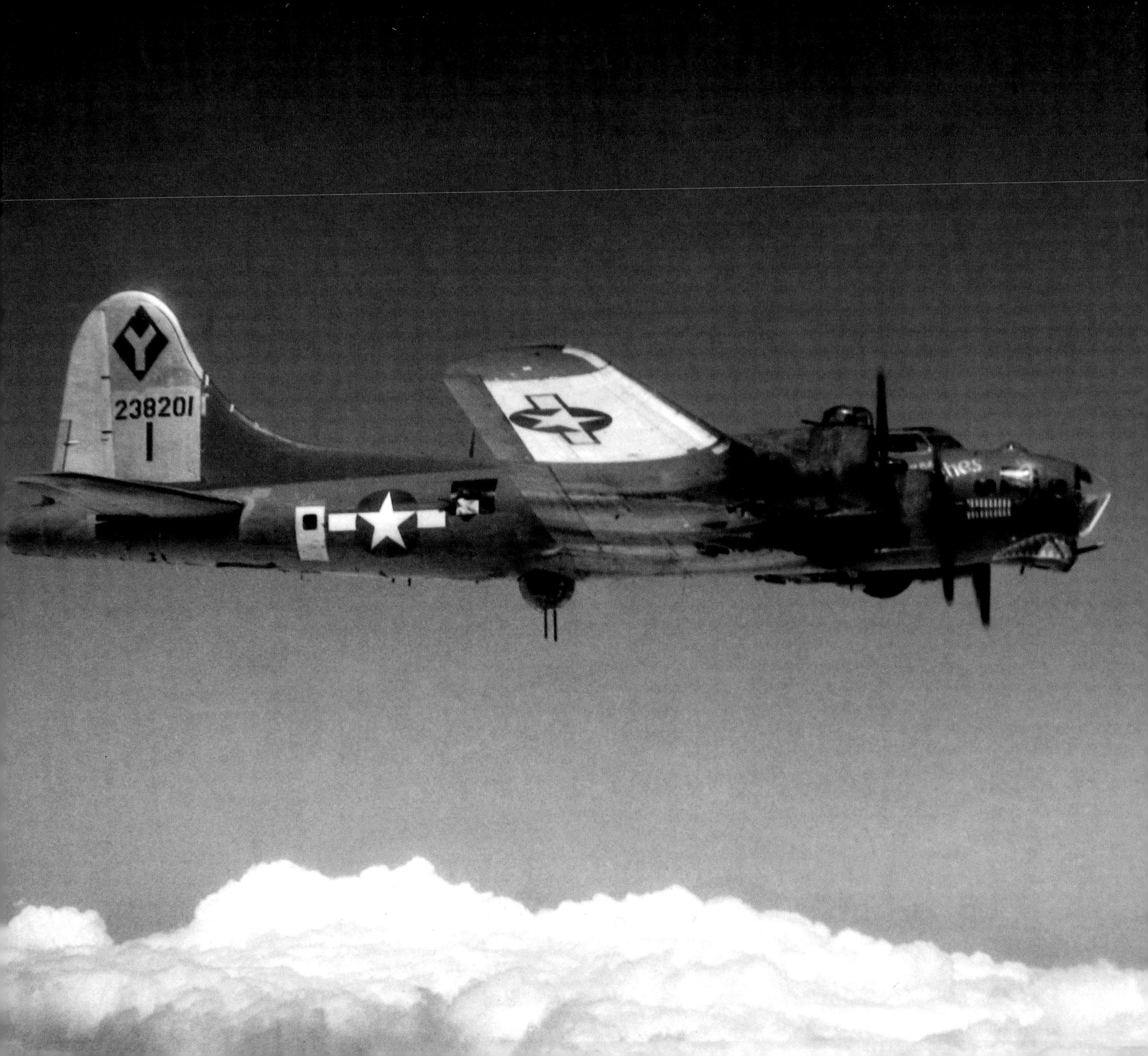
Y
238201
I

CHAPTER 9

OPERATIONAL DIFFICULTIES

Enemy action was not the only cause of bomber losses. A number of aircraft went down over occupied territory from mechanical failure or problems that led to increased fuel consumption. Maintenance crews in Italy labored under harsh conditions, always working outside in hastily constructed airfields with few amenities. Such rough conditions led to the loss of a 483rd Bomb Group B-17 when an onboard fire downed the plane over Yugoslavia.

Opposite page: A fine view of the Flying Fortress. This B-17G, nicknamed *Patches,* flew with the 346th Bomb Squadron, 99th Bomb Group. The aircraft completed forty-one missions before it crash-landed at Amendola in August 1944.

A 99th Bomb Group Fortress over the oil refinery at Moosbierbaum, Austria, during the raid of August 28, 1944.

A 97th Bomb Group B-17 flies past the burning synthetic oil refinery at Moosbierbaum, Austria, near Vienna, during the attack of August 28, 1944. A plume of smoke from fires started by the bombing at the refinery can be seen rising through the smoke screen that covered the refinery.

Flying Fortress 42-97913 was over Yugoslavia on the way to bomb the oil refinery at Moosbierbaum, near Vienna, on August 28, 1944, when a fire suddenly broke out under the top turret. The fire quickly spread to the cockpit and radio room; it was too strong to fight, and the pilot, Capt. Jonas Blank, gave the order to bail out. As the crew began to leave the aircraft, the bombardier salvoed the bombs. A crew member in another aircraft in the formation reported, "I looked at the plane and thought the cockpit windows and turret were all frosted over. Then the pilot opened his window to let the smoke out. [The] tail door flew off and [the] tail gunner bailed out . . . then the waist door flew off. . . . [The] bomb bay doors were opened. . . . Immediately afterward two men bailed out. Two men went out the waist door and two men went out the nose hatch."[lxviii] The Fortress circled several times as the crew bailed out, then crashed. Fortunately, all crew members got out of the stricken aircraft. Three of them, 1st Lt. Harry Whye, tail gunner Staff Sgt. James Tucker, and waist gunner Staff Sgt. Kenneth Cunningham, reported their experience: "As we neared the ground, several cars full of German soldiers were seen to be following us along the roads. One farmer drove a herd of goats in front of one car and another farmer drove some cattle in front of another car. The Germans then shot at Sergeant Cunningham, shooting one panel out of his chute and cutting one shroud line. . . . [The] three of us landed safely and were hidden by the Partisans. The other seven were captured within four hours after they hit the ground."

After hiding in a cornfield for four days, until the search for them ended, they then proceeded, on foot, on a week-long trek through German lines until they reached a British mission with the Partisans. Transferred to an American Office of Strategic Services (OSS) unit shortly thereafter, they flew back to Italy about two weeks after they were shot down.[lxix]

Liberators were, if anything, slightly more likely to have mechanical trouble than Fortresses, and one from the 454th Bomb Group also went down over Yugoslavia. On the way to bomb the sought marshalling yard at Linz, on January 20, 1945, the Liberator flown by 1st Lt. Paul Cash and his crew ran into trouble when its three engines began to run away intermittingly. The crew turned around and began to head for Italy, hoping to reach the Adriatic, and the pilot asked the navigator, Flying Officer Samuel Rosenberg, to come to the cockpit to assist. On the way forward, Rosenberg's chute opened accidently. After flying for about half an hour without reaching the sea, the engines really began to give trouble. The propeller flew off the number three engine and hit the number four engine, stopping it. The Liberator, with only two working engines, began to lose altitude. Cash gave the order to bail out, and the six men in the rear of the plane—the gunners, flight engineer, and radio operator—all did so. As luck would have it, they descended into a firefight between Partisans and German soldiers. All reached the ground, but two, the nose gunner and a waist gunner, were killed in the crossfire. Partisans rescued the remaining four and took them to a British mission the next day.

The four officers remained in the plane, as Rosenberg couldn't bail out with his open parachute and elected to make a wheels-down landing on a flat area covered by a foot of snow. The fuselage buckled during the landing, and the nose dug itself under snow and earth. Initially stunned, the four men soon got out the plane, but Cash and the copilot, 2nd Lt. Claude James, were both injured. Within twenty minutes, a German patrol captured all four and held them at a

Opposite page top: The engines and the tail are all that remain of a B-24 that crash-landed near Anzio in early June 1944.

Opposite page bottom: A 451st Bomb Group B-24 with bomb-bay doors open over Vienna on January 15, 1945.

A 2nd Bomb Group B-17, flown by Maj. Bradford Evans, makes a forced landing at Amendola, Italy, after one of the engines blew up on the return from a mission to Toulon in early 1944.

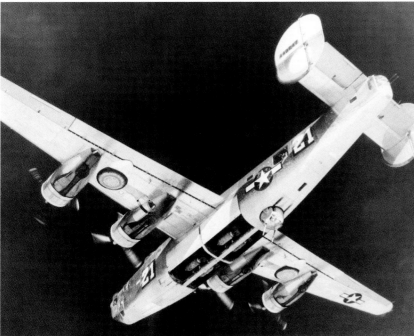

nearby village, in a barn, overnight. In the morning, the Partisans attacked and liberated them from captivity and took them to a Partisan hospital for treatment, where the other four crew members joined them on January 23. The uninjured crewmen were taken to Split and returned to Italy on January 30. The injured pilots remained behind for hospitalization, but both fortunately survived.[lxx]

Mechanical problems on a 97th Bomb Group Fortress, however, did not force the crew to take the long way home, as Lieutenant Cash's crew did. The oxygen system was a vital necessity for the airmen's survival at the high altitudes frequented by the Fifteenth in their unpressurized aircraft, and its failure could lead to serious problems for the crew. On the mission to Maribor on November 6, 1944, a crewmen on a B-17 44-6328 had a close call, but one not caused by enemy action. The plane, which would later be shot down in April 1945 with another crew, dropped its bombs as the lead ship in the formation did. The bombardier, Staff Sgt. Frank Antonucci, was a "togglier," an enlisted man trained to drop the bombs on target without using a bombsight, an innovation introduced in the fall of 1944 to deal with a shortage of trained bombardiers. The radio man, Sgt. Donald Fry, checked the still-open bomb bay to ensure that all the bombs were gone. He discovered that they were still there, hung up. Fry contacted Antonucci, who asked the pilot, 1st Lt. Walter Welch, to hit his emergency bomb release, which he did without effect. The ball-turret gunner, Sgt. Donald Miller, joined Fry in the radio room and plugged in his oxygen hose, and both men entered the catwalk in the bomb bay to dislodge the bombs. Sergeant Antonucci came back from the nose, through the cockpit, and entered the bomb bay, too. He worked on the manual release, and eventually all the bombs fell away. Antonucci began to return to the nose when he suddenly collapsed with his legs dangling from the catwalk into the open bomb bay. His "walk around" oxygen bottle was empty, and he had passed out from lack of oxygen. The flight engineer, Sgt. John Thurston, got his legs onto the catwalk and dragged him onto the flight deck behind the cockpit. Miller entered the bomb bay to help, but his parachute harness snagged in the bomb bay and his oxygen hose became disconnected. As he, too, passed out, he imagined himself falling through the still-open bomb bay doors. Fry came to his rescue, freeing the tangled

parachute harness from the beams in the bomb bay, and dragged him to the radio room. All the while, the semi-conscious Miller was moving around, trying to step off the cat walk and through the open bomb bay. Both Antonucci and Miller were quickly revived by connection to the oxygen system again, and the trip home was made without further incident.[lxxi]

Another peril faced by Fifteenth aircrews, besides the enemy and the possibility of mechanical failures, was the danger of damage from friendly aircraft. This could be in the form of friendly fire, collisions, or being hit by bombs dropped by another aircraft in the tight formations flown by bombers for protection. The latter occurred on the 449th Bomb Group's fourth combat mission, to Mostar, on January 14, 1944.

A Liberator nicknamed *Blind Date*, flown by 1st Lt. Vincent Isgrigg, dropped its bombs while another aircraft, *White Fang*, flown by 2nd Lt. Harold Pickard and his crew, flew directly underneath it. At least two bombs, possibly three, hit *White Fang* in the nose turret, the fuselage above the ball turret, and the right wing, setting the fuel tanks on fire. The flight leader, 1st Lt. John Wood, reported the result: "I heard a muffled explosion and looked out my left window and saw ship 606 [*White Fang*] burst into flames. I turned my head away for a few seconds and when I looked again, I saw the tail end completely break away from the rest of the ship."[lxxii]

Two crewmen—the tail gunner, Sgt. Robert Hansen, and a photographer assigned for the mission, Sgt. Charles La Marca—were able to bail out. Hansen went out a hole in the fuselage near the tail, while La Marca jumped through the now-open end of the fuselage. A crewman

Above: Bombs dropped from a Liberator fall toward a B-24 below them in a formation during a mission.

Opposite page top: The instant the bombs struck the tail of the B-24 shown in the previous photo. It crashed soon afterward.

Opposite page bottom: The Liberator *V Grand* of the 465th Bomb Group under repair at the island of Vis, after an emergency landing in early November 1944.

in another Liberator actually saw one smoke-blackened chute open. Both men reached the ground safely to become prisoners of war.

The explosion knocked Isgrigg's Liberator out of formation and damaged the bomb bay. The pilot reported the plane was out of control, and the copilot, bombardier, navigator, radio operator, and flight engineer headed for the bomb bay to jump as the aircraft plummeted several thousand feet. Isgrigg managed to regain control of the ship, however, and told the crew to "hold it." The five men in the bomb bay, however, were no longer connected to the intercom and did not hear the good news. All five jumped. Isgrigg flew the Liberator back to base himself, with the gunners who had remained in the rear of the aircraft.

Chetnik Partisans rescued two who jumped, the bombardier, 2nd Lt. Stanley Grezik, and radio operator, Staff Sgt. Ottaro Tosti, but the other three crewmen, who landed farther away, were taken prisoner. Tosti and Grezik were reunited the next day and taken to a Partisan head-quarters, where they stayed overnight before continuing on with a small Partisan band to a combined OSS-SOE (Britain's Special Operations Executive) mission working with the Partisans, near the town of Kosalin. Navy Lieutenant Holt Green, the OSS man who organized a rescue network for American flyers downed in Yugoslavia, and later in Slovakia, took them to the town of Berane. Sergeant Tosti returned to Italy with several other Americans in an Italian aircraft used to drop supplies and agents and pick up escaped Allied prisoners and evading flyers in Yugoslavia before a regular shuttle service was established by American C-47s in mid-1944. Grezik remained in Yugoslavia, working with the OSS team.[lxxiii]

A 97th Bomb Group crew also avoided the prospect of evading the enemy after they experienced the effects of "friendly fire" while on the April 6, 1945, mission to bomb German positions around Bologna in preparation for the impending final Allied offensive. While on the bomb run, the fragmentation bomb load of another Fortress in the formation dropped onto Lt. John DeMont's aircraft. The first bomb hit the number three engine, knocking it out. More bombs damaged the main spar on a wing and holed the fuel tanks in both of them, as well as damaging the flaps. The propeller on the number four engine began to windmill and vibrate, shaking the entire aircraft, and the pilots were unable to feather either of the two engines on the right wing. Another falling bomb penetrated the radio operator's cabin and his table, but fortunately his flak suits prevented any injury. To make matters worse, when the crew dropped their own load of fragmentation bombs, one exploded prematurely in the bomb bay, creating heavy smoke that filled the aircraft.

A Liberator from the 49th Bomb Wing burns on Bron Airfield, near Lyon, France, in mid-September 1944. These aircraft were used to ferry badly needed supplies to Allied forces that had outrun their supply lines during the swift advance up the Rhône River after the invasion of southern France the previous month.

Right: The 463rd Bomb Group pummels the marshalling yards at Mestre, Italy, on June 10, 1944. The Fortress in the foreground was shot down by flak a few weeks later over Budapest.

Below: Ground crewmen extinguish the fire that destroyed a Fifteenth Air Force Fortress on a field in Italy in early March 1945. An engine on the B-17 caught fire during landing, but the crew got out safely before flames consumed the bomber.

DeMont told the crew to prepare to bail out of the stricken Fortress, as he attempted to reach a friendly field nearby. They soon reached the airfield and flew over it with their wheels extended, shooting off recognition flares. As they made their approach to the runway, they shot red flares to indicate an aircraft in distress, to ensure that the runway would be kept clear since they didn't know what radio frequency to use to contact the field's tower. DeMont landed safely, without flaps, and using his brakes stopped just before the end of the runway. Ground crews later counted more than four hundred holes in the Fortress.[lxxiv]

The third danger not presented by the enemy, but a constant threat to the formations of bombers flying in close proximity to each other for mutual protection, was collision. Collisions occurred throughout the operational life the Fifteenth Air Force, often involving two bombers or fighters. In early 1944, however, a more serious incident occurred that cost three Fortress groups eight airplanes in a single mission, during the raid on Piraeus, Greece, on January 11.

Bad weather dogged the mission, and a third of the bombers and all the escorting Lightnings from the 14th Fighter Group turned back before reaching the target. The remainder continued on, but collisions began before the formation reached the target.

The 301st Bomb Group lost five B-17s. The nose of Fortress 42-30466, flown by 1st Lt. Richard Williams, hit another aircraft, and began to fall, the front portion of the aircraft gone. Three of the crew managed to bail out to reach the ground safely. A second Fortress from the group, manned by the crew of 1st Lt. Wayne Cherrington, collided with yet another Fortress as the pilot said over the intercom, "I'm going to get above these clouds if it is the last thing I do." It was, as the nose struck the other Fortress and burst into flames. Cherrington's Fortress broke into two parts and plummeted to the ground, but three crewmen survived: the radioman and two gunners. A third 301st

Ground crewmen take a break from maintenance early in 1945 at the base of the 99th Bomb Group. Poor weather greatly reduced the number of missions flown by the Fifteenth during January.

Despite the collisions that cost the mission eight aircraft, other Fortresses pressed on and successfully bombed the target at Piraeus on January 11, 1944.

Fortress suffered the same fate, with only one extremely lucky survivor. Flown by Capt. Robert Goen, the Fortress collided with another ahead of it in the formation. The tail broke off from the rest of the fuselage, and the tail gunner, Sgt. James Raley, couldn't bail out as the tail began to spin. It fell nineteen thousand feet but landed in a group of trees that miraculously broke his fall sufficiently so that he survived with only minor injuries. A fourth 301st bomber lost in the collisions also had survivors. The plane, piloted by 2nd Lt. Donald Ready, broke apart after the collision, and the navigator, Lt. Aaron Siegel, and the radio operator, Tech. Sgt. Samuel Schursky, both managed to escape. The collision knocked Siegel unconscious and he came to in the air, in time to open his parachute and reach the ground safely. Schursky also was able to open his chute in time. In the fifth aircraft lost, flown by the crew of Lt. Joseph Dunbar, the entire crew was unfortunately killed.

The 97th lost two bombers that collided with each other, and 1st Lt. Herbert Easterling's crew all perished. In the other aircraft, flown by Flying Officer Roy Mayo, three men managed to escape when the bomber broke apart in midair.

The last plane lost, the 99th Bomb Group Fortress flown by 1st Lt, Joseph Donahue, flipped over on its back and a wing came off when another Fortress collided with it. Three of the crew got out, but the remaining crewmen perished.

Greeks civilians buried many of the crewmen killed in these collisions and some of the survivors had the opportunity to attend the funerals. All evaded capture with the help of Greek civilians and resistance members and returned to Italy in March and early April.[lxxv]

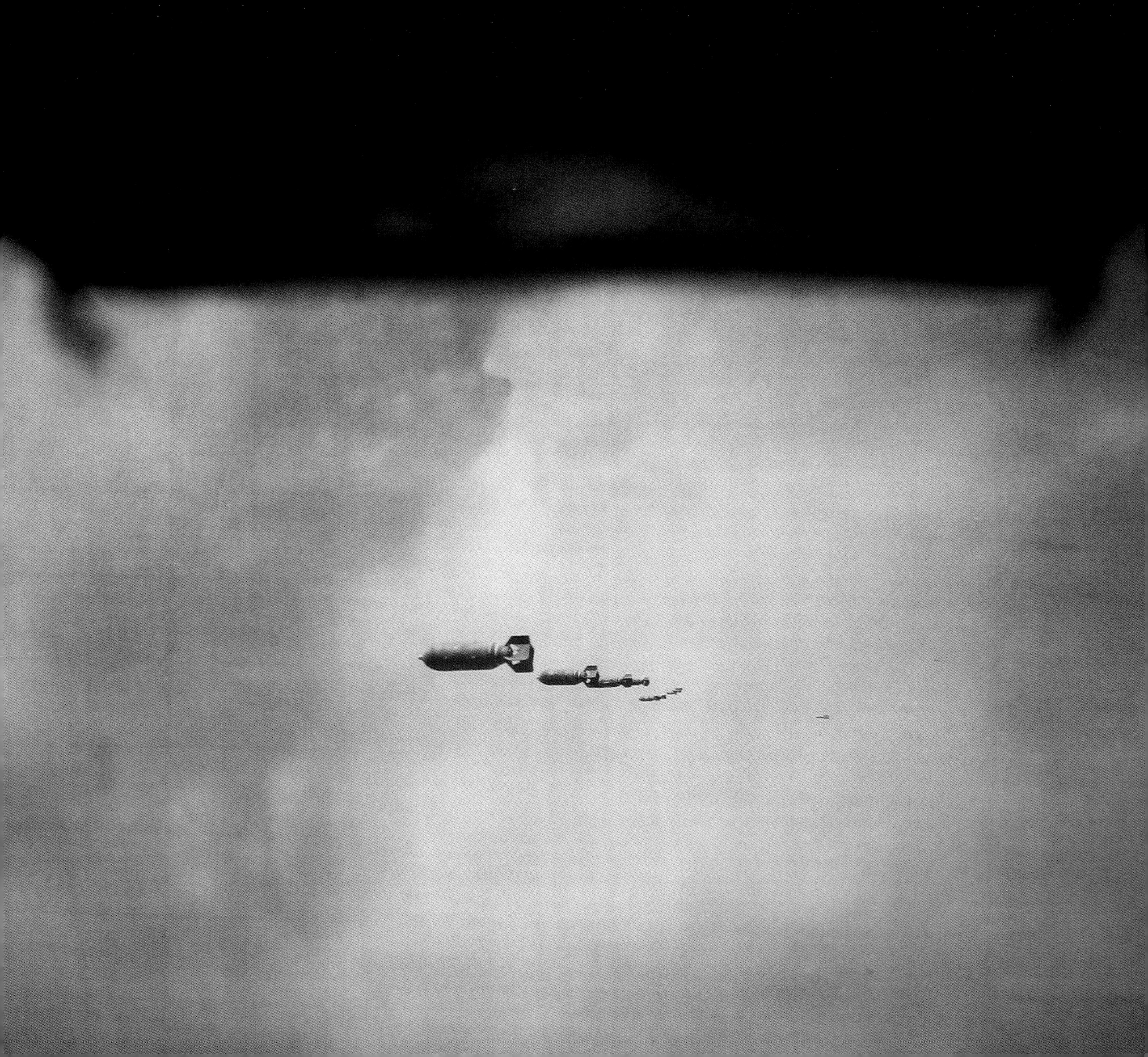

CHAPTER 10

LONE WOLF

Some of the most unusual and innovative operations flown by American air forces during World War II were the Lone Wolf missions of the Fifteenth Air Force. The idea began after lone bombers successfully reached German targets at night on missions to locate and map German radar during the summer of 1944, without loss. This proved that small numbers of bombers could reach targets in occupied territory at night and return safely.

Opposite page: Bombs dropped by the 2nd Bomb Group fall toward the synthetic oil refinery at Blechhammer, Germany, during the Lone Wolf mission of December 12, 1944. The total overcast illustrates the difficulties crews encountered during the winter months in locating and bombing their targets.

Such missions were first flown in late October 1944 to targets in southern Germany and Austria and continued until March 1945. They were initially mounted at night, but soon during the day, too, to keep pressure on German targets as increasingly bad fall weather prevented bomber formations from flying many scheduled missions during these months. The use of small numbers of bombers would keep operations from coming to a standstill and also harass the enemy, even if they could not inflict major damage.

A B-17 from the 99th Bomb Group drops its bombs through total cloud cover using PFF radar, as Lone Wolf aircraft did on both night and daylight missions.

The 5th Bomb Wing sent thirteen Fortresses on such a mission during the night of November 12 to 13, 1944, to bomb the synthetic oil refineries at Blechhammer, Germany. One of them was from the 2nd Bomb Group and flown by Lt. Sterling Trump on his last mission. The flight to the target was uneventful, but as they neared the target, the H2X equipment began to act up, and they had to search for the target without the aid of radar as German searchlights began to play around the sky, searching for them. Trump later reported, "As we were trying to find the target, Jerry started in with his searchlights and flares." They flew in the vicinity of Blechhammer for about half an hour but couldn't readily identify the refineries. On the recommendation of the bombardier, the crew then headed for the city of Gleiwitz, the scene of the German provocation that began the Second World War. Encountering more searchlights, they dropped their bomb load over the city as the fighter-detection radar that scanned the rear for approaching aircraft flashed green in the instrument panel in the cockpit, indicating that a German night fighter was in their vicinity. "Our night fighter detector gave warning of fighters all the way down from Gleiwitz to the Yugoslav coast." Fortunately, no attacks materialized.

By this time, their fuel supply was becoming dangerously low, depleted by the additional half hour searching for their target. After they had crossed the Adriatic, fortunately avoiding a night-time ditching or bailing out over the sea that would have most certainly been fatal, the number two engine stopped, followed by the number four. Shortly thereafter, the other two engines stopped; the Fortress was completely out of fuel. With little altitude left with which to reach their field, the crew prepared for a crash-landing. Trump recalled, "The next few seconds were the longest of my life. I kept thinking 'either way this is my last mission.'" They came in over a highway and crash-landed near Lake Lesina in Italy. None of the crew was injured. Another of the four Fortresses the 2nd dispatched on these missions ditched off the coast of Italy, where the entire crew was picked up by Italian fishermen, including a correspondent for *Yank* magazine who was also on board.[lxxvi]

The experience of another Lone Wolf crew that did return to base provides an insight into the hazards of these nighttime missions during winter. Such missions were particularly arduous for pilots and navigators, as the former had to fly by instruments alone. There were two navigators, a radar navigator and dead-reckoning navigator, who had to locate the target using only rudimentary radar-navigation aids. Their Liberator, by the nature of the mission, was a "Mickey" ship, containing the Gee and H2X radar equipment necessary to carry out a radar bombing attack. The navigators used the Gee receiver to take readings from several ground stations and determine the position of the plane during the flight, while H2X radar was used to identify the target. The latter could also be used as a rudimentary navigational aid when Gee signals could no longer be received deep in German-controlled territory.

The Fifteenth Air Force mounted the last Lone Wolf mission of 1944 on December 12 in daylight. First Lieutenant Winton Reynolds's crew, of the 455th Bomb Group, was among those dispatched. Their Liberator was painted a blue-gray color, without any markings, to make it less distinguishable from the clouds as it traversed the night skies.

After takeoff, the aircraft climbed steadily, reaching fourteen thousand feet while over the Adriatic Sea. When it reached eighteen thousand feet, the temperature was thirty-two degrees Fahrenheit below zero, and it began to snow. The crew soon left the snowstorm behind, but then the number four engine began to run hot, necessitating an increase in power on the other three

engines and increasing fuel consumption. At twenty-four thousand feet, the bomber emerged from the clouds, but the tail gunner reported that they were leaving a vapor trail behind that would advertise their presence to any German night fighters roaming about. It soon became apparent that the increase in fuel consumption would prevent them from reaching their assigned target, the refineries at Blechhammer, so the crew chose an alternate target, the city of Neisse, which was in the vicinity. The crew put on their flak suits and helmets during the long bomb run, necessary as the radar used to identify the target could be tracked by the Germans. Chaff was dispensed to confuse German flak radar. Flak began to come up through the clouds below, but the chaff confused the radar about the bomber's altitude, and the rounds exploded safely below them. Reynolds took some mild evasive action by skidding the Liberator as the flak came closer, announcing over the interphone, "The Jerry has got our course okay, but he hasn't quite got our altitude." As they approached the aiming point to release the bombs, flak gunners began to gauge

B-17s from the 301st Bomb Group fly over the Alps on the way to bomb a target in Austria in March 1945. The Fortress in the foreground has a PFF radar dome fitted in place of the ball turret on the underside of the bomber.

their altitude accurately, and flak bursts began to appear in the bomber's vicinity. "It's coming up to us now. It's pepping off our tail," remarked the tail gunner. Reynolds replied, "Okay, I'll skid her over a bit," then the bombardier chimed in, "Steady, hold her—that's it." They then dropped the bombs, including two containing leaflets that would open before reaching the ground. As the Liberator turned away from the target, a crew member exclaimed, "I hope we blew the hell out of 'em down there."

During the return flight, they slowly lowered their altitude to stretch out their flight time and flew into a snowstorm again. Ice began to form on the wings at seventeen thousand feet. When several navigational checkpoints were missed, the two navigators on board found that the wind had shifted and they were now flying into a strong headwind, rather than the forecast tailwind, and still several hundred miles from home. The ice continued to build up over the entire aircraft, but as they were flying over the mountains of Yugoslavia, they couldn't drop down to reach warmer air.

The coast finally appeared on the Mickey radar scope, and the radio operator contacted Big Fence and got a bearing to confirm their position.

Reynolds told the gunners to come out of their turrets as even more ice appeared, although they had now cleared the mountains and could fly at lower altitude: "We are in heavy weather and picking up clear ice very fast. I don't know if it can be broken off or not [by the rubber de-icing boots on the wings]. Better get ready for an emergency in any event. Check the spare raft and 'Gibson Girls' [hand-powered emergency radios]."

As the icing got worse and it became clear they would not reach Italy, they began to look for the island of Vis, off the Yugoslav coast, with its emergency landing field,. The plane began to run out of fuel, and the number one engine failed when they were only ten miles from Vis. Reynolds told the crew over the interphone, "Pilot to crew. We are running out of fuel. Standby to bail out!" The radio operator sent a mayday message, and the crew began to prepare to bail out over Vis, preferable to ditching or bailing out over the Adriatic Sea in winter. The copilot radioed their distress call: "Mayday! Mayday! This is St. Nick V for Victory going down. Out of fuel! We will try to reach the coast!" The number one engine stopped, then the number three engine. Reynolds announced, "Pilot to crew. Open the hatches and stand by. We are running out of fuel! If we break out of the clouds near the island we will bail out over it. We have two engines."

Yugoslav women and children look on as mechanics repair a B-24 on the island of Vis, where Lieutenant Reynolds and crew crash-landed at the end of the Lone Wolf mission in December 1944.

At five thousand feet, they broke out of the clouds and could see the island as the ice on the wings and fuselage melted, some hitting the cockpit windshield. They tried to make the emergency field as the radio operator sent "SOS" and screwed down his transmitter key, to send a continuous signal of their position. As they approached the strip, they saw another aircraft had crashed and blocked it. Then the number four engine stopped, leaving only one engine, which could barely keep them in the air. Reynolds headed for a valley between two nearby ridges. The Liberator glided between them, and the pilots spotted a vineyard, dead ahead. Reynolds shouted to the copilot: "Watch the wings. Will they clear the canyon walls?" They did, and he lowered the landing gear and, as the gear contacted the ground, cut power to the remaining engines and applied brakes. The B-24 jumped a fence in its path, then the nose landing gear broke away and the nose dug into the earth, filling the cockpit with mud and vines as the plane ground to halt. The crew all exited the plane, an operation that one crew member likened to "men escaping from an asylum." As they gathered, uninjured, in the rain near their B-24, one observed, "Guess we were pretty lucky." Reynolds later received a well-deserved Distinguished Flying Cross for the flight.[lxxvii]

A Liberator from the 484th Bomb Group makes an emergency landing on the island of Vis, off the coast of Yugoslavia. The island was taken and held by the Allies in early 1944 and provided shelter for many Fifteenth Air Force aircraft that would otherwise have been lost. Many of the aircraft landing on the island later returned to Italy.

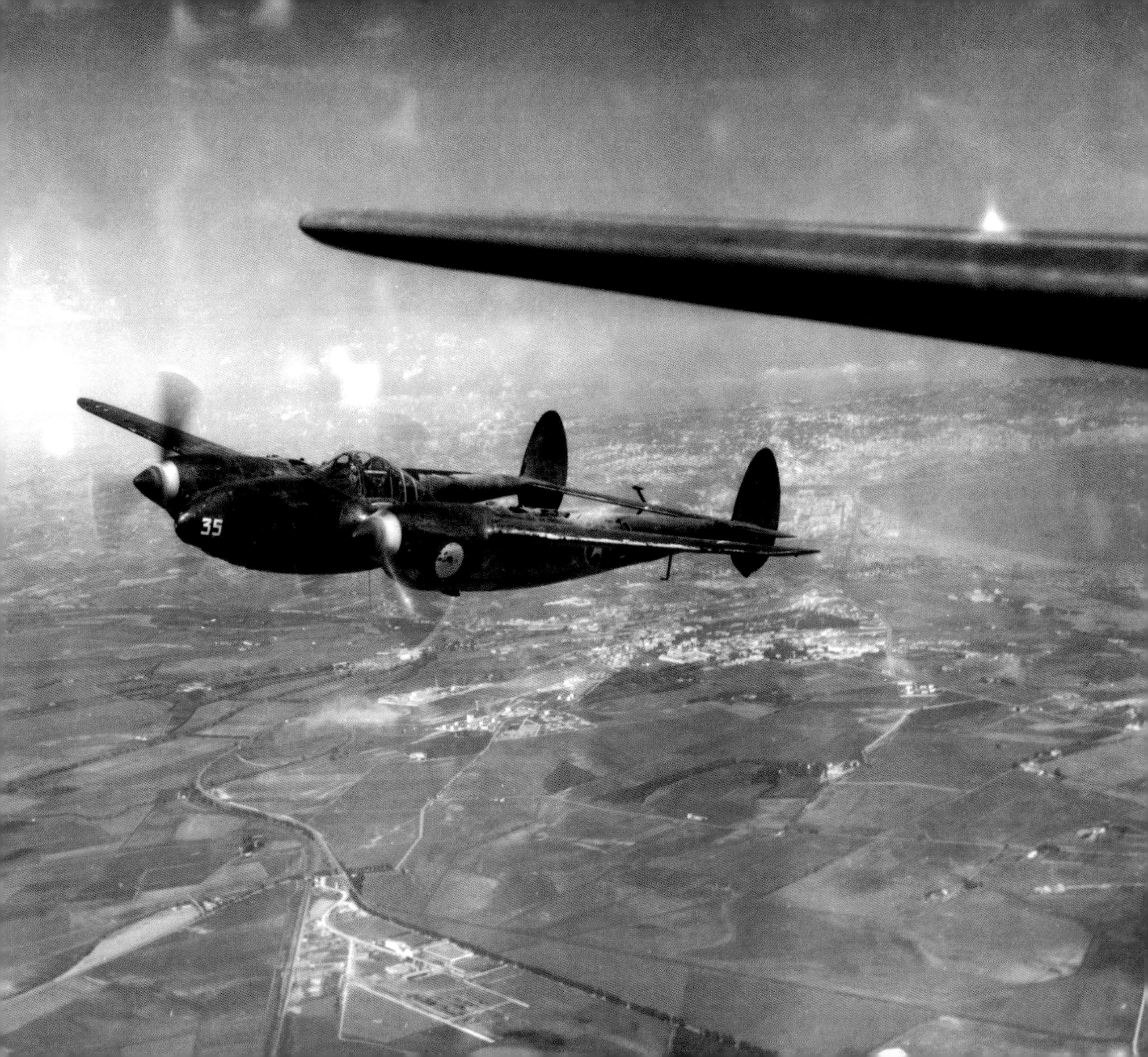
35

CHAPTER 11

RECONNAISSANCE MISSIONS

Besides fighter and bomber missions, aircraft of the Fifteenth also flew daily reconnaissance missions through the skies of German-occupied Europe. Many were photo-reconnaissance missions, vital to identifying targets before they were bombed and to assessing damage after bombing missions. Others were weather-reconnaissance missions, vital in obtaining accurate reports of weather over targets for mission planning as well as weather forecasting. Interception by German fighters was initially rare, but with the advent of operational German jets in the fall of 1944, photo-reconnaissance missions became increasingly more dangerous.

Opposite page: An F-5 Lightning, the reconnaissance version of the P-38 Fighter.

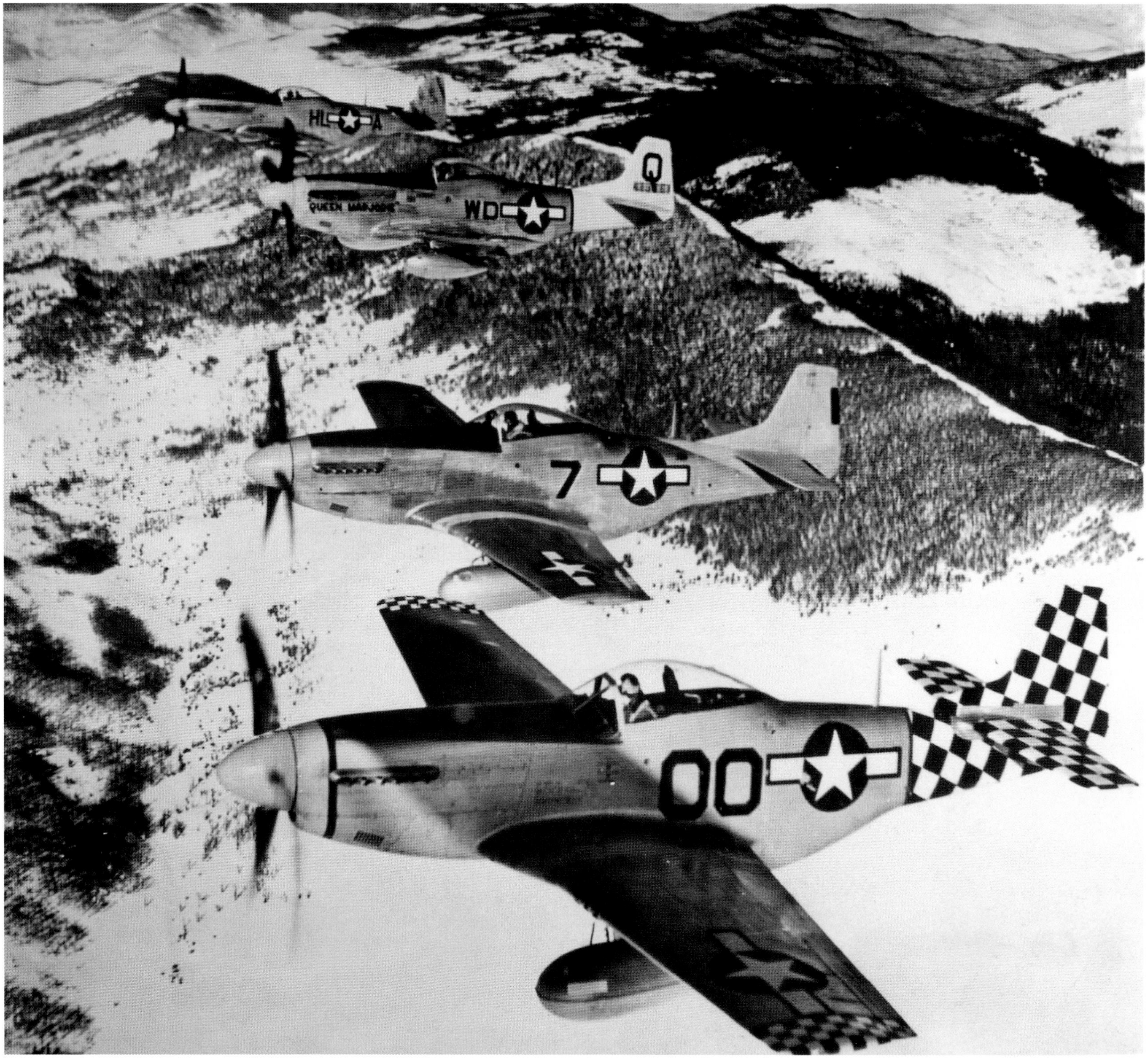
HL A
Q
QUEEN MARJORIE
WD
7
00

An early encounter with fighters took place during the bombing of Cassino on March 15, 1944. A photo-reconnaissance F-5 Lightning from the 15th Photo Reconnaissance Squadron was assigned to take photos of airfields and marshalling yards in northern Italy, as well as the town of Cassino. While the plane was over the town on his camera run, an Allied aircraft controller told the pilot, Captain Ballard, that radar had detected three aircraft in his area. When he had completed the photography, he dipped his right wing and saw three Me 109s below his tail, climbing to attack. The first enemy fighter fired and missed, but before the F-5 could

Opposite page: Mustangs representing three of the four P-51 fighter groups assigned to the Fifteenth Air Force. From top to bottom 31st, 52nd, and 332nd Fighter Groups. Mustangs usually escorted reconnaissance missions in the final months of the war, as German jets became a menace to unarmed reconnaissance Lightnings.

Right: A reconnaissance photo taken by a Fifteenth Air Force reconnaissance F-5 showing a large German transport, a Ju 390, at Letany Airfield near Prague. Reconnaissance played a vital role in Fifteenth Air Force operations, in photographing targets before a raid so important features could be identified and then photographing the damage inflicted by bombing raids for damage assessment by photo interpreters.

take evasive action, the second hit the Lightning in the left engine and the cockpit, destroying the radio and wounding Ballard in the back. He succeeded in diving the Lightning to escape, reaching airspeed "off the clock," and only pulled out after diving almost twenty thousand feet. Feathering the left engine, Ballard flew to an airfield at Naples and managed to land on one engine, wounded. He taxied the Lightning off the runway and then lost consciousness. He was taken to a hospital, and the film was taken to a photo lab and processed.[lxxviii]

The pilot of another reconnaissance Lightning escaped harm in an early encounter with a German jet during a photo mission later the same year. After several photo-reconnaissance pilots failed to return in the early fall of 1944, the Fifteenth Air Force began to assign fighters to escort missions in areas where German jets were believed to roam—northern Austria and southern Germany.

The first such encounter from which American pilots returned safely to base took place on November 12, when a jet approached an F-5 and its escort near Gunzburg, Germany, but dived into the clouds below when the escort approached. The same day, Lieutenant T. L. Franklin of the 15th Photo Reconnaissance Squadron met a jet over northern Italy, where the latter were not believed to operate. He saw a pair of contrails from an Me 262 approaching him from below; the jet easily climbed to within five thousand feet as Franklin pushed his throttles forward and escaped. About a week later, Lt. Elmer Majeske of the 32nd Photo Reconnaissance Squadron had a close encounter with an Me 262. He was taking photos of the marshalling yard at Weilheim, Germany, as the escorting fighters were climbing to rendezvous with him. Suddenly, an Me 262 approached, and he turned his F-5 into the attacker. "I turned into the attack and dived down whereupon the jet overshot and dove after one of the escort" he reported. The jet had enough, however, and flew away.[lxxix]

By the end of the month, on November 26, an Me 262 succeeded in firing on a reconnaissance flight. Lieutenant George Renne was taking pictures over Munich when he spotted an Me 262 only five hundred feet below, flying toward him. He notified the escorting fighters, Lightnings from the 1st Fighter Group, as the Me 262 climbed and made an attack pass. Renne dropped his external fuel tanks, opened his throttles, and turned into the jet. He later reported: "He [the jet] opened fire while we were flying head-on to each other. I dropped maneuver flaps and broke sharply to the right. The Me 262 made a wide, 180 degree, turn to start another pass. . . . I turned left and then joined the fighters while they chased the Me 262 . . ."[lxxx] The Messerschmitt streaked into the clouds. The American aircraft then began the flight home, to Italy, but just as they reached the Alps, another Me 262 approached them from the rear. One of the fighter escorts, 1st Lt. Guy Thomas, was lagging behind when the escort leader called for them to break to intercept the Me 262 while Renne continued on course. The Me 262 went into a steep, climbing turn and disappeared. Thomas did not rejoin the others when they re-formed and was later reported as killed in action. A German jet squadron, III./JG 7, claimed two Lightnings destroyed on the twenty-sixth, and Thomas may well have been one of them.[lxxxi]

The jet menace to reconnaissance aircraft, even with fighter escort, became more evident when an F-5 of the 32nd Photo Reconnaissance Squadron was shot down on December 2, 1944. First Lieutenant Keith Sheetz was flying near Munich, under the overcast so he could take his photos, with four Mustangs of the 31st Fighter Group as escort. An Me 262 suddenly attacked the flight from behind, diving out of the overcast, firing at Sheetz's Lightning. Sheetz radioed, "I have been hit by a jet and am going into the clouds and going home."[lxxxii] He disappeared

continued on page 154

P-38 Lightnings of the 1st Fighter Group peel off in formation. The Lightning in the foreground belongs to the 27th Fighter Squadron.

RIMINI M/Y.

M.A.P.R.C. D.B.30. 25/3/44.

ATTACKED 22/3/44.

4020   NA 956   NA 956. 682 Sqdn. MAR. 25th. 4 4 / 13·30. F/36. 22,000'SECRET.

Left: A photo interpreter's damage assessment of a raid on the marshalling yards at Rimini, Italy, using a post-raid reconnaissance photo taken by a reconnaissance aircraft. The arrows and number on the photo refer to specific points of damage noted on the accompanying damage assessment.

Opposite page: Pilots of the 15th Photo Reconnaissance Squadron, the main photo reconnaissance unit of the Fifteenth Air Force for much of 1944 until the 5th Photo Reconnaissance Group was assigned to the Fifteenth that fall.

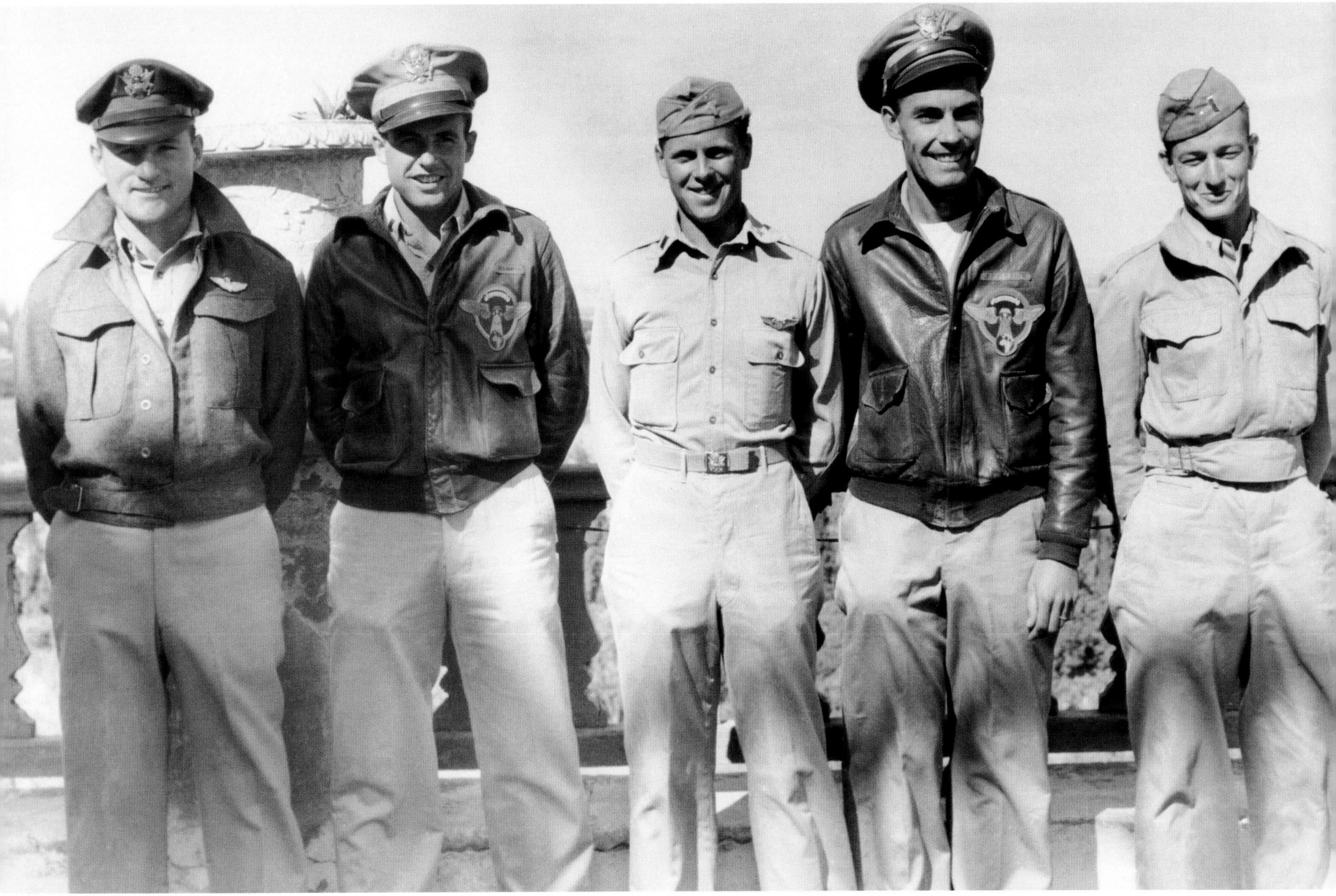

into some nearby clouds below, but the fighters were unable to locate him again, although they heard him radio once more that he was headed for Ancona. Unfortunately, he never arrived and was later reported as killed in action. The shoot down of a Lightning by an Me 262 of III./JG 7 was reported by the Germans on December 2, credited to a *Leutnant* Weber.[lxxxiii]

On December 14, a P-38 from the 82nd Fighter Group, escorting a photo-recon mission, tangled with two Me 262s over Munich. The pilot, Lt. Walter E. Camper, reported that two jets zoomed past the escort and opened fire on the recon Lightning at twenty-five thousand feet. After the first pass, one turned right, got between the two flights of the escort, and made a head-on pass at them, passing underneath them. Both jets then zoomed up and attacked again, as the recon Lightning joined the escort formation. The Americans then turned into the two jets, and both flew off in different directions without opening fire again.

An Me 410 now joined the fray, attacking the Lightnings head-on and closing to only fifty yards as it fired; the Lightnings returned fire. The two jets suddenly reappeared and took up formation with the Americans about two thousand yards away. One closed with the Lightnings again, firing from three o'clock, then disappeared.

The Americans turned for home and yet another jet attacked them. The jet pilot made the mistake of turning, to get into a better firing position, and lost speed so the Lightning was able to keep up with him. Lieutenant Camper turned inside him and opened fire at six hundred yards, but he was not in a good firing position and missed. The jet disappeared, and the Americans returned to base without loss or damage.[lxxxiv]

Only a short time later, however, the first destruction of an Me 262 by the Allied air forces in the Mediterranean took place, on December 22, 1944. The victory was shared by two pilots of the 31st Fighter Group escorting a photo-reconnaissance flight over southern Germany. After taking photos around Munich, the flight headed to Regensburg, where 1st Lt. Eugene McGlauflin spotted a jet just before it climbed to attack the flight. When in range, the jet fired at one of the two Mustangs flying to the right of the recon Lightning. McGlauflin later recalled:

> After the jet made his first pass, hitting my element leader's wingman's plane [it overshot and] immediately turned left. I . . . with my wingman [Flying Officer Roy Scales] turned sharply left. The Me 262 then climbed to 8,000 feet. I followed him, staying out of range, but didn't lose sight of him because I kept cutting him off on the turns. He then dived down to 16,000 feet and climbed up again to 28,000 feet . . . by cutting him off sharply on a turn, I got within 200 yards . . . 90 degrees from the jet. . . . I fired about five bursts and saw a red ball of flame appear momentarily. . . . The jet immediately dived down from 28,000 feet and seemed to glide for about five or ten minutes before it leveled out at 5,000 feet. . . . The pilot bailed out . . .

The jet crashed. McGlauflin and Scales were each officially credited with half a kill for their victory.[lxxxv]

*****

The 154th Weather Reconnaissance Squadron flew the daily weather-reconnaissance missions crucial to the Fifteenth Air Force. They flew at high altitude in the worst weather and rarely met enemy aircraft, but when they did, the encounter could become difficult for the American pilots, as their Lightings were unarmed.

One such encounter took place on October 31, 1944. First Lieutenant Daniel Dixon was on a reconnaissance mission over Yugoslavia when an Fw 190 appeared suddenly and attacked him. He was northwest of the city of Zagreb, writing notes of the weather he encountered for his report, when he glanced up and saw a Focke-Wulf heading toward him from eleven o'clock, firing at him. "I snapped into a left bank and he went by," he described. "Looking back over my right boom [tail] to see where he went, I noticed my right engine losing coolant, hydraulic fluid . . . [and it] was on fire. I dropped my belly tanks and 'split S'd' through a cloud layer at 12,000 feet and feathered my engine. . . . I flew for about three hours on a single engine."

During the return flight, he discovered that the attack had also shot out his hydraulic system. When he reached a field at Bari, he had to manually pump his landing gear down. He landed on the strip, but without hydraulics he could not brake, so the aircraft sped down the entire length of the runway, crossed a road, and stopped only feet away from a stone wall. Daniel walked away and filed his weather report, the end of another mission.[lxxxvi]

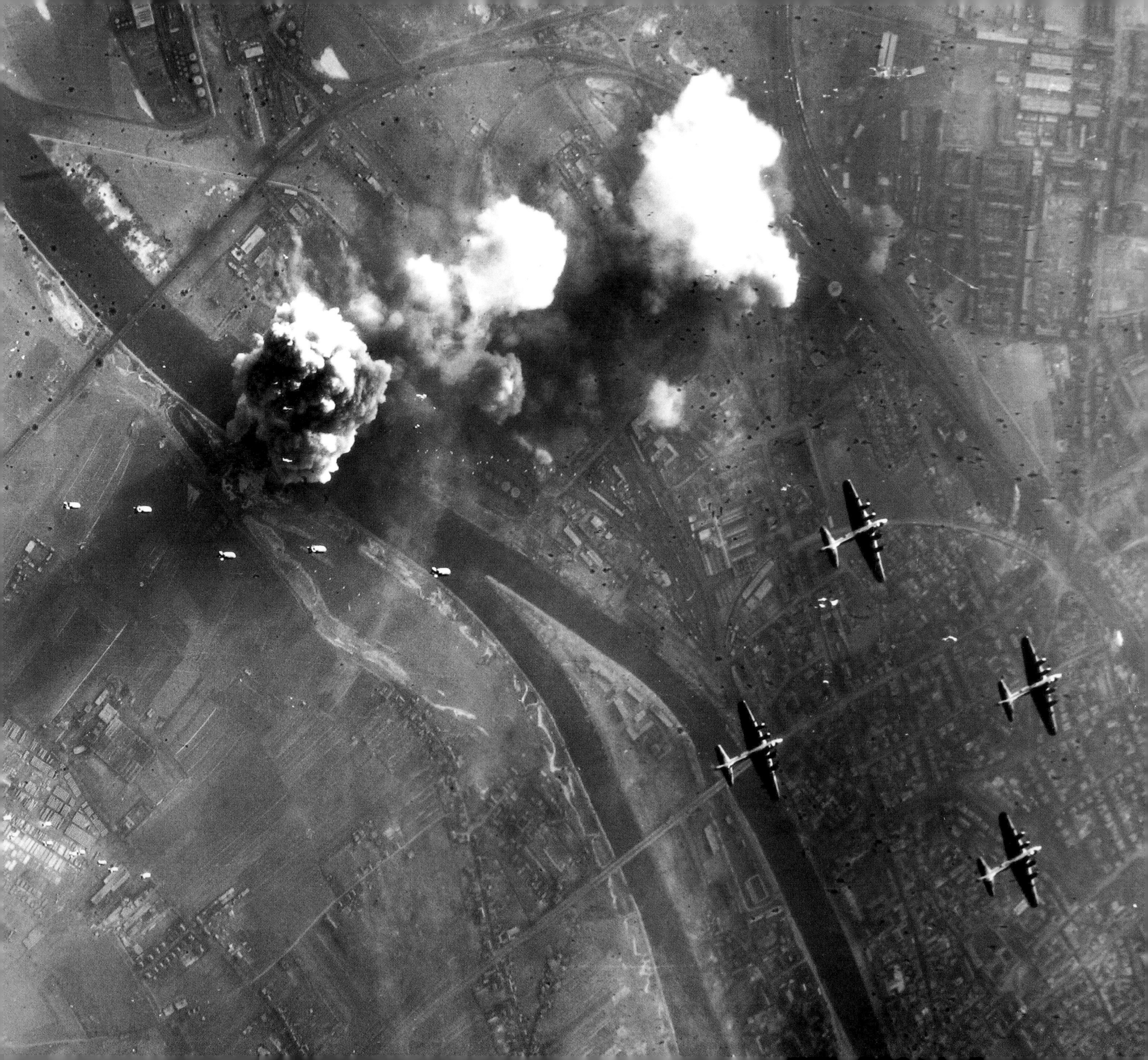

CHAPTER 12

EVADERS AND GUESTS OF NEUTRALS

The Fifteenth Air Force lost more than two thousand aircraft, many behind enemy lines, during its one and a half years in combat. Some of the crews managed to evade capture and return to Allied lines, but the Fifteenth was unusual among American combat air forces in the number of crews able to do so. More than six thousand airmen succeeded, primarily because some of the countries the Fifteenth flew over on its missions had well-organized resistance movements. Several Allied clandestine organizations initially aided evading Fifteenth crewmen: the American Organization of Strategic Services (OSS), the British Special Operations Executive (SOE), and the British organization dedicated to helping Allied evaders and prisoners, MI9. Eventually the Fifteenth organized its own unit to assist evaders, called Air Crew Rescue Units, working with the organizations just mentioned.[lxxxvii]

Opposite page: Bombs fall as others have already hit their target at Regensburg, Germany, during the raid by B-17s of the 5th Bomb Wing on December 25, 1944.

Evading crews were rare in the early days of Fifteenth Air Force operations. One such crew was that of a 2nd Bomb Group Fortress piloted by 1st Lt. William Slaughter. During the mission to bomb Eleusis Airfield, near Athens, Greece, on December 20, 1943, the 2nd Bomb Group lost three Fortresses, including Slaughter's. On the bomb run, the tail gunner called out German fighters attacking from the rear, and soon afterward, a barrage of flak hit the formation, just after bombs away. Slaughter's Fortress, number 42-25345, was hit in three engines; number four caught fire and was feathered. The ball-turret gunner, Tech. Sgt. Durwood Clem, described the effect of the enemy onslaught: "The metal was peeling off the right wing like paper." Soon the entire right wing was ablaze, and the Fortress began to lose altitude. Cockpit electricity was cut off, the bomb-bay doors were partially blown off, and the radio no longer worked. As the formation made their turn to head for home, 42-25345 turned in the opposite direction, forced to do so as only one engine on the left wing was working. It began circling before returning to the formation with its left wing dipped and right wing on fire, losing altitude quickly.

During the circle, three to four more Me 109s attacked the crippled Fortress. Two made a single pass and were gone, but a third came in from behind, firing repeated bursts of cannon and machine-gun fire. The tail gunner, Tech. Sgt. Stanley Owiek, returned the fire. He reported, "The third fighter came in, in trail, and shooting long bursts. I returned the fire and kept shooting as he came in. He spun past us, out of control, and went down. After I bailed out, I saw the same enemy fighter in a right spiral and a little later, I noticed where it had crashed." Slaughter also confirmed the enemy fighter's crash after he bailed out, about thirty seconds before the Fortress exploded. All crewmen bailed out, only about ten miles from the Eleusis, and reached the ground safely, although the flight engineer, Sgt. William Buell, had been wounded.

Slaughter recalled: "I delayed opening my chute until I had dropped about 5,000 feet, as enemy fighters were circling the chutes of the men in my crew. . . . [They] shot at several of the crew . . . and Lieutenant Lanham, my bombardier, had two panels shot out of his chute." The copilot, 1st Lt. Robert Ogletree described his landing: "I landed on a barren hillside and while I was getting out of my chute, a Greek shepherd approached me. He appeared very friendly, kissed me, and shook my hand. . . . [He] led me up the hill to . . . a small group of armed Greeks [who] were waiting to cover our escape from a German patrol that was out searching for those of us who parachuted down."

Sergeant Clem described his experience when he encountered a Greek civilian after he reached the ground: "I hid my chute and started running up the mountain side." Three other crewmen soon joined him: "We could see two truckloads of Germans coming up the valley on the road. They were armed with high-powered rifles equipped with telescopic sights. . . . We could see the Germans unload from the trucks and [they] deployed along the road. They were close enough so that we could single out the officers and see them hiding in the shade of olive trees and scanning us with field glasses. The boys and myself ran like hell over the mountain, dodging from boulder to boulder, while the Germans were taking pot shots at us. The Greek soldiers [resistance] stayed behind to cover our retreat and they told us later their ambush had wiped out the entire German patrol."[lxxxviii][lxxxix]

Although the crewmen landed in different places, they reunited that evening at a resistance camp in the mountains.

Opposite page: A Flying Fortress bombs the airfield at Eleusis, Greece, on December 8, 1943, a week before Lieutenant Slaughter's B-17 was shot down over the same target.

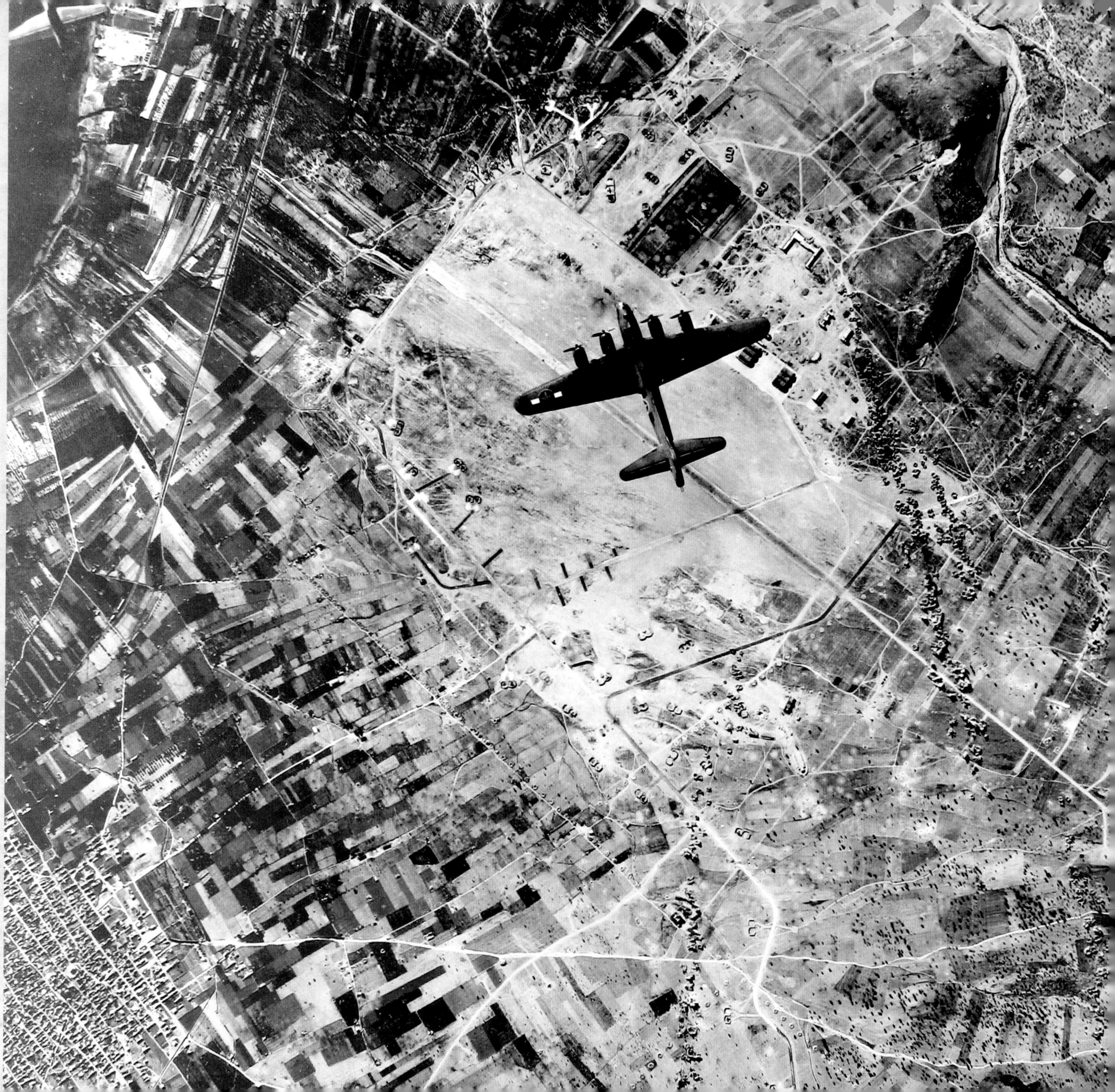

Most of the crew walked for a month through the mountains of Greece, aided during the journey by members of the Greek resistance. They traveled during the day except when crossing major roads and rail lines, which they did at night, and encountered German patrols on occasion. Each night the crew stayed in Greek villages, split up among peasants' homes.

At one point during the month-long trek, Lieutenant Slaughter became ill and had to remain in a Greek village. While recuperating, he was joined by another crewman from the 2nd Bomb

A navigator examines holes made by flak in the nose of his 450th Bomb Group Liberator over Mostar, Yugoslavia, after one of the early missions flown by the group in January 1944.

A 465th Bomb Group Liberator flies over the Alps on the way to bomb a target in Germany.

Group, Staff Sgt. Frank Naro, whose Fortress had been shot down by flak on a previous raid on Eleusis, on December 14. Naro evaded capture, as did his pilot, 2nd Lt. Walter Ward, but one crewman was killed and the others taken prisoner. Naro himself narrowly avoided capture just after he landed on Greek soil.

He landed close to a Greek farm, and farmers gave him peasant clothes just as a German patrol arrived, obviously looking for him. The farmers gave him some tools and led him to a vineyard, where he posed as a worker until the Germans had searched the farm and left empty handed. As they drove away, he saw two members of his crew in one of the vehicles.

The farmers then gave him a jug and a pick to complete his disguise and led him up a mountain, where he hid for several days. His journey across Greece then began, during which he stayed in villages, like Slaughter's crew. In one home, where the family could speak English, he stayed in a room next to one occupied by a German officer. At another village, where he remained for more than a week, he received more presentable civilian clothes and a forged identification card with his photo. He left by truck and passed safely through several German checkpoints. Reaching a British mission to the resistance in early January, he received a British battledress uniform to replace his civilian clothing. He then set out with a Greek guide and encountered Lieutenant Slaughter, who was now fit to travel again, shortly afterward. They both set out to reach safety with two Greek guides and equipped with passes signed by the Greek resistance.

It took the pair about two weeks to reach the coast and a small seaport, where several other American airmen and escaped British prisoners of war were already waiting for transport to Italy. The remainder of Slaughter's crew arrived shortly thereafter. On the last day of January, the Fifteenth Air Force crews and the others set sail in a *caique*, a small Greek fishing craft, and after a two-day voyage reached a small port on the Turkish mainland, near Izmir. Civilian clothing now replaced their uniforms again, and the British and American consuls arranged for accommodation in a local hotel. The American airmen then traveled by train to Ankara and flew to Allied territory a few days later. The navigator of Slaughter's crew, Lt. William Nehila, was the only member who did not return to Allied lines. He was separated from the rest of the crew and eventually captured, like the majority of Naro's crew. He spent the rest of the war in prisoner-of-war camps.[xc]

Two months after the Slaughter crew's adventure began, another Fortress crew began a similar ordeal behind enemy lines, following the last mission of Big Week to Regensburg on February 25. While the 449th Bomb Group was over Regensburg, flak damaged two engines on the B-24 nicknamed *Sophisticated Lady*, flown by 1st Lt. Gilbert Bradley. Savage fighter attacks followed that lasted over an hour. Their onslaught raked the fuselage of the Liberator, killing one waist gunner, Staff Sgt. Paul Biggart, and wounding the other, Staff Sgt. Roland Prescher, in both legs. Enemy fire also knocked out all three turrets, riddled the rear of the fuselage, and damaged the rudders. Another 449th Liberator flew alongside the stricken bomber, helping defend against the enemy fighters. *Sophisticated Lady's* ball-turret and tail gunners, Staff Sgts. Franklin Grubaugh and Irving Mills, each claimed a Ju 88 shot down and the navigator, 2nd Lt. Joseph McMenimem, an Me 210 before the turrets were knocked out. Grubaugh later recounted the action in a diary: "The fighters (Me 210a, 110s, 109s, and Ju88s) hit us as we crossed the Alps, going to the target. Had a flying battle from them until we got across the Alps. They left us just as my turret went out. All the other turrets had been out for at least fifteen minutes. Lieutenant Kenneth Ebersole and Mills were firing [the] waist guns. . . . We had a running fight that lasted about two hours."[xci]

The crew threw loose equipment out of the B-24, but a third engine, with a damaged oil line, stopped over Yugoslavia. Bradley ordered the crew to bail out, and all who could did so, just before the bomber crashed near a farmhouse.

Grubaugh, Prescher, Mills, and Ebersole landed close together. Partisans met them and took them to a village, where Bradley and McMenimem joined them. On February 27, Partisans started the group on a hike to a British mission in the area. On the way, four 450th Bomb Group crewmen from the crew of 1st Lt. John Giraudo, also shot down on February 25, joined

Opposite page: Bombs strike the fighter factory at Regensburg on February 25, 1944. Lieutenant Bradley's *Sophisticated Lady* was badly damaged on this mission, and the crew bailed out over Yugoslavia.

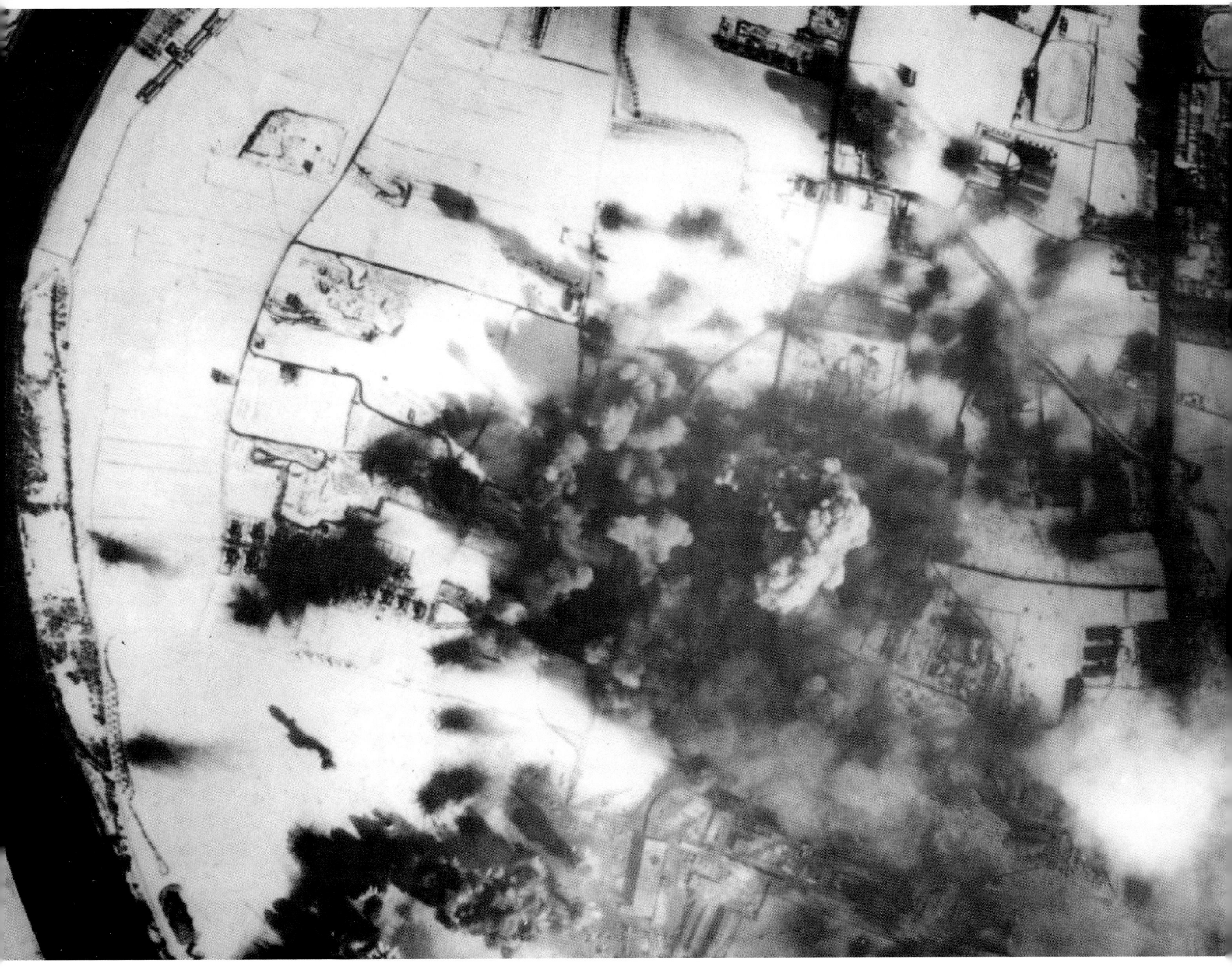

them. Flak had damaged their Liberator at the target, and then fighters had attacked the ship over Yugoslavia on the flight home, forcing the crew to bail out. Two others from the crew, separated from the four who joined Bradley's crew, also evaded, but Giraudo and four others were taken prisoner.

During the trek, Prescher's wounds forced him to stay behind, and Lieutenant McMenimem stayed with him. The remaining members of the fugitive band continued on to the British Mission, where they arrived on February 29. The group rested at the mission, commanded by a British major who had news of some of the others in their crew, scheduled to join them in the near future.

An Me 410, far left center, chasing a Liberator, far right center, over the Alps during the February 23, 1944, mission to bomb the aircraft factory at Steyr, Austria. Lieutenant Bradley's crew was also attacked by fighters over the Alps two days later, during the mission to Regensburg.

Grubaugh's diary recorded the arrival of 1st Lt. Robert Kotard and six of his crew from the 2nd Bomb Group on March 3: "Last night seven men who had bailed out of a B-17 on 31 January came to the village. They're all in pretty bad shape. We doubled up on beds last night, everyone sleeping in one room."[xcii] Flak had damaged Kotard's Fortress during the second raid on northern Italian airfields on January 31. The crew bailed out over the Adriatic Sea, near the port of Pola. Two drowned and a third was taken prisoner, but Partisans rescued Kotard and the others.

Two days later, Slaughter's copilot, 2nd Lt. Anson Hughes, and radio operator Staff Sgt. Herbert Clements, from Bradley's crew, joined the group at the British mission, as did Lieutenant McMenimem. The three and their Partisan escorts were delayed by an encounter with a German patrol on the way, forcing them to hide for a day.

The fliers stayed with the British mission for several days awaiting evacuation by air from a crude landing strip nearby. Grubaugh again: "We have to wait for the snow to melt so a plane can land. . . . The snow is six feet deep in the timber, about two and half feet in the open. Last night we got about another eight inches of snow. It is snowing and blowing terribly this morning."[xciii] By March 13, Sergeant Prescher, with the last member of their crew to turn up, Sgt. Joseph Montagna, had joined them. During their wait, two men from the 2nd Bomb Group crew became so ill they were taken to a Partisan hospital and did not rejoin the others.

For the next few days, it continued to snow, and food became short as the party awaited an airdrop of supplies when weather permitted. The British mission was able to send some clothing, although food was still in short supply. The men suffered badly from lice, which, combined with hunger, made them very uncomfortable. Only a few of the men had boots; most others still had only the fleece-lined flight boots, necessary for high altitude flying but most unsuitable for walking.

The weather finally improved, and on the March 16 the group began their trek to a landing field that wasn't snowed in. They arrived at the British mission near the field on the twentieth, just missing an evacuation flight the previous day. Prescher went to a Partisan hospital on March 21, and the rest of the group moved on, arriving that night at the headquarters of Josip Tito, where they met the Partisan leader. The headquarters had a shower, and the men could wash properly for the first time in almost a month.

On March 24, German Do 217 bombers appeared overhead but did not bomb the area. Grubauch recorded in his diary: "Two Do 217s were over today. . . . Another plane over at 1700. It did some strafing from about 1,500 feet. No apparent damage." Two days later, three of the group left for Italy in a Russian aircraft that had landed on the crude landing strip, part of an Allied agreement that permitted Russian aircraft to use airfields in Italy to supply Tito's Partisans.

A few days later, another Liberator crew, a Fortress pilot, and two escaped British prisoners of war appeared at the headquarters for evacuation to Italy as well. As even more evading fliers arrived, twenty of the American airmen hoped to catch an evacuation flight, but German bombers attacked the airstrip and fighters strafed the area, so they were unable to leave.

Snow prevented any more flights until the night of April 2, when more than thirty of these airmen flew to Italy. Another Allied aircraft returned to drop supplies on the fifth but did not land. The remaining crewmen, including several from Bradley's crew, did not fly to Italy for several more days, but all eventually reached Allied control.[xciv]

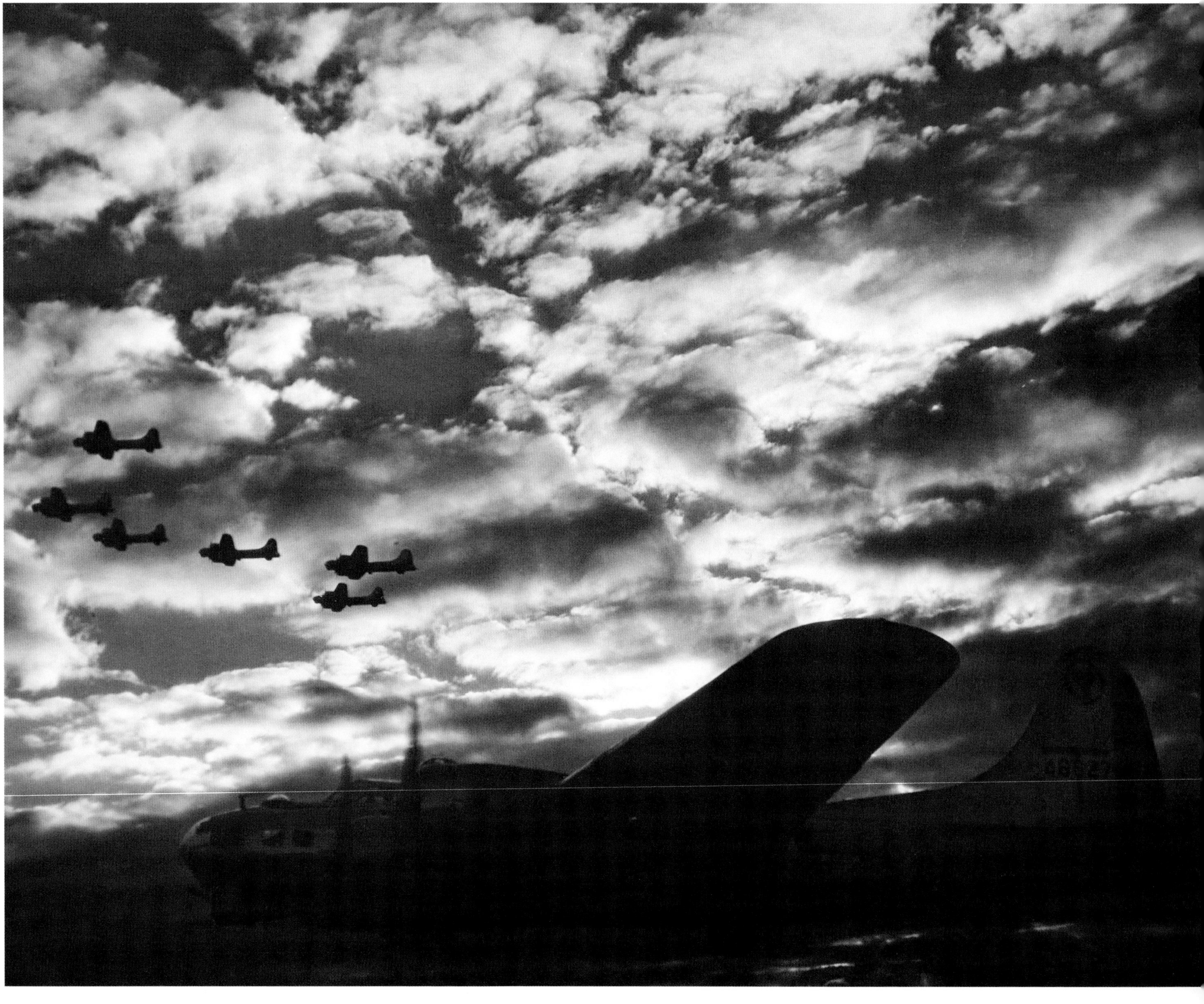

During the first half of 1944, more than fifty downed Fifteenth Air Force airmen successfully evaded capture and returned to Italy. In July, as mentioned at the beginning of this chapter, the Fifteenth formed its own unit to assist its downed flyers, called the Air Crew Rescue Unit. It helped a number of evading Fifteenth airmen, with the able assistance of other Allied organizations working behind the lines in Yugoslavia.[xcv]

On November 7, during the raid on the marshalling yards at Maribor, flak hit a 99th Bomb Group Fortress flown by the crew of 2nd Lt. Edward Wiketh in the left wing just after bombs away, and the propeller of one engine flew off. Immediately after this, another burst hit the nose, killing the navigator-bombardier. The bomber dropped back in the formation, then turned away and lost altitude. Wiketh ordered the crew to bail out, and the ten remaining crewmen left the stricken bomber. All but two of them were taken prisoner. Sergeants Thurston Medlin and Jack Cooke landed close together in a wooded area. Yugoslav civilians immediately surrounded the pair, and an elderly man came up to them and shook their hands. A young girl then took them to her home, where her father, who spoke English, told them that no Partisans were in the area and they should turn themselves in to the Yugoslav police, who would not turn them over to the Germans.

The girl's father told them not to worry about anything and, with two other men, began to walk with them through the countryside. When they came to an inn, their escorts left them at the door. Another young girl, from this neighborhood, pointed to a nearby building and exclaimed "Gestapo!," gesturing for them to run for it.

The pair took off into the woods and the second girl joined them, leading them to a home a few miles away, where they met two Partisans. The quartet left the home that night, stopping at barns as they wandered the area for several days with the Germans searching for them. The Partisans eventually found new places for the pair to hide until an elderly man was able to take them by cart across the Drava River. They stopped at an inn overnight and then continued to walk, stopping at different houses on their trek. An Italian now joined the group, and they all continued to move from house to house as the Partisan pair attempted to contact couriers who could take them to Partisan-controlled territory. This took several more days, and it was not until November 19 that they met a Partisan group to escort them to safe territory. After an encounter with a German patrol, the two airmen finally reached a local Partisan headquarters three days later and a British mission to the Partisans the following day. The British immediately turned them over to an American mission whose evacuation airstrip was threatened by the Germans, so Medlin and Cooke traveled with the Americans and several more evading airmen to a mountaintop, where they stayed for a few days. Partisans then moved the group toward the Sava River, which they crossed, defying German patrols, on December 14. A collaborationist Yugoslav unit attacked their Partisan escort, but the airmen escaped and continued their journey, finally reaching a British mission with an open airstrip on December 20. A week later, on December 27, an American C-47 flew them back to Italy.[xcvi]

Of course, Yugoslavia was not the only country outside the Reich in which Fifteenth Air Force aircraft went down. Neutral countries—Spain, Turkey, and Switzerland—also became emergency destinations for damaged aircraft and those low on fuel that couldn't make the flight back to base. Switzerland received most of these aircraft, crews that either landed or bailed out over the country to avoid becoming prisoners of war.

Fate gave a 450th Bomb Group crew such a Christmas present after flak badly damaged their Liberator during the December 25, 1944, mission to bomb the marshalling yards at Innsbruck,

Austria. On the bomb run, flak damaged the number one and two engines on the left wing, the number four engine on the right wing was smoking, and fuel lines in the bomb bay were punctured and leaking. A flak burst hit the cockpit, destroying most instruments and wounding the pilot, 1st Lt. Vincent Fagan; the copilot, 2nd Lt. Nicholas Mackoul; and the flight engineer, Tech. Sgt. James Estes.

Despite the damage, the Liberator stayed with the group formation and bombed with them. Soon after bombs away, attempts to feather engines one and two failed, and the Liberator fell out of the group formation, losing altitude. After briefly considering flying back to Italy, the absence of a working compass and the loss of altitude quickly led to the decision to try to reach Switzerland.

Within half an hour, Lake Constance came into view, and the crew tried to locate the airfield at Zurich. While doing so, they strayed back over Germany, and flak began to burst around them. It continued as they turned for Switzerland again, and Swiss antiaircraft fire also began to bracket the Liberator. As more flak hit the bomber, the damage prevented the pilots from lowering the landing gear to signal their desire to land at the nearest Swiss airfield, so they rang the bail-out alarm.

All but one crewman bailed out. A waist gunner, Sgt. Ralph Coulson, who had earlier told his crewmates that he would never bail out, went down with the ship. The parachute of the navigator, 2nd Lt. Martin Homistek, caught on the tail of the Liberator and he also went down with the aircraft. Both were killed when it crashed near the town of Wureligen, in Switzerland. Copilot Mackoul did bail out successfully but landed in a river and drowned.

The remaining crewmen landed safely and were taken to the airfield at Dubendorf for interrogation, then to an internment camp at Abelboden. The radio operator, Tech. Sgt. Vernon Leitch, escaped from the camp on January 23 with ski clothes and train tickets that would get him to Berne and the American consulate. He journeyed by bus and train to Berne, where he spent several days with American military attaché in the company of other escaping airmen. Directed to take a train to Lausanne, near the French border, he missed the train and returned to the military attaché. His next attempt used a Polish escape route through the town of Neufchâtel, where he stayed at a safe house with Polish soldiers also trying to escape.

Three crewmen from the 484th Bomb Group Liberator flown by Lt. R. A. Dean that went down over Yugoslavia from engine failure on November 20, 1944, prepare to board a C-47 for the flight to Italy a few days later.

B-17s of the 99th Bomb Group drop their bombs on target.

He joined a group of almost thirty Poles, and another American, during an attempt to cross the border into France, but a Swiss border guard challenged them. The two Americans and some Poles bolted, and although the guard shot at them, he missed. The American duo escaped from another Swiss guard as they wandered the area trying to find the border, then decided to return to the safe house. As they neared the house, two Swiss policemen, who were watching the house, caught them. Leitch and the other American were sent to a punishment stockade at Hunenberg.

On January 31, Lieutenant Fagan, nose gunner Staff Sgt. Thomas Owen, and waist gunner Sgt. Claude Hunt got away from the internment camp on a sled, then hailed a cab that took them to an inn. Here, a Swiss policeman nabbed them. While he was phoning for instructions, they decided the jig was up and returned to Abelboden.

Left: A Flying Fortress from the 340th Bomb Squadron, 97th Bomb Group, bombs marshalling yards in Subotica, Yugoslavia, on September 18, 1944. This aircraft ditched in the Adriatic in on January 21, 1945, but all the crew were saved.

Opposite page: The first Fortress lost by the 483rd Bomb Group, over Nis, Yugoslavia, on April 15, 1944. Flak hit a wing fuel tank, and the aircraft burst into flames. All aboard were killed.

Sergeants Owen and Hunt made a second escape attempt on February 4, with the aid of a Yugoslav officer. They skied over a mountain, then got on a train. The same Swiss policemen who had captured them a few days earlier saw the trio but failed to recognize the two Americans. He did, however, recognize the Yugoslav officer, who held all their tickets, as an escaped internee and arrested him. Without tickets, the two Americans were soon rounded up, too. All found themselves in the Hunnenberg punishment stockade.

continued on page 174

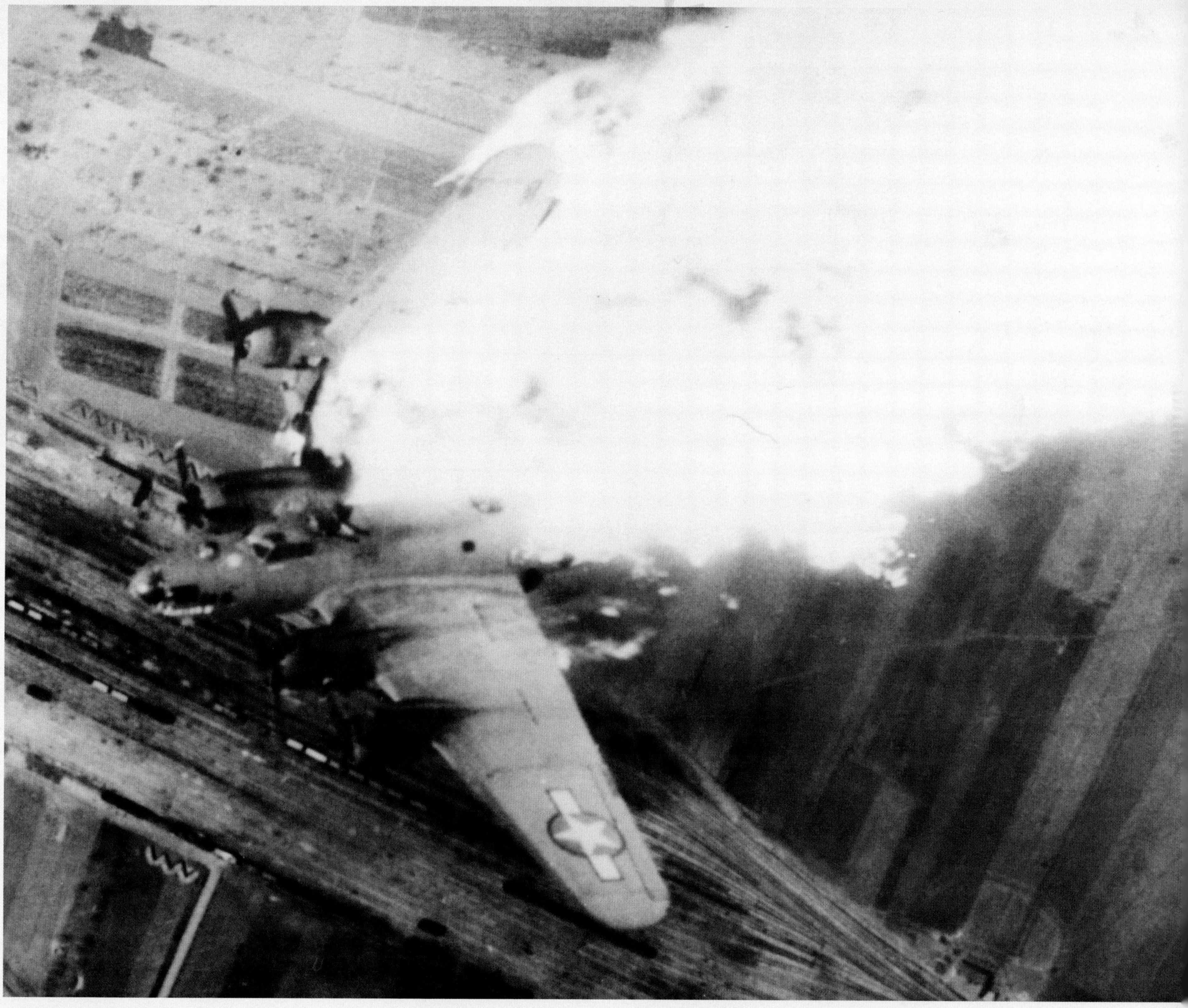

A 449th Bomb Group Liberator struck by flak in the waist during a mission to bomb a bridge in Yugoslavia in the fall of 1944. A waist gunner was killed, but the pilot managed to bring the damaged B-24 safely back to base.

Lieutenant Thomas Smith of the 14th Fighter Group examines damage inflicted to his P-38 after a collision with a German fighter on January 16, 1944. Despite the severe damage, he was able to crash-land in a wheat field near his base.

On February 15, all the members of the crew, including those punished for escape attempts, were sent to Berne, where the Swiss had gathered other aircrew. All had been designated for repatriation to the Allies and soon left by train for France and Allied control.[xcvii]

Of course, fighter pilots, as well as bomber crews, also evaded capture, and one early Fifteenth Air Force evader was Maj. Horace Hanes. Bad weather on January 7, 1944, prevented the bombing of the aircraft factory at Wiener Neustadt, and some of the escort fighters, briefed to escort the bombers on the return flight, fought a thirty-minute air battle with enemy fighters. During the dogfight, the 1st Fighter Group lost seven Lightings, including those flown by Major Hanes and his wingman, 1st Lt. Horace Corbett. Both were shot down near Bedjna, Yugoslavia, close to the border with Austria. Corbett crashed with his plane and was killed. Hanes bailed out and landed in a tree on a hilltop. He slipped out of his harness and tried to remove the canopy from the tree, so his location would be less obvious, but was unable to do so. Fortunately, a Yugoslav woman soon appeared, with her daughter and an axe, and chopped the tree down. They took him to their home, and, after a short time there, other civilians took him to a nearby town, where a woman spoke English. From here, three young men escorted him to a Partisan detachment in nearby mountains, then to a division headquarters the next day. After a few days here, he set out with a Partisan escort on a hike that lasted five days, to a Partisan general staff headquarters, near the town of Rasinja. Here he received shoes and other equipment necessary for more walking, then proceeded with a party to the Sava River. The Germans were moving many troops through the immediate area, so his party doubled back, then found another part of the river where they were able to cross safely. After crossing a heavily guarded highway and rail line, Hanes was taken by truck to a British mission serving with the Partisans. From here, his party began to hike to the town of Mizin. Heavy snow held them up for several days, but they finally reached the town in late February and then continued on to Tito's headquarters, where they arrived on February 28. From here, Hanes moved to the town of Petrovac, where he waited for a plane to return him to Italy. The C-47 arrived on March 19 and returned to Italy.[xcviii]

Another fighter pilot who spent unanticipated time in Yugoslavia did so following a strafing mission, one of the most dangerous tasks undertaken by fighter pilots, as we have seen. Light flak, and even small-arms fire, at low altitudes could be deadly. The flyers of the 52nd Fighter Group flew a strafing mission on September 3, 1944, during which six of their Mustangs went down. Fortunately several of these men survived this ordeal, evaded capture, and reached Italy.

The P-51s met stiff opposition strafing roads and railway lines in Yugoslavia, south of Belgrade, and small-arms fire hit the Mustang flown by 2nd Lt. Lloyd Hargrave. The engine began to smoke, so he jettisoned his canopy in order to see and climbed to eight hundred feet with the intention of flying back to base. Only a few minutes later, however, his engine began to lose power, so he crawled out of the cockpit and jumped. Hargrave had trouble gripping the ripcord, and when he was finally able to pull it, his parachute opened when he was only twenty feet from the ground. His fighter crashed only one hundred yards away, but he landed safely and began to gather his parachute canopy when two farmers appeared, followed by a Chetnik Partisan. The trio took him to a nearby farm, gave him water and a snack, and then led him a short distance to a wagon, which transported him to a local Chetnik headquarters, where a Chetnik officer gave him a statement to sign indicating they had assisted him. He gave the .45-caliber pistol he carried as part of his escape equipment to the officer in a gesture of thanks. The officer then took him, by buggy and auto, to a major Chetnik headquarters. They arrived that evening.

An English-speaking Chetnik began to interrogate him, but he gave little information. The Chetniks treated him well. A tailor attached to the headquarters made him a warm coat, and the staff even shined his shoes each day. On September 5, Hargarve left this headquarters by cart for a small town in the area, where a Chetnik major commissioned him as an officer in the Chetnik Air Force and gave him rank insignia. He was the guest of honor at a banquet that night and a celebration of the Yugoslav king's birthday the next day. On the seventh, he left, with an escort, for an American mission in the area and, after two nights there, returned to Italy by C-47 on September 17.[xcix]

The crew of a bomber that crash-landed on the island of Vis prepare to return to Italy in a C-47 transport in November 1944.

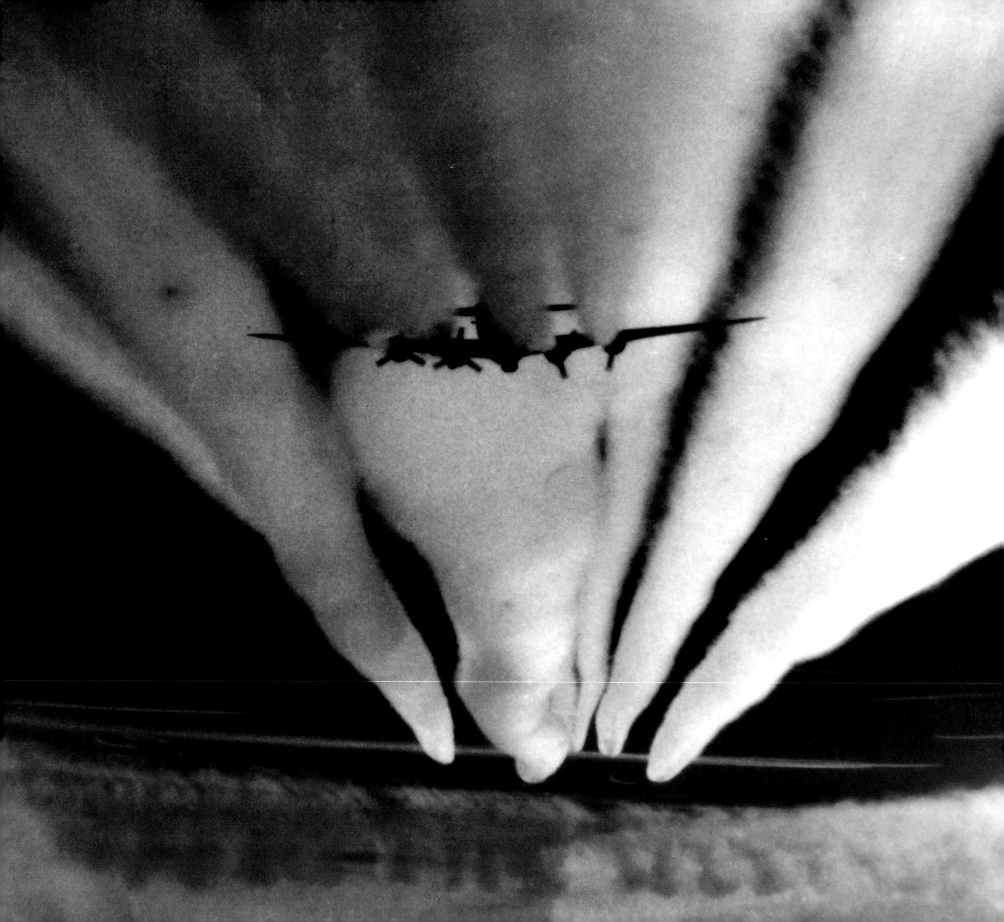

CHAPTER 13

SLOVAKIAN RESCUE AND PRISONERS OF WAR

As Fifteenth Air Force missions turned increasingly to central Europe, beginning in the summer of 1944, more crews went down in areas not controlled by Yugoslav Partisans but in countries allied with Germany. One of the latter was the Slovak portion of Czechoslovakia, temporarily a self-governing satellite of Nazi Germany. Crews that bailed out or crashed here during much of that summer usually found themselves prisoners of the Slovaks. Once the Slovak Army revolted against their collaborationist government at the end of August, however, these men were released. Those crews shot down after the uprising began could evade with the help of the burgeoning Slovak Partisan movement. Many of these crewmen eventually returned to Italy in several of the more dramatic rescue missions organized by the Fifteenth Air Force.

Opposite page: A Flying Fortress flies through the contrails left by bombers ahead in the formation during a mission in the winter of 1944.

Two of these lucky individuals were part of the crew of a Liberators lost by the 459th Bomb Group during the mission to bomb the oil refinery at Moosbierbaum, Austria, on June 26. The B-24, flown by 2nd Lt. Lincoln Artz, had engine trouble and left the formation after bombing the target. The crew bailed out near the border of Czechoslovakia and Hungary. Hungarian troops captured them and stripped them of shoes and all personal possessions, but two, Staff Sgts. Edward Donatelli and Frank Fuquay, had landed just inside the Slovakian border, and Slovakian border guards demanded the Hungarians turn them over to them. The Hungarians complied, and the Slovakians took the pair to a hospital in Bratislava, where they remained for two weeks until transferred to a military barracks and finally the prison camp at Grinava, in mid-August. After the Slovak National Uprising broke out, both men escaped from the camp with other American prisoners and soon encountered Slovak Partisans who took them to Banska Bystrica, the headquarters of the uprising.[c]

Another airman who reached Banska Bystrica was 2nd Lt. Frank Soltesz, a fighter pilot with the 325th Fighter Group. During the July 7 mission to bomb the refineries at Blechhammer, his flight attacked some Me 109s near Bratislava. During the dogfight an Me 109 got on his tail and hit his Mustang, blowing off the canopy. The fighter went into a dive, a wing came off, and Soltesz bailed out at five thousand feet, landing in a Slovak village. He spoke Slovak, so the villagers took him to a nearby town, where he received medical attention for injuries sustained in the jump. Turned over to Slovak police, he used his language skills to convince them not to turn him over to German soldiers, who appeared soon after. The police took him by car instead to a hospital for more treatment and, the next day, to a government ministry in Bratislava. Attempts to question him were unsuccessful, and after more medical treatment, Soltesz ended up in a prisoner-of-war camp. Quartered with other American officers, he stayed in this camp for about a month, until mid-August, when the Slovaks transferred all the prisoners to another prison camp, at Grinava. A day after the Slovak Uprising started, the camp commandant attempted to find transport to move the prisoners, but without success. The guards deserted, so the prisoners then left the camp in small groups. Soltesz and his companions, 2nd Lts. Earcel Winberg and Neal Cobb, procured civilian clothes and met a civilian who led them on September 5 to Slovak Partisans, who offered to take them to Banska Bystrica. After a few days, they met a dozen more American prisoners from Grinava, and with the aid of several guides they soon reached the insurgent-held town.[ci]

Lieutenants Winberg and Cobb were the navigator and bombardier on a 464th Bomb Group Liberator flown by Lt. Earcel Green, which also went down during the Blechhammer mission on July 7, one of four B-24s lost by the 464th on the mission. Flak hit an engine just after bombs away, and the Liberator fell out of the formation. Several more flak bursts hit the bomber as it rapidly lost altitude. Winberg tried to stem fuel leaks, and Cobb manned a waist gun as the flight engineer, Sgt. Claude Davis, helped the wounded tail gunner, Staff Sgt. John Schiana, from his position and bandaged his wound. Green then ordered to the crew to bail out, and Cobb and Staff Sgt. Jesse Houston, a waist gunner, tossed Schiana from the aircraft and then jumped themselves. Winberg, Davis, and another gunner, Staff. Sgt. Gerald Howland, also succeeded in jumping before the bomber crashed, killing Green and two other crewmen. Two other gunners jumped as well, but one was killed when his chute opened too close to the ground.

Moosbierbaum Oil Refinery under attack on June 26, 1944. The smoke is only partially effective, as much of the refinery is still visible.

Bombs fall from a B-17 of the 340th Bomb Squadron, 97th Bomb Group, over Pardubice, Czechoslovakia, on the August 24, 1944, attack on the oil refinery in the city. The 97th lost one Fortress on the mission.

Slovak police rounded up the unwounded survivors, but a civilian found Schiana and carried him to the local gendarmes. Taken to a hospital for treatment, he rejoined his crewmen in late August in Grinava Prison Camp, where his comrades had been imprisoned after interrogation in Bratislava. When the Germans approached Bratislava in early September, Slovak guards disappeared from the camp, and the crew escaped with the other American prisoners. Of the six crewmen who bailed out, Howland was the only one captured to become a prisoner of the Germans. Schiana's group of prisoners joined Slovak soldiers and went through several towns before reaching Banska Bystrica on September 11.[cii]

The crew of another Liberator, from the 454th Bomb Group, also became Slovak prisoners on the same mission. Flak damaged two engines over their target, the synthetic oil refinery at Odertal, Germany, and slightly wounded the pilot, 1st Lt. John Wilson, and the copilot. A third engine soon developed a problem with a propeller. Their bomber lost altitude on the flight home, and to compound their problems, fighters attacked them for half an hour. The attack inflicted more damage to the aircraft and wounded several crewmen, but the gunners claimed two Me 109s and three Fw 190s shot down. Eventually Wilson lowered the landing gear to signal

Flying Fortresses over Blechhammer during the September 13, 1944, the mission on which Lieutenant Artz's aircraft went down over Slovakia. The white cloud at left is from the explosion of an antiaircraft rocket.

surrender, and the attacks ceased. He immediately raised it again and the attacks resumed, so he lowered it once again and the crew bailed out over Czechoslovakia. One crewman hit the tail when he jumped from a waist window; knocked unconscious, he could not pull his ripcord and fell to his death. Although one man evaded capture for two days, Slovak gendarmes captured the surviving crewmen, taking the wounded to a hospital and the others to Pesnick Prison Camp, where they remained until early September. Like other American prisoners, they escaped captivity when the uprising began. Helped initially by Slovak civilians, they soon met Slovak soldiers fleeing the advancing Germans, and the escapees formed small groups to continue their flight. Six of them eventually managed to reach Banska Bystrica.[ciii]

The next month, on August 22, the 459th Bomb Group lost seven Liberators when the 304th Bomb Wing attacked the oil refineries at Blechhammer, Germany. Flak hit one of the seven, flown by 1st Lt. William Sykes, after bombs away, holing a fuel tank and damaging an engine that had to be feathered. With another engine out of control and fuel low, Sykes ordered the crew to abandon the bomber over the Czech Protectorate portion of Czechoslovakia, then part of the Third Reich. Five of the crew were captured and became prisoners of war in Germany, but two more, Staff Sgts. Ralph Fuchs and Clyde Thompson, landed close together and hid in woods. An old man and boy found them and saved them from Germans soldiers searching for them. The

Czechs then pointed them in the direction of Poland, and Russian lines. After two days on the run, a peasant agreed to guide them across the border into Slovakia instead. They succeeded in crossing the border, but Slovak soldiers soon arrested them, and they found themselves in Grinava Prison Camp with other American prisoners. An interpreter told them not to reveal that they had initially landed in the Czech Protectorate, and not Slovakia, so they wouldn't be turned over to the Germans. After only a few days in the camp, the beginning of the Slovak Uprising led to their release. Over the next three weeks, they, too, journeyed through Slovakian towns and villages until reaching Banska Bystrica.

German troops examine the wreckage of a Fifteenth Air Force Flying Fortress shot down over Slovakia in the late summer of 1944.

A Liberator catches fire after flak hits it over the oil refinery at Blechhamer in August 1944. Three crewmen bailed out before the bomber exploded moments after this photo was taken.

Two other members of this crew, 2nd Lt. Walter Leach and Sgt. Delos Miller, also landed in the Czech Protectorate. Leach sprained his ankle on landing but immediately received help from some locals, who hid him in a field, then brought him food and civilian clothing. Later, he received first aid at a farmhouse, and farmers hid him from a police patrol looking for him and his comrades. A young man, one of those who had found him, offered to guide him to Russian lines, and they walked into the mountains, sheltering in a barn overnight. An older man met them the next day and led them on a three-day journey to the town of Presov. During this outing, a car stopped and picked up Leach. Miller was picked up by the same car a short time later.

Miller had evaded capture after landing by hiding in some woods until evening, when he set off in the direction of Poland. He encountered a man who pointed the way to Slovakia, so Miller went in this direction until he met a boy on a bicycle. Directing him to hide near a house, the boy later returned with food, accompanied by an older man. He spent the night outside, and the next morning, the man returned with civilian clothes. Then several Czechs took him to the location of his crashed aircraft on the way to Slovakia. On the journey, he met two more Czechs, who gave him food and who walked with him for part of the day. When they left him, he continued on alone, reaching an inn, where he met two more young men who accompanied him to another village. There, he slept in a barn for two nights, until the mayor of the village arranged for a car to take him to a train station. When the car arrived, escorted by civilians on bicycles, Miller found it contained Lieutenant Leach. They both drove to a hotel, where they spent the night, then proceeded to the train station, each escorted by a Czech civilian. The Americans waited in the station, surrounded by German soldiers getting onto and off of the numerous German troop trains that passed by, until a civilian train arrived. After changing trains, they reached the town of Vrutky, where they spent the night in another hotel. They met a Russian officer working with the Partisans in the hotel who arranged for a car to take them to a Slovak Partisan unit deep in the mountains. After arriving at a Partisan headquarters with an interpreter, they set out for Banska Bystrica. When they arrived at a village with train station, a crowd of villagers gathered to gape at the foreigners, and one of them, a woman who spoke English, invited them to her home. Here the mayor of village told them he would personally take them to a Partisan headquarters. In his company, they traveled to the headquarters in the town of Martin, as Soviet Air Force planes were alleged to land there to supply the Partisans. When the Germans troops approached the town, Miller and Leach moved with the headquarters as it retreated to Banska Bystrica, where they joined other Americans waiting to be evacuated by air.[civ]

The Slovak Uprising provided an immediate change in circumstances for airmen downed over Slovakia. If not immediately captured by the Germans, they could now expect assistance from Slovak insurgents. The 2nd Bomb Group Fortress flown by 2nd Lt. Daryle Stuckey's crew had engine trouble on the way to bomb the oil refinery at Blechhammer during the mission of September 13. Forced to turn for home shortly before reaching the target, three of the four engines stopped over Slovakia, and Stuckey ordered the crew to bail out. A waist gunner, Cpl. Paul Reinhart, described what happened: "I was last out of the ship, as far as I know, and I fell at least 1,000 feet before pulling the rip cord and noticed the other chutes in the distance."[cv] All crewmen succeeded in jumping, but six of them were captured. Four, however, evaded capture with the help of Slovak Partisans.

Corporal Robert Hare landed near Slovak peasants, who pointed the direction to take, along a road, to avoid capture. After hiding from a car and walking for several hours, he met two small boys who took him to a Slovak home where he changed into civilian clothes. The next day, he went with a Russian he encountered, who was working with the Partisans, to another home whose owner spoke English. After two days here, he and the Russian doubled back to reach the town of Zapolchavy, where another boy led them into the mountains. The following day, the trio arrived at a town held by Slovak troops, and Hare continued on from there to Banska Bystrica.

Another crewman from Stuckey's Fortress, Staff Sgt. William Spruce, landed close to Hare but did not meet him. He immediately headed up a mountain after landing, hiding there overnight. The next day, two Germans with a dog captured him. As they escorted him to captivity, Slovakian Partisans ambushed the trio, killing the Germans and freeing Spruce. They took him to a nearby village, where a civilian took him in. Taken to another home the next day, he met another Partisan, who told him of the airfield at Banska Bystrica. With two more Partisans as escorts,

Liberators from the 55th Bomb Wing over the synthetic oil refinery at Blechhammer at the beginning of the raid of October 13, 1944. The smoke generators have gone into action, but no bombs have yet burst on the target.

Left: A 451st Bomb Group Liberator plunges earthward after a collision with another aircraft during the attack on the synthetic oil refineries at Blechhammer, Germany, on December 17, 1944. Unfortunately, all crewman were killed in the crash. The other B-24 returned safely to base.

Opposite page: Fifteenth Air Force B-24s, believed to be from the 465th Bomb Group, over the smoke-covered synthetic oil refinery at Blechhammer, Germany, in late 1944.

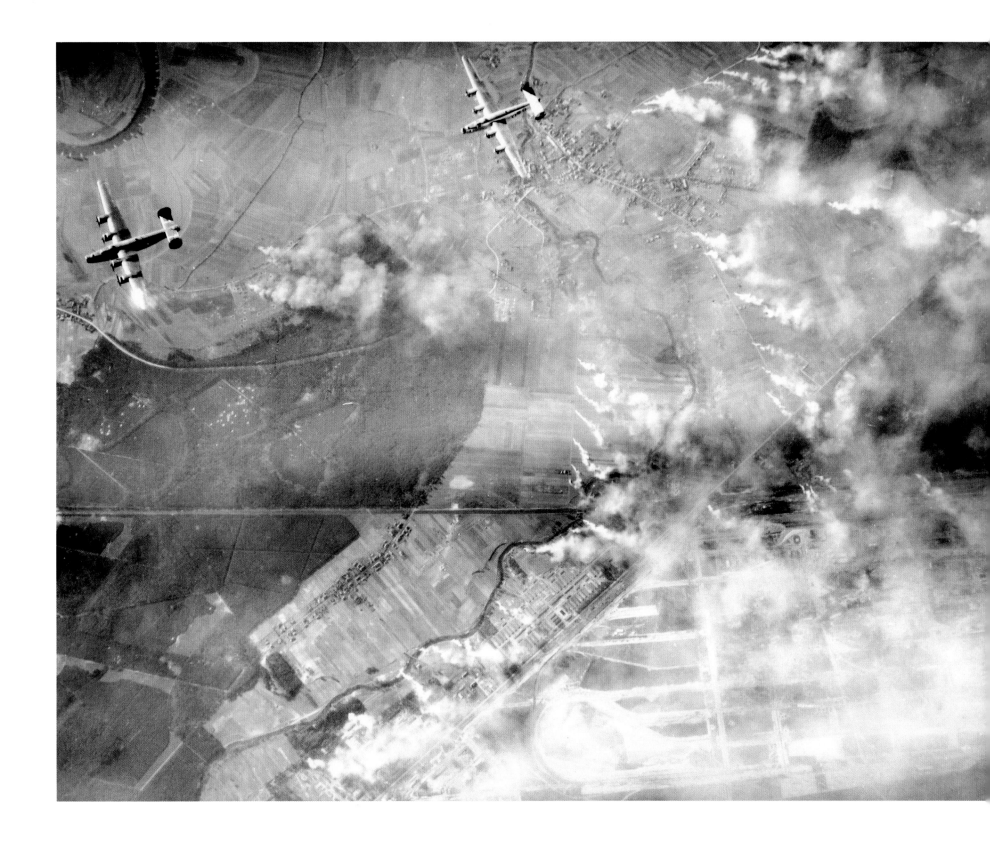

Fifteenth Air Force Liberators bombing the city of Bratislava, Slovakia, in June 1944.

he passed through German lines and soon encountered a Russian Partisan commander with a motorcycle who drove Spruce to Banska Bystrica, where he joined other members of his crew, including Corporal Reinhart.

After he jumped, Reinhart landed near some peasants gathering hay and immediately ran into nearby woods, then moved on. Eventually reaching a dirt road, he spent the night and the next day in the woods, until he met a farmer who brought him food and drink, then started with him for Banska Bystrica. That night, they encountered a Slovak Partisan road block. He recalled: "I ran into a barrier across the road and figured out something was up. About midnight I came across a big cut in the road and went down along the bank. . . . [W]hen I got on the road again, someone said something to me. They were in a small hut along the road

Sergeant Kenje Ogata, a ball-turret gunner, receives the Air Medal from Lt. Col. James B. Knapp, commander of the 451st Bomb Group, in late 1944. His crew crash-landed in Hungary after losing two engines on the December 26, 1944, mission to bomb the synthetic oil refinery at Oswiecim, part of the infamous Auschwitz concentration camp. The crew returned to Italy and continued their combat tour. He was one the few Japanese Americans to serve as a combat air crewman with the Army Air Force.

. . . [with] rifles pointed at me. [One of the Partisans] called out [to] several of this buddies and they asked if I were Russian, German, or French. . . . I asked if [this] . . . was Czechoslovakia and one said 'Ja' . . . I said I was an American. One patted me on the back and said 'Comrade.'"[cvi]

He was identified as an American and taken to a local Partisan headquarters, where he met his copilot, Lt. Henry Tennyson. Tennyson had landed in a tree when he bailed out and, like the other crewmen, hid from the Germans who were searching for him. During the night he began to move through several villages, entering one the next morning upon finding no Germans there. He went to the church and a villager there motioned for him to go into the town square, where a crowd of villages had gathered. One of them spoke English and took him to a house where he was fed before being taken to the local school teacher, who set out with him to find Slovak Partisans. After a journey across several mountains and through several towns held by German troops, the pair arrived in St. Benedickt, held by Slovak troops, a Partisan headquarters. Here he met Reinhart, and the pair was taken by mule to Banska Bystrica.[cvii]

The arrival of Corporal Reinhart and the other evaders at Banska Bystrica, eighteen American airmen by mid-September, led the Slovak insurgents to inform the Czech government in exile in England of their presence. The Czechs radioed this information to Fifteenth Air Force headquarters on September 14, asking for the airmen to be evacuated as soon as possible. Soviet Air Force aircraft had been landing at Tri Duby Airfield near Banska Bystrica for several weeks to bring supplies and personnel to support the Slovak Uprising, so the mission was a definite possibility.

The Fifteenth planned a mission for three days later, and two Flying Fortresses from the 483rd Bomb Group landed at Tri Duby that morning. The two aircraft carried six OSS men, four of them with orders to set up an Air Crew Rescue Unit, called the Dawes Mission, to facilitate the evacuation of these airmen and others expected to arrive in the near future. Navy Lieutenant Holt Green, whom we met in chapter 8, headed the mission. The two other men comprised an OSS intelligence mission. The flight also carried a British intelligence agent and more than four tons of ammunition, arms, and radio equipment for the Slovak insurgents.

Russian officers and Slovak Partisans met the two aircraft, and a crowd of Partisans and civilians gathered. A truck soon arrived with the American airmen awaiting evacuation. The Fortresses remained on the field for only half an hour, and then took off with twelve airmen, three British soldiers, and a Czech. Lieutenant Tennyson, Reinhart's copilot, remained at Tri Duby at OSS request to help them organize their rescue operation.

A Mustang from the 52nd Fighter Group fighter escort, flown by 2nd Lt. Ethan Smith, crash-landed near the field during the mission. His Mustang's engine malfunctioned near Banska Bystrica, and he had to made a forced landing, but hit a ditch, tearing off the landing gear. The impact broke his seat harness, and he hit his head on the gun sight, rendering him unconscious for several hours. Taken to a hospital for treatment, he returned to the OSS mission and waited until the second evacuation flight, on October 7, to return to Italy. His Mustang remained at Tri Duby, but it was never repaired.[cviii]

Bad weather delayed a second evacuation mission to Tri Duby until October 7, when six Fortresses from the 483rd Bomb Group, escorted by 52nd Fighter Group Mustangs, reached the field early in the afternoon. Overcast covered the area, but the bombers found a hole and got underneath it, although Tri Duby was not in sight. After about fifteen minutes, the field came into view, and the Fortresses landed. They stayed on the ground more than an hour this time as the Mustang escort buzzed the field at low level for protection. They brought fourteen more OSS men, reinforcements for the Dawes Team and several more OSS intelligence missions; an Associated Press war correspondent, Joseph Morton; and more arms, ammunition, and other supplies for the insurgents.

The return flight carried thirty evading airmen—twenty-eight Americans and two New Zealanders—as well as five Frenchmen, two representatives of the Slovak National Council, and a Czech resistance officer. Tennyson made the trip, too, as the Fifteenth Air Force now insisted on his return to Italy for debriefing. Five of the Fortresses took off, but the sixth, mired in mud on landing, only took off several hours later. The crew refused to abandon their aircraft, and with the efforts of many Partisans pulling on ropes and some fine throttling by the pilot, the bomber eventually took off safely, arriving in Italy after nightfall.

Three former prisoners of the Romanians, one wearing a Romanian Air Force cap, hold the homemade American flag they raised over their prisoner-of-war camp after Romania surrendered to the Allies in August 1944.

Bad weather delayed a third flight, scheduled for the next few days. By the time the weather cleared, German forces had captured Tri Duby, so it never took place. The airmen gathered for evacuation retreated with Slovak forces, as did the OSS missions, but the Germans captured them all later. Most of the OSS men on the mission were also captured and executed at Mauthausen concentration camp in January 1945.[cix]

Most captured Fifteenth Air Force crews didn't have the good fortune to be flown from enemy territory, instead becoming prisoners of the Germans or their allies. One such prisoner, Staff Sgt. Leonard Bernhardt, experienced the siege of Budapest by the Russians and witnessed the effects of the Holocaust on Hungarian Jews firsthand.

On the way to bomb the oil refineries at Blechhammer, on June 30, 1944, German, two-engine fighters attacked the 460th Bomb Group over Hungary. The enemy was very aggressive, closing to within 150 feet of the Liberators and firing all the way with cannons and machine guns. On the Liberator flown by 2nd Lt. Elder Erfeldt, Staff Sgt. Martin Troy, the tail gunner, succeeded in downing one enemy fighter, but an engine on the bomber caught fire during the attack. To add to the crew's problems, the bomb bay and flight deck began to burn, setting off .50-caliber ammunition feeding the top turret. The flight engineer, Tech. Sgt. John Lenburg, continued to fire at the attackers until the fire burned him badly and forced him out of

A formation of P-39s flies over Northern Italy in 1945.

the turret. On the pilot's order, the copilot rang the bailout alarm as the damaged bomber lost altitude, with the left wing and fuselage on fire. Staff Sgt. Leonard Bernhardt, one of the waist gunners, tried to help Sergeant Troy but found him dead in his turret. He had to fight flames to return to the waist to put on his parachute and was badly burned in the process. The other waist gunner, Tech. Sgt. Ralph Wheeler, pushed Bernhardt out of the waist window when he got stuck while trying to jump, but Wheeler could not get out himself. He was killed, as were Sergeant Troy and the tail gunner. Seven of the crew bailed out of the inferno and all reached the ground safely, landing near Lake Balaton.

Sergeant Bernhardt had a harrowing experience as he descended in his parachute. A twin-engine fighter flew directly at him, and he only managed to escape by spilling the air from his chute and plummeting out of the way. He landed in a wheat field, where Hungarian farmers immediately began to beat him. The arrival of Hungarian gendarmerie saved him, but after marching him to the police station, they refused to provide first aid for his burns. Other members of his crew, along with other airmen, also arrived at the police station. Later a truck took them all to a hospital in the town of Veszprem. Here the injured were hospitalized, while the others departed for a Hungarian prison camp and later a prisoner-of-war camp in Germany.

The injured, including Bernhardt, stayed in Veszprem for a week, after which they traveled by train and streetcar to a hospital in Budapest. The staff of the hospital treated him well, and while there, he learned of the roundup of Hungarian Jews around the country that had begun in April and the creation of ghettos for the Jews of Budapest. As the Russians fought their way into the city, the hospital became a target and was heavily shelled as German artillery was dug in around it. When Russian troops entered the hospital, Bernhardt was able to save several of the nurses from assault. He was then transferred to several Russian hospitals, where he also received good treatment.

He finally returned to Italy in early March and reported what he had learned of the deportation, mistreatment, and murder of Hungarian Jews by the Germans, as well as the impressment of Hungarian civilians for labor by the Russians. He also carried a letter written by a Jewish family in Budapest to relations in the United States that described their deportation from their home in the country to Budapest and the murder and mistreatment they witnessed of Jews in the city by the Hungarian Arrow Cross.[cx]

The shot-down crewmen who ended up in Romanian and Bulgarian hands were more fortunate than Sergeant Bernhardt, or those who fell into German hands, as both countries surrendered in the late summer of 1944 and freed all their Allied prisoners. The aircrews of the Fifteenth Air Force in Romanian captivity had the unusual experience of an airlift rescue to Italy while the war was still raging. The story began when flak shot down the commander of the 454th Bomb Group, Col. James Gunn, on the August 17, 1944, mission to Ploesti. His Liberator led the 304th Bomb Wing, but after experiencing some equipment problems, it dropped back to deputy lead. Heavy flak hit a wing of the Liberator, setting the number one engine on fire and damaging the number three and four engines. Gunn feathered the burning engine just as more flak hit the number two engine. The nose of a plane alongside them in the formation blew off, and Gunn had to drop from the formation to avoid a collision as it became difficult to maintain altitude. With the bomb bay filling with gasoline, he ordered the crew to bail out. After the copilot told him that all the crew had bailed out, Gunn jumped after the co-pilot. He later recalled: "My first sensation upon bailing out was relief . . . because I was worried about an explosion. . . . As I neared the ground, I could see people running towards me from all directions. . . . I got underneath a shock of wheat and covered myself up as best I could. . . . [Soon] I heard voices [and after an hour's search] a fellow poked me with a stick and found me. [He saw two Romanian soldiers and] . . . some thirty civilians. . . . They appeared to be farmers."[cxi]

The Romanians took him first to Ploesti, where he spent a few days with other prisoners at a Romanian headquarters. Later he moved to a prison camp in Bucharest. When the Romanian government surrendered to the Allies, the Luftwaffe bombed Bucharest. Attempts by the Americans to radio their situation to Fifteenth Air Force headquarters in Italy were unsuccessful, and Gunn met with the Romanian Minister of War on August 25 and asked for an aircraft to fly him to Italy. The flight was agreed upon the next day, and on August 27, he took off in a Romanian twin-engine Savoia-Marchetti with a Romanian crew, but engine trouble soon forced them to return. He tried again the following day, this time crammed into the fuselage of an Me 109 flown by a crack Romanian fighter pilot, Capt. Buzu Cantacuzino, who had fifty-four enemy aircraft to his credit. Gunn recalled:

> We finished preparing the Messerschmitt and painted the American flag on both sides of the fuselage and also put American markings on the wings. . . . We got on our way for Italy at 1720. The night before, I had thoroughly briefed this pilot on the method of crossing the coast line, how to avoid flak, etc, and how to find our field. . . . I had no oxygen in the back [of the Messerschmitt] so I was forced to lie still through the entire flight. . . . The lack of oxygen made me rather dopey, but I fought off sleep. . . . As soon as we had started moving down, I could feel that we were losing altitude. I peeked out of the hole at the front of my compartment and saw that we were over the Adriatic. . . . About the time we began to lose altitude, I felt the engine begin to sputter . . . but it didn't sound too bad. The crossing of the coast [of Italy] and the entry to the field was done so fast that no interception [by Allied fighters] was encountered. As we approached the field, he rocked the wings . . . so the flak gunners on the ground could see the flags and markings . . . [and] lowered the wheels. . . . No shots were fired at us and it was a great relief to me when I felt the wheels touch the ground. I heard him stop the engine and a few moments later heard him say to someone: "I have a surprise for you." After the plate on the side of the fuselage had been removed, I got out. . . . A good-sized crowd [surrounded the plane, including] . . . members of my former group. After the hurrahs and cheers, the Lieutenant Commander and I had a bite to eat and I quickly changed from the clothes I had worn for the past ten days . . . we [then] left for Fifteenth Air Force headquarters.[cxii]

Gunn's flight was the aegis of Operation Reunion, which began the next day when two B-17s from the 2nd Bomb Group took an Air Crew Rescue Unit party to Bucharest to organize the repatriation of the prisoners by air. The first mission to do so took place on August 31 when thirty-eight Fortresses from the 2nd and 97th Bomb Groups, refitted to accommodate the prisoners in their bomb bays, landed in Bucharest and returned to Italy with 739 prisoners. The flight was not uneventful, as the escort shot down two German Me 109s that tried to interfere with the mission.

As the Fortresses landed on the large, grass-covered field, Mustangs of the 52nd Fighter Group flew top cover over the field, joined by Romanian Me 109s that only a few days ago had been their foes. After the Fortresses landed, they taxied toward lines of former prisoners on the edge of the field, many dressed in variety of uniforms, including German and Romanian, as well as civilian clothing. The freed prisoners immediately began to climb into the Fortresses, and before the operation ended on September 3, more than 1,100 former American prisoners of the Romanians returned to Italy.[cxiii]

In the final days of the war, a Fifteenth Air Force pilot found himself in a different situation: that of liberating himself as he accepted the surrender of his captors. The incident began during an armed reconnaissance mission over northern Italy on April 22, 1945, as Allied troops advanced quickly into northernmost Italy.

With the war drawing rapidly to a close, fighters ranged freely over northern Italy and Austria, undertaking armed reconnaissance missions that often involved strafing ground targets. On April 22, all Fifteenth Air Force fighter groups flew armed reconnaissance missions over northern Italy. The 82nd Fighter Group lost three Lightnings on the mission, including one flown by 1st Lt. Pren Hollingsworth. As the Group returned to base, at the low altitude necessary for an armed reconnaissance mission, intense, light flak greeted them over the town of Ostiglia. One Lightning went down over the town, and flak hit another, flown by Hollingsworth, in the right engine. He feathered it, gained altitude, and flew away from the town, but the engine soon caught fire and the blaze spread to the fuel tank, so he had to bail out.

Opposite page: Fifteenth Air Force crewmen, former Romanian prisoners of war, on their arrival in Italy during Operation Reunion, which repatriated more than 1,100 former prisoners by early September 1944.

Fifteenth Air Force crewmen recently liberated from Bulgarian prisoner-of-war camps arrive back in Italy, September 1944.

Hollingsworth landed hard and injured his leg and his back. Members of a German flak battery immediately surrounded him and took him to a farmhouse. That evening, a German lieutenant escorted him to a small town in the area, where a captain searched him and tried to interrogate him, without success. During the night, the Germans took him farther behind the front lines, but the confusion from the Allied advance made it impossible to send him any farther, so they returned him to the flak unit's headquarters and his original captors. A German signal unit finally took him with them when they retreated on the night of April 25. American Thunderbolt fighter-bombers strafed and bombed the area the next day, as the advancing British Eighth Army drew near. That night, the Germans destroyed all their equipment and attempted to cross the Adige River, taking Hollingsworth with them, but British shelling thwarted their attempt. They all took cover in a farmhouse, finding other Germans already there. Soon after their arrival, the Germans agreed among themselves to surrender to Hollingsworth. He then took command of the group, and during the night, more Germans arrived at the farm and surrendered to him.

On the morning of the April 27, Hollingsworth donned civilian clothes over his flight suit and began to walk toward British lines with an Italian civilian, holding a white flag. After a few miles, he reached British troops. When it was announced that he was an American, they immediately recognized him. He told them of the Germans awaiting them at the farmhouse and then proceeded by truck to Forli, where the RAF debriefed him. The next day, Hollingsworth hitched a ride on an RAF C-47 and flew to Foggia and Fifteenth Air Force headquarters.[cxiv]

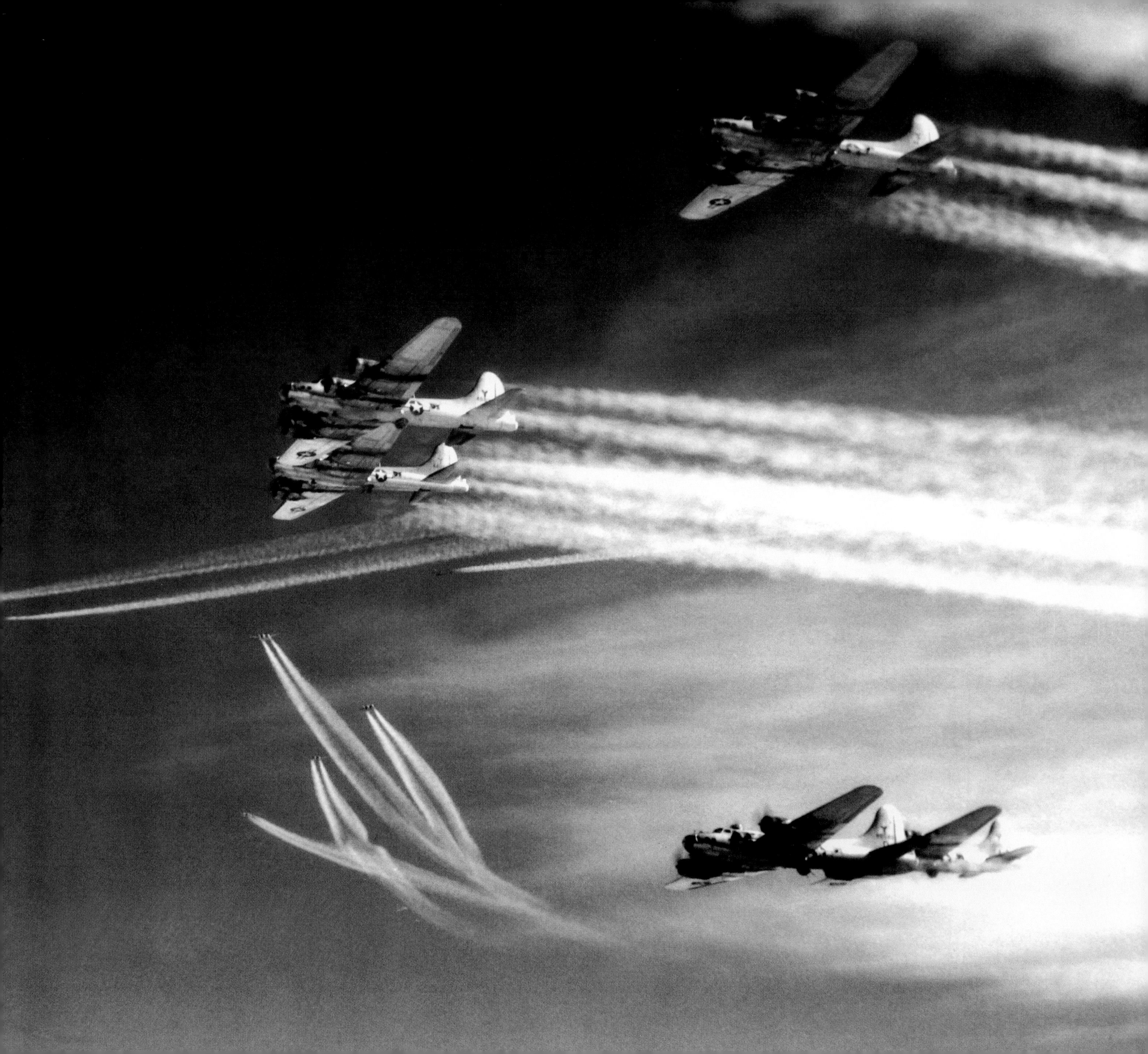

CHAPTER 14

WAR CRIMES AGAINST AIRMEN

Fifteenth aircrews not only had to contend with the perils of combat and death in the air, but also with the prospect of brutal treatment on the ground if they fell into enemy hands, as we have already seen with Sergeant Bernhardt in chapter 13. Once an airman reached the ground in enemy-controlled territory, either by parachute or in a crash-landed bomber, this was no guarantee that he would end up as a prisoner of war. There are a number of documented cases of civilians and soldiers beating, or even killing, American airman after their harrowing escape from a damaged aircraft.

Opposite page: 340th Bomb Squadron B-17s from the 97th Bomb Group head toward their target while escorting P-38s leave contrails behind them.

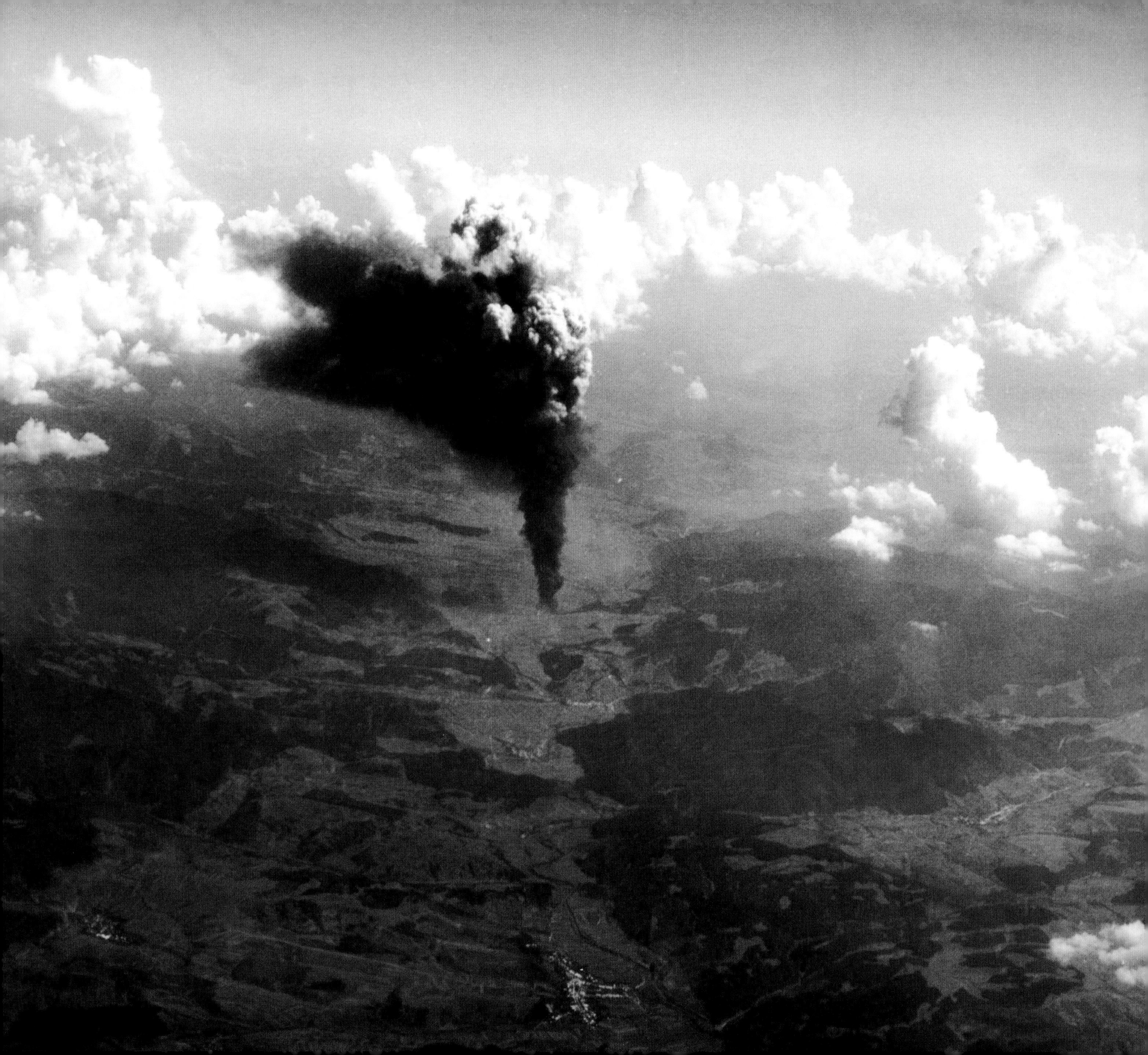

During the mission to bomb the synthetic oil refinery in the Auschwitz concentration camp complex on August 20, 1944, two German Me 109s shot down a 2nd Bomb Group B-17, *Silver Streak*, as it straggled behind the formation after flak damaged two engines. Early on the flight home, the Messerschmitts made several passes at the Fortress, flown by 1st Lt. Robert Lambert. Their cannon and machine-gun fire knocked out another engine and wounded the navigator, 1st Lt. Robert Erickson; a waist gunner, Staff Sgt. Charles Robinson; and the tail gunner, Staff Sgt. Joseph Nargiso. The bomber began to lose altitude and drifted even farther from the formation, so Lambert gave the order to bail out. All crewmen left the ship and reached the ground safely, near a village about forty miles from Budapest. Lambert broke his ankle on landing, but the others landed uninjured as their bomber crashed nearby. Despite having narrowly escaped death in their stricken bomber, their trial had only just begun, as all crewmen suffered beatings at the hands of Hungarian civilians and police.

Lambert landed in a farmyard, and farmers took him to the courthouse in the village nearby. From what he could gather, they wanted to put him on trial. Several Hungarian policemen intervened, and he eventually found himself in the charge of a civilian who escorted him to a jail in the town, where he met the navigator. He later recalled: "We were marched across a courtyard to another building of the jail and up some stairs, being kicked and beaten all the way. Upstairs, we were forced to undress and stand against a brick wall. While we were standing against . . . [it], the guards and civilian proceeded to beat us with shoes and belts."[cxv] The ordeal lasted about twenty minutes.

Sergeant Nargiso landed in a field, and Sergeant Robinson landed in the same area. Hostile civilians threatened Nargiso as soon as he reached the ground, so when a car drove up, he surrendered to the occupants. With doors locked, the car drove through the threatening crowd and took him to the same jail holding Lambert and Erickson, where men in civilian clothes initially interrogated him: "There was also a civilian interpreter in the room and the two started questioning me. . . . Every time the civilian asked me a question through the interpreter, he would take a swing at me. I was hit a number of times . . ." When Nargiso was not forthcoming with information, "they called in three gendarmes who stripped me naked and then proceeded to beat me up. One gendarme tied my feet and held them in the air while the other beat the soles of my feet with a rubber hose. While this was going on, the civilian, who had been questioning me, kept punching me in the face. This lasted for about half an hour."[cxvi] Threatened with execution and pistol-whipped, he was thrown in a cell, then beaten again.

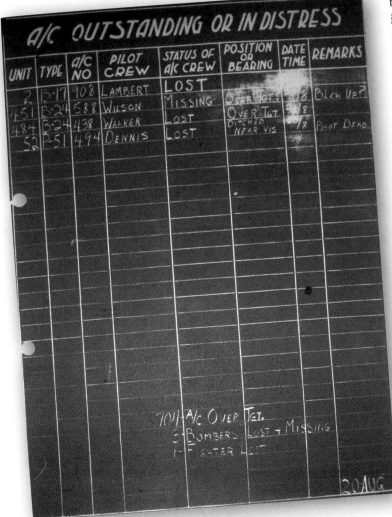

Below: The list of aircraft lost or missing on the blackboard in the operations room at Fifteenth Air Force headquarters, August 20, 1944. Lieutenant Lambert's crew is listed as lost.

Above: A Flying Fortress flies home with the burning refinery at Oswiecim behind it on August 20, 1944.

Left: A Fortress from the 416th Bomb Squadron, 99th Bomb Group, drops its bomb load on a railroad bridge in the city of Szob, Hungary, on September 20, 1944.

Robinson landed safely, but farmers beat him, too, using rakes, sledge hammers, and pitch-forks. He passed out from the beating, but came to a few minutes later as the crowd took him to the jail.

The radio operator, Tech. Sgt. Robert Larson, was chained when he was captured and then marched to the same jail by soldiers and civilians. During the march, civilians beat him with clubs. At the jail, he and Robinson were beaten during interrogation, then put in cells.

Later, the entire crew—which also included the bombardier, 1st Lt. Thomas Wilson; the ball-turret gunner, Staff Sgt. Thomas Kirk; and the flight engineer, Tech. Sgt. James Lang—were beaten yet again. Guards forced the men to line up and stand at attention in the jail, then beat them with fists, belts, and rifle butts.

The entire crew soon traveled by truck to Budapest, where the wounded men and Sergeant Robinson, still suffering from his beating, were taken to a hospital. In mid-September, the Hungarians took Lambert to a house in Budapest and interrogated him there for several days. Afterward, he was transferred with the rest of his crew to Germany, where they spent the rest of the war in prisoner-of-war camps.

The identities of the perpetrators were unknown to the airmen, and a thorough postwar investigation in Hungary was restricted, as the country soon came under Communist control. Because American investigators were unable to gather more evidence to identify the perpetrators, the case was never brought to trial.[cxvii]

The perpetrators of a more heinous crime, the murder of two Fifteenth Air Force crewmen, also escaped punishment, not because they could not be identified but because they were never apprehended. During the raid on the synthetic oil refinery at Blechhammer on October 14, 1944, flak badly damaged Fortress 44-8004 of the 97th Bomb Group, piloted by 1st Lt. Victor Beiniek. Flak shot up one engine, the fuel tanks began to leak, and a fire broke out. Three crewmen were wounded: Beiniek, navigator 1st Lt. Arthur Sanders, and waist gunner Sgt. Wesley Bangs. Over Czechoslovakia, the pilot warned the crew to be ready to bail out, but the B-17 lost altitude so quickly that the only way to save the crew was to crash-land. A small, grass-covered airstrip, apparently used by German Ju 87 *Stuka* dive-bombers, suddenly came into view, and Beiniek made a successful crash-landing on the strip, located near the town of Napajedla. The crash injured a waist gunner, Staff Sgt. Howard Ott, but all crewmen got out of the bomber.

After they got away from the Fortress, several Mustangs from the escort who had followed the bomber down strafed it, starting a fire that destroyed it, obscuring evidence of the Americans' landing. The strafing also enabled the crew to get away from the scene of the crash before German troops arrived. They reached a woods, where they encountered a man they took to be a Partisan but who was actually a Czech gamekeeper. He told them to hide in the woods until nightfall, when he would return. The bombardier, 1st Lt. Raymond Winters, the only crewman who was armed, gave his pistol to the man, who promptly buried it.

The crew then split into two groups. Pilot Beiniek; the copilot, 1st Lt. Howard Nefe; a gunner, Staff Sgt. Edward Grant; the radio operator, Staff Sgt. William Lawrence; and the flight engineer, Sgt. Howard Ott, were in one group. The second comprised bombardier Winters, navigator Sanders, bombardier-navigator 1st Lt. James Johnson, Sergeant Bangs, and flight engineer Staff Sgt. Daniel Smith.

The second group moved off and hid in the woods until a civilian came upon them. The man spoke some English and told them he would help them escape by taking them to his home to hide overnight. Winters and Johnson agreed to accompany him to his house, planning to return for the enlisted men later, so they left with the civilian. Sergeant Grant later recalled, "As the

465th Bomb Group B-24s bombing the synthetic oil refinery at Oswiecim, part of the Auschwitz concentration camp complex, during the second attack on the refinery on September 13, 1944. The German smoke screen can be seen covering part of the refinery.

second group attempted to make their way out of the woods, I heard quite a bit of shouting, and then shooting. I did hear someone holler, 'Don't shoot Americans.' Everything went quiet for a while and then our group was surrounded by German soldiers. Lieutenant Nefe, our copilot, spoke German and he shouted to the Germans not to shoot as we were Americans and wished to surrender."[cxviii] German soldiers, commanded by a Gestapo man, also captured the first group of airmen, who heard the murder of Lieutenants Winters and Johnson.

The English-speaking civilian turned out to be one of several Gestapo agents, American investigators later learned, dispatched to crash sites with German police and Luftwaffe and Army troops. Immediately after the shooting of the two unarmed American flyers, several more Gestapo men arrived at the scene of the murder, and the Gestapo agent who shot the two Americans suggested to another Gestapo man that they also shoot the three enlisted men nearby. The second Gestapo man answered that there were too many witnesses present, so they took the three prisoner. One of the Gestapo men later claimed to a Czech that the two men killed had been shot while trying to escape, but he was later overheard telling another Gestapo man that he had simply shot the two men after they came from hiding in some bushes. Some Czechs claimed that Luftwaffe officers reported the murders to higher headquarters and that an investigation ensued. The Gestapo man responsible, however, was not charged with a crime but apparently decorated instead.

The Czech manager of a local cemetery buried the two slain airmen and noted at the time that they had both been shot in the back of the head. Luftwaffe officers from an airfield nearby and several Czech officials of the local government were present during the interment. In October 1945, American war crimes investigators exhumed both airmen and confirmed how they had been shot. The pair were then reburied in a ceremony, and many Czechs attended the service to honor them.

The burial of Lieutenants Winters and Johnson in October 1945, after war crimes investigators complete the investigation of their murder.

The airmen who survived were initially taken to a local police station, then to the Luftwaffe base in the vicinity. After transfer to Germany and interrogation at the Luftwaffe interrogation center in Frankfurt, they all ended up in prisoner-of-war camps until the war's end.

The Gestapo men involved in the murder were identified by the Allies, but never apprehended, so the case was never brought to trial.[cxix] The same outcome also occurred after the investigation of another crime against airmen of the Fifteenth that occurred at a notorious German concentration camp just as the war was drawing to a close.

This photo is believed to show Liberators of the 461st Bomb Group leaving contrails behind them on the way to their target in October 1944. Contrails were disliked by flyers as enemy fighters could easily locate the bombers.

The Fifteenth Air Force flew its last large bombing raid on April 25 to the marshalling yards at Linz, Austria. Losses were heavy—a dozen Liberators and three Fortresses, including *The Anthony* from the 483rd Bomb Group, piloted by 1st Lt. Robert Sinton. Flak was intense over the marshalling yard and hit the number four engine and the right wing of this B-17, which immediately caught fire. The bomber lost a few thousand feet of altitude but initially kept up with the formation until crews in other Fortresses saw crewmen bail out. The aircraft stayed with the formation for about three more minutes until it suddenly began to spiral toward the ground, exploding in the air. The explosion killed Sinton and the tail gunner, who could not get out of his turret in time to jump.

A B-17 with fighter escort in the background, over Linz during a mission several months before *The Anthony* went down on the bombing mission of April 25, 1945.

Unfortunately, the eight crewmen who had bailed out had the bad luck to land near the notorious concentration camp at Mauthausen, less than ten miles east of Linz. One crewman, Tech. Sgt. Bernard Brach, was killed when his parachute failed to open and he plummeted to the ground. Another crew member reported that his parachute had caught fire.

SS guards from the concentration camp and *Volkssturm* members shot at the airmen as they descended near the camp. The copilot, 1st Lt. Joseph Nolan, was struck in the head and killed. The rest of the crew who bailed out—waist gunners Tech. Sgt. Charles Chaney and Staff Sgt. Samuel Rhodes, togglier (enlisted bombardier) Staff Sgt. Robert Zinn, flight engineer Tech. Sgt. William Gable, ball-turret gunner Staff Sgt. William Campbell, and navigator Flying Officer Herbert Westerlund—all landed safely.

Three, Lieutenant Westerlund and Sergeants Zinn and Chaney, were captured together and driven by car to the main camp at Mauthausen. Here, guards led them into a courtyard and lined them up against a wall. Zinn later recalled:

We were lined up against a wall . . . [and were] subjected to the laughs and taunts and threats of enlisted personnel of the SS stationed at the camp. After standing about ten minutes, everybody in the courtyard were snapped to attention by the appearance of an SS captain. We came to attention as he approached. He walked first to Chaney and spit on his left cheek. He asked me where we were from. When we refused to tell him, he slapped Chaney and Westerluand. He then called us Roosevelt gangsters and murderers. He showed us small photographs of homes which appeared to be destroyed by bombs. He then walked up and down in front of us and slapped us at will. Two SS men (enlisted men) joined in the slapping.

After we stood there getting slapped for about forty-five minutes, two political prisoners approached, carrying a large crate containing a body. . . . The SS officer . . . told us to take him out and sit him against the wall. We bent over him and saw it was first Lieutenant Joseph Nolan.[cxx]

They were able to examine his body and noticed an entry wound under his neck, indicating he had been shot from below. One of their guards boasted they had shot Nolan as he neared the ground, still in his chute. Shortly after this, the Germans brought in Sergeant Rhodes. Guards ordered the four Americans to face the wall; fortunately they were not shot, but ordered to carry Nolan into another courtyard in the camp, where they found Brach's remains. Both dead men were stripped of their clothing, taken to the camp crematorium, and cremated. Sergeants Campbell and

continued on page 209

Opposite page: A Flying Fortress, flying in formation, leaves contrails behind it on a mission to bomb the marshalling yards at Linz, Austria, on January 8, 1945.

The Fifteenth Air Force headquarters tally of losses for the last large bombing raid in Europe, on April 25, 1944. *The Anthony,* flown by Lieutenant Sinton's crew, is listed as "blown up." *US Air Force*

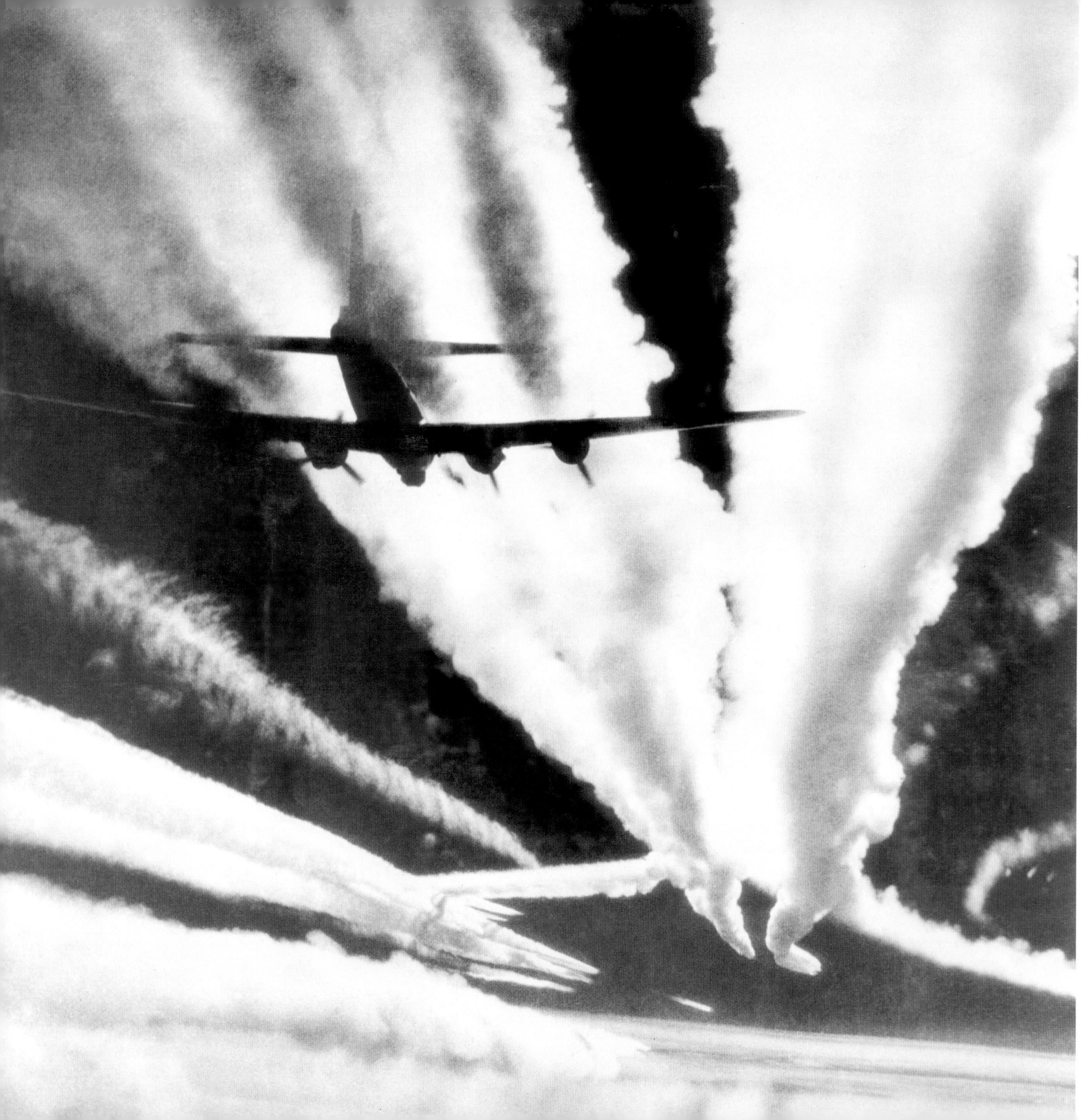

Liberators attack the marshalling yards in Munich in the fall of 1944.

Gable were already in the courtyard, and all six crewmen were searched again and then put in a small cell. They remained here until May 1, receiving only one bowl of thin soup and a piece of bread each day, similar to the rations for prisoners of the camp. On May 1, the Germans transferred them to Luftwaffe control and the airbase at Horsching. Soon afterward, they traveled to a prisoner-of-war camp near Salzburg, from which they were liberated on May 8. The SS troopers who killed Nolan were never identified, and the case was eventually closed by war crimes investigators.[cxxi]

The perpetrators of the murder of a 97th Bomb Group flight engineer, however, were tried for their crime. The 97th was part of a large raid on the marshalling yards at Munich, Germany, on November 16, 1944. A Fortress flown by 2nd Lt. Donald Keerwitz experienced engine trouble while over Austria on the way to the target. It caught fire, and Keerwitz ordered the crew to bail out. Seven of them did so. As the radio operator and a gunner, Sgts. Eugene Troutman and Austin Fauret, were preparing to do so, the pilot regained control of the B-17, and they stayed with him. Keerwitz headed for Italy and managed to crash-land at an Allied airfield.

All seven of the men who jumped reached the ground safely, near the town of Greifenburg, in southern Austria. Only six, however, were captured. The Germans reported that the flight engineer, Tech. Sgt. William J. McCurdy, had been killed during the jump, but postwar investigation revealed that Austrian civilians shot him.

A member of the local home guard saw the crew descending in their parachutes, one near a neighbor's house. He picked up a rifle and went to the house, where he met a friend who was visiting the neighbor. The friend armed himself, and the pair then positioned themselves behind a tree and barn to watch McCurdy land. Once on the ground, McCurdy shed his chute and began to walk toward them, hands raised. Both men fired, and one hit him in the chest. The pair then approached the fallen airman, and one exclaimed, "You should die like a dog!" They then picked him up, and he died as they carried him to the house. Soon afterward, Wehrmacht soldiers and a policeman arrived. They took the body to a local cemetery and buried it, with a wooden marker reading GRAVE OF AN UNKNOWN AIRMAN U.S.A.

Reports of the crime reached war crimes investigators, and four men were arrested—the two perpetrators and two accomplices alleged to have ordered the Allied flyers shot. At their trial the accused tried to defend themselves by saying that McCurdy had tried to flee and they had shot him only after warning him to halt. There was eyewitness testimony from other Austrians of their crime, however, and the tribunal convicted the two shooters, sentencing them to life in prison. The two accomplices, however, were found not guilty.[cxxii]

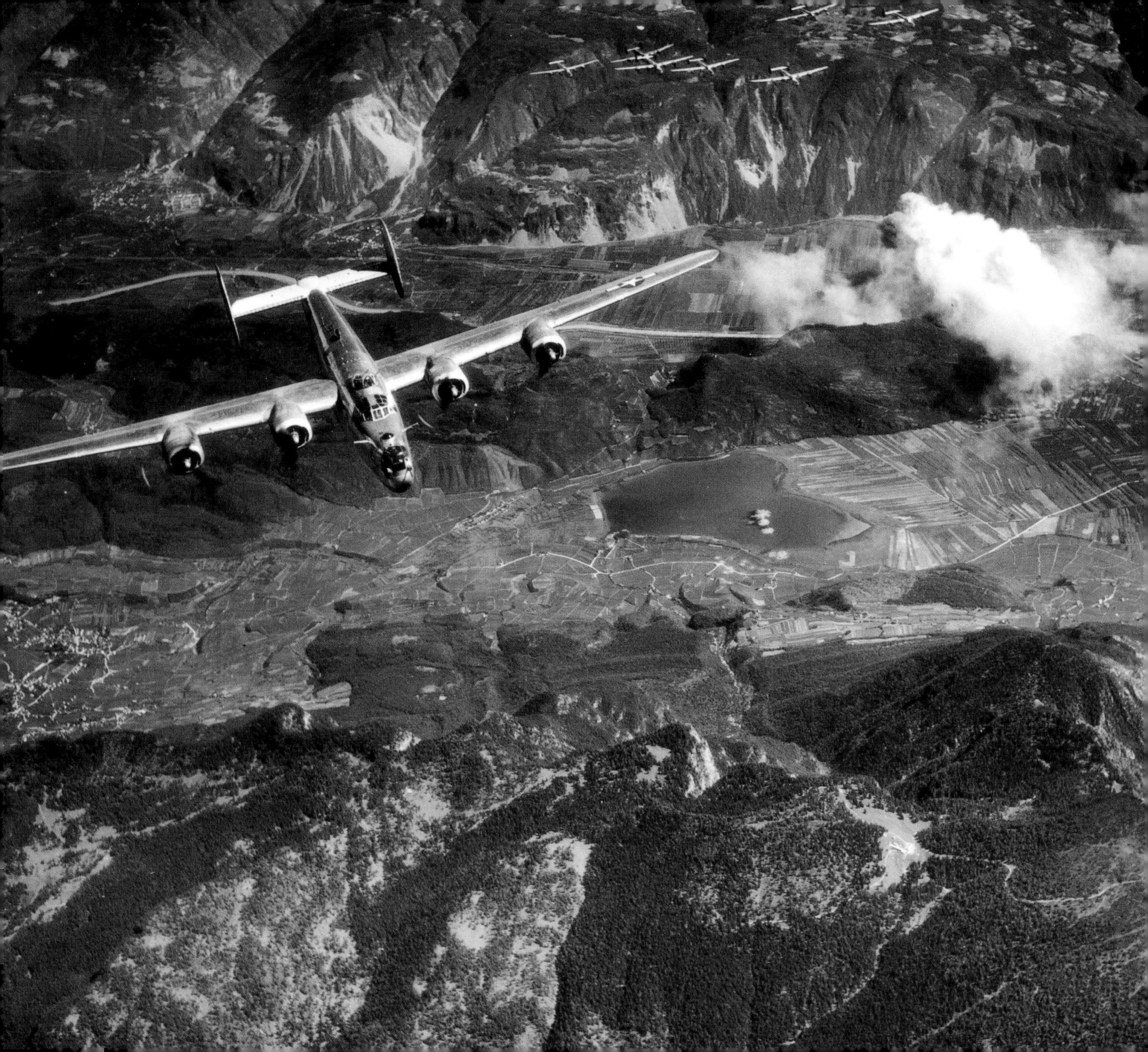

CHAPTER 15

THE END
OF THE
CAMPAIGN

During the late winter of 1945, as the American and British armies prepared to cross the Rhine River and enter the heart of Germany and the Soviet Army drove into eastern Germany, the Fifteenth continued its pounding of southern Germany and Austria and bridges and marshalling yards in northern Italy. Flak continued to be the primary menace to bomber crews and accounted for a number of aircraft and crews.

Opposite page: Liberators over the town of Ora, Italy, after bombing rail lines near the town that were part of the famed Brenner Line, the main supply line for German troops in Italy. Such rail lines were important targets of the Fifteenth Air Force in the last months of the war.

B-17s from the 97th Bomb Group in formation over the marshalling yards at Graz, Austria, on March 3, 1945. The Fortress nicknamed *Kwiturbitchin II* is in the foreground.

Bridges in northern Italy, in particular, proved costly as they required bombing from lower altitudes than usually flown by bombers of the Fifteenth, to improve accuracy. The German flak could be lethal at these lower altitudes, as the 47th and 304th Bomb Wings discovered during the mission to bomb the bridge at Albes, spanning the Isarco River, on February 28. Flak cost the two attacking wings ten aircraft. One of them was a Liberator in the lead box of the 450th Bomb Group flown by 2nd Lt. Edward Lee's crew.

Flak had struck their plane only a minute before the bombs away on the bridge. A burst hit the number four engine, which caught fire, causing the Liberator to lose altitude and fall out of the group formation before the pilots could regain control. Flak also hit the bomb bay, and the fuselage soon caught fire, but attempts to extinguish it were fruitless. Lee told the crew to bail out, and five managed to do so before the Liberator exploded in the air. Lee, copilot 2nd Lt. John Caldwell, and flight engineer Staff Sgt. Russell Hicks were still in the plane when it exploded. Their bodies were found in the wreckage. As the surviving five crewmen descended to the ground, German troops fired at them, and the ball turret gunner, Sgt. Richard Moshier, was hit when about five hundred feet from the ground. He later described the experience: "I bailed out, my chute opened, and I looked back and saw the ship explode in [the] air. I lost consciousness at about 500 feet and woke up in an Italian hospital two days later" with a fractured skull. All the crewmen who reached the ground became prisoners of war in northern Italy until liberated two months later.

Another of the Liberators lost on the mission was from the 456th Bomb Group. Flak bursts hit number 42-51688 badly in the bomb bay and waist. Shrapnel blew away the top of the fuselage, the aircraft immediately caught fire, and the plane went into a spin. The pilot, 1st Lt. Donald Trepte, immediately realized that the ship was mortally wounded. He tried to use to intercom to tell the crew to bail out, but flak had shot it away. He and copilot 1st Lt. Robert Walker attempted to fight the controls a little longer, to allow others to bail out.

The top turret gunner, Tech. Sgt. William McAteer, later recalled: "When the ship was hit, I saw the top blow out and the ship burst into flames immediately. I called over the interphone advising the crew to bail out, but . . . the interphone was inoperative. . . . I got out of the turret . . . my clothes and oxygen mask were burning, so I took off the mask and waited a while to see what the pilot and copilot were doing. I thought they were dead because of their slumped position, so I bailed out through the forward bomb bay. I opened my chute immediately and then I looked up and saw a ship, which I thought was ours, blow up. . . ."

Their clothing on fire, Trepte and Walker had only seconds to leave themselves, as the controls were no longer responsive. Both bailed out, and as they descended in their parachutes, the Liberator blew up. Shrapnel wounded the left waist gunner, Tech. Sgt. Erwin Dodge, but he also managed to bail out. Unfortunately, however, he was dead when he reached the ground. The wreckage of the plane spun to the ground and crashed, and the surviving three crewmen became prisoners of the Germans.[cxxiii]

These two bombers were from different groups, but of course bomber and fighter groups could, and often did, lose more than one aircraft on a mission. The loss of two bombers by a group on a single mission was not uncommon, and the Germans did, on occasion, shoot down ten, twelve, or even sixteen bombers from a single group.

continued on page 217

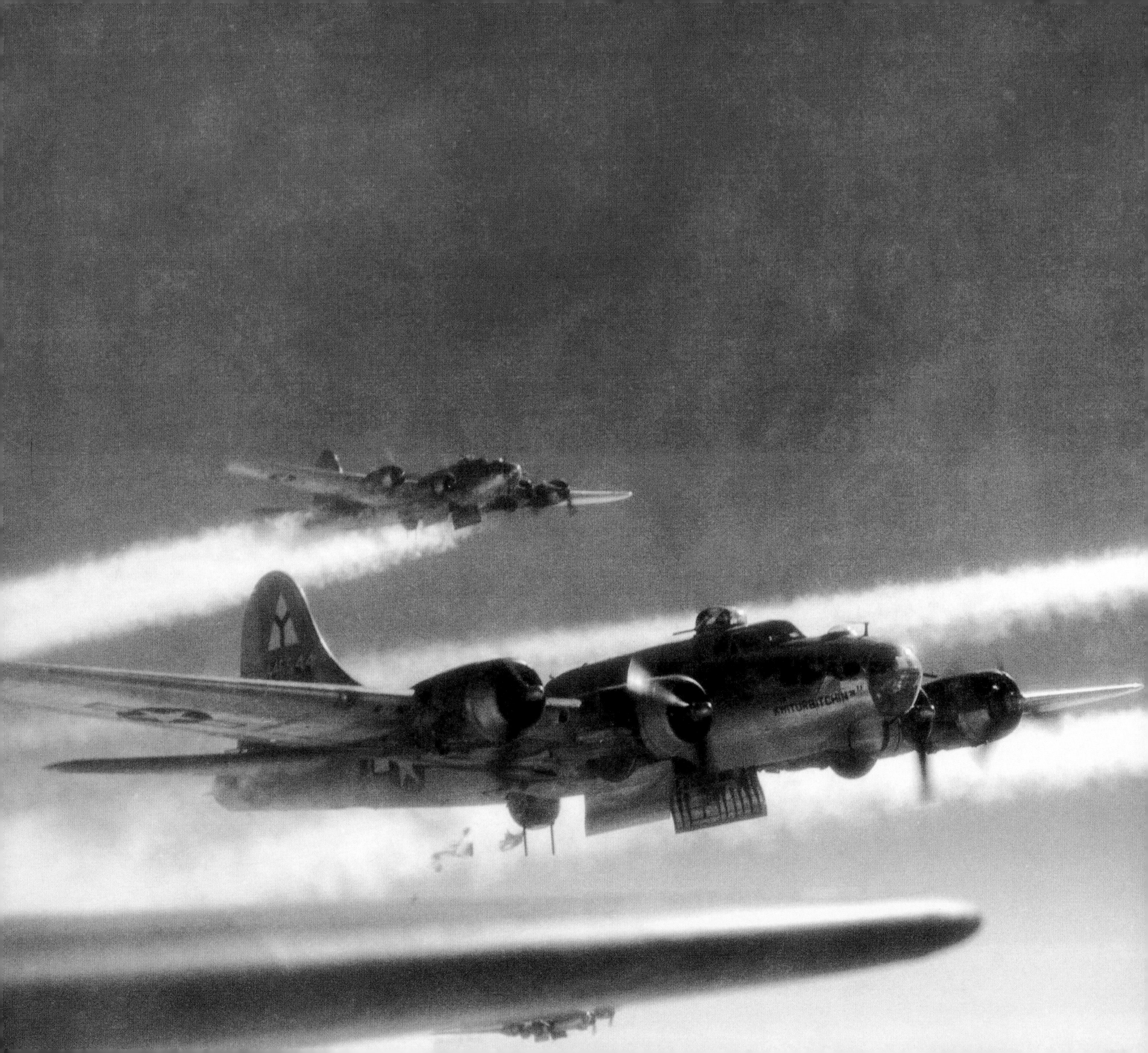

Clouds from flak bursts, in the background, provide a backdrop for *Kwiturbitchin II* during the March 3, 1945, mission.

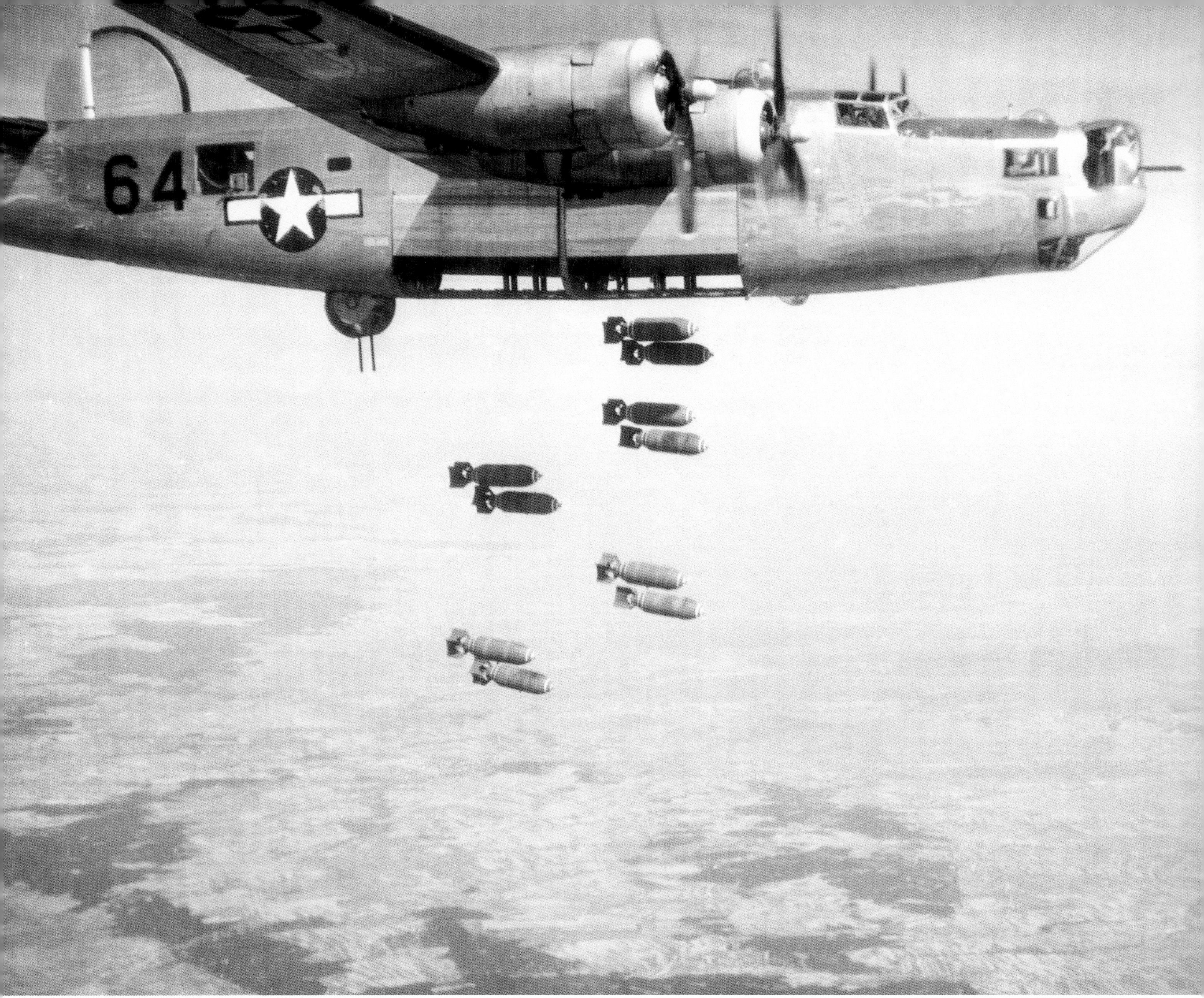
64

Four Liberators from the 484th Bomb Group went down during the February 21, 1945, mission to bomb the marshalling yards in Vienna. A deadly flak-box barrage shot down four of their aircraft, including the group lead and deputy lead Liberator, on the bomb run. This was the most hazardous portion of a mission. To ensure the most accurate bombing, they could not take evasive action.

Two flak bursts hit Liberator number 42-50526, flown by 1st Lt. Charles Marshall, before bombs away. The copilot, 2nd Lt. John Gross, later recalled: "There were about three bursts of flak directly ahead [of our Liberator], then two bursts hit us. The tail gunner was hit, just above the hip, [the] radio operator through the right shoulder, and one navigator [there were two on board] in the leg. . . . The radio was shot out, hydraulics shot out, and two engines out; . . . rudder and elevator control cables severed. . . . We made a turn out and away from the formation. A waist gunner thought every one was shot and bailed out. We lost altitude fast. . . . We headed for Lake Balaton and threw out everything we could." Marshall headed east to Russian lines, and the crew began to bail out over Yugoslavia, in the vicinity of Subotica.

The wounded tail gunner, Staff Sgt. Robert Richmond, was unable to pull his ripcord, so the pilot told the crew to fashion a static line and bail him out. Unfortunately, his wound was so severe that he was dead when he hit the ground. The remainder of the crew was able to bail out, Marshall last. The wounded navigator, 2nd Lt. James Cummins, broke his leg in landing and was hospitalized. Four of the crew landed in German-controlled territory and became prisoners. The pilot and copilot reunited at a farmhouse soon after they hit the ground. Partisans picked them up and took them to Belgrade within a few days. Soon after that, they flew back to Italy. Bulgarians initially took the other three evading crew members and turned them over to the Russians. They, too, eventually reached Belgrade, and later Italy.

Flak hit another 484th aircraft, piloted by 1st Lt. Eugene Frazier, in four bursts on the way to the target, severely damaging the nose, tail turret, and bomb bay and buckling a wing. Fuel began to leak as well. The Liberator immediately left the group formation and headed for Russian lines, but it lost altitude before it could reach them, and Frazier immediately ordered the crew to bail out. They all did so, over eastern Austria, and the B-24 blew up just after Frazier, the last man out, had jumped. All became prisoners of war. On the way to Vienna, a hostile crowd threatened them; a woman actually attacked one crewman, but he was not injured, a more fortunate outcome than other crews experienced, as we shall see. They continued on to Germany for interrogation and transfer to a prisoner-of-war camp where all were liberated in April.

The same fate awaited the crew of Capt. Percy Kramer's Liberator, the group's lead aircraft, which was badly hit just after the bombs had been released. Losing altitude, it dropped out of the formation outside Wiener Neustadt, and all of the crew bailed, to become prisoners.

The Liberator of 2nd Lt. Chad Ikerd had already dropped its bombs when flak bursts hit it and damaged the aircraft, including the intercom. The crew attempted to reach Russian lines but couldn't quite make it, and after flying into Hungary for about twenty minutes, Lieutenant Ikerd ordered the crew to bail out when the plane was at five thousand feet. Most of them did, through the nose hatch or the bomb bay, and Hungarian troops immediately captured them near the city of Gyor, still held by Axis forces. But three men in the waist—the top-turret gunner, ball-turret gunner, and a photographer assigned to the crew for the mission—did not. Although they were last seen wearing their parachutes, they were found dead in the wreckage without them.

Just before he jumped, the tail gunner, Sgt. Benjamin Pettry remarked to the trio, "Goodbye, boys; I'll see you on the ground." It is possible the three may have thought the plane was going to crash-land, since it was flying straight and slowly descending to the ground. The men who did bail out spent the next two months as prisoners of war.[cxxiv]

* * * * *

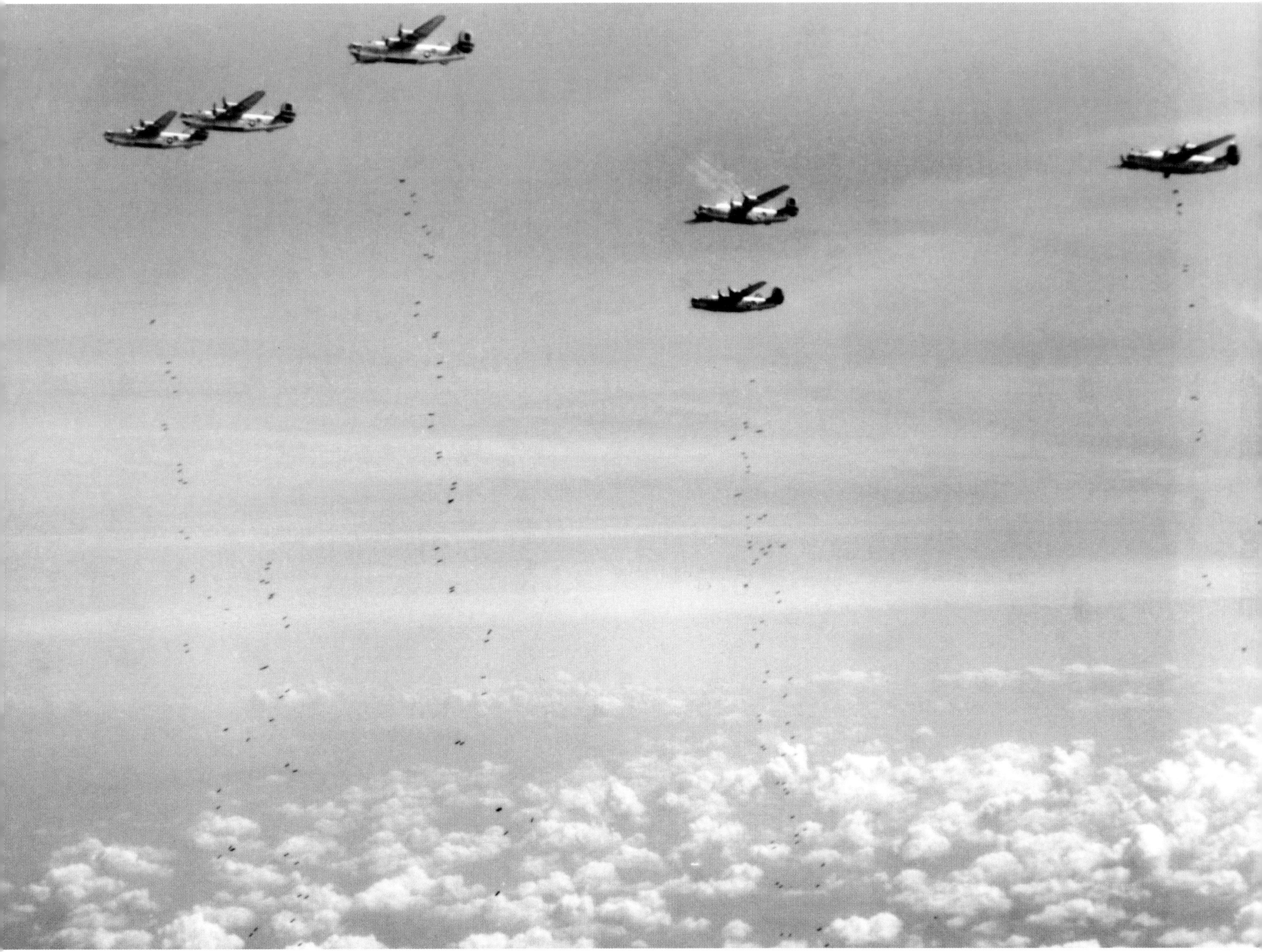

As the war in Europe sped to its conclusion in April, the fighting remained as fierce as ever, and the Fifteenth continued to have losses, often while attacking Italian bridges as they turned most of their attention to Italian targets to support the Allied offensive that ended the war in Italy in early May. Only a week before the 98th Bomb Group returned to the United States for redeployment to the Pacific, one of the group's Liberators went down attacking an Italian bridge during the April 8 mission against the railroad bridge at Vipiteno. Flak hit one of them, number 44-50654, flown by 1st Lt. Le Mert Wade, as it was about to drop its bombs. Shrapnel punctured the fuel tanks, and gasoline began to stream from one wing. Flak bursts also damaged the waist and tail, cutting the intercom and wounding at least one of the waist gunners. The Liberator plane turned out of the formation and slowly lost altitude, flying for about five minutes before Wade motioned for the crew to bail out, since he couldn't use the intercom. The flight engineer, Tech. Sgt. William Survilla, looked into the waist of the aircraft before he jumped, but saw no one and assumed the crewmen in the rear had already jumped. The tail gunner, two waist gunners, and the radio operator, however, had not bailed out and were found in the wreckage of the Liberator by the Germans. Germans captured the rest of the crew. The Liberator hit a mountainside, and the bombs still aboard exploded when it crashed.

The bombardier's view from a B-17 of the 301st Bomb Group flying over northern Italy on a mission to bomb bridges at Bressanone on April 8, 1945.

Missions to Italian targets continued as the Allied offensive in the north pressed on during April, culminating in the last, massive mission flown by the Fifteenth on April 25 to bomb the marshalling yards at Linz, Austria. Losses were high, and flak shot down one bomber, a 461st Bomb Group Liberator nicknamed *Miss Lace*, piloted by 2nd Lt. Lawrence Toothman, before bombs away. Shrapnel wounded the navigator, Flying Officer Paul Ashworth, and then traveled through to the cockpit, where it exploded between the pilot and copilot, instantly killing the latter, 2nd Lt. William Jones, and wounding Toothman in the arm. The ball-turret gunner, Corporal Howard Acheson, described the damage: "One AA shell entered our ship near [the] bombardier's window, penetrating to the cockpit and exploding between [the] pilot and copilot. Lieutenant Jones' chest was crushed, [with] wounds in [the] head and abdomen." The flight engineer, Sgt. Oscar Scogin, took a look at Jones to confirm he was dead. Toothman told the rest of the crew to bail out; they did so, all landing near each other, and were immediately captured. Most had been wounded by flak or injured during the parachute descents. They remained prisoners only a short time, until the war ended early in May.[cxxv]

A Flying Fortress bombs the bridges at Vipiteno, Italy, during one of several missions to destroy the bridges in April 1945.

Another 461st Liberator may have been the last Fifteenth Air Force bomber attacked by a German fighter on the Linz mission. At one point on the mission, a lone Fw 190 attacked the Liberator but did not press its attack as a German fighter would have a year earlier. The Luftwaffe pilot opened fire when six hundred yards away from the bomber, but the return fire of the Liberator's gunners forced him to abandon the attack, and he was last seen heading toward Germany. The attack did not inflict any damage. *Miss Lace* was the only 461st bomber lost on the mission; the last lost by the group during the war.[cxxvi]

The next day, the Fifteenth Air Force lost the last of the more than two thousand bombers that went down from November 1943 through the end of April 1945. This last bomber went down the

continued on page 225

Right: A B-24 from the 451st Bomb Group flying over Linz, Austria, on April 25, 1945.

Opposite page: Bombs fall from a 463rd Bomb Group B-17 toward the marshalling yards in Linz, Austria, during the last major bombing mission flown by the Fifteenth Air Force on April 25, 1945.

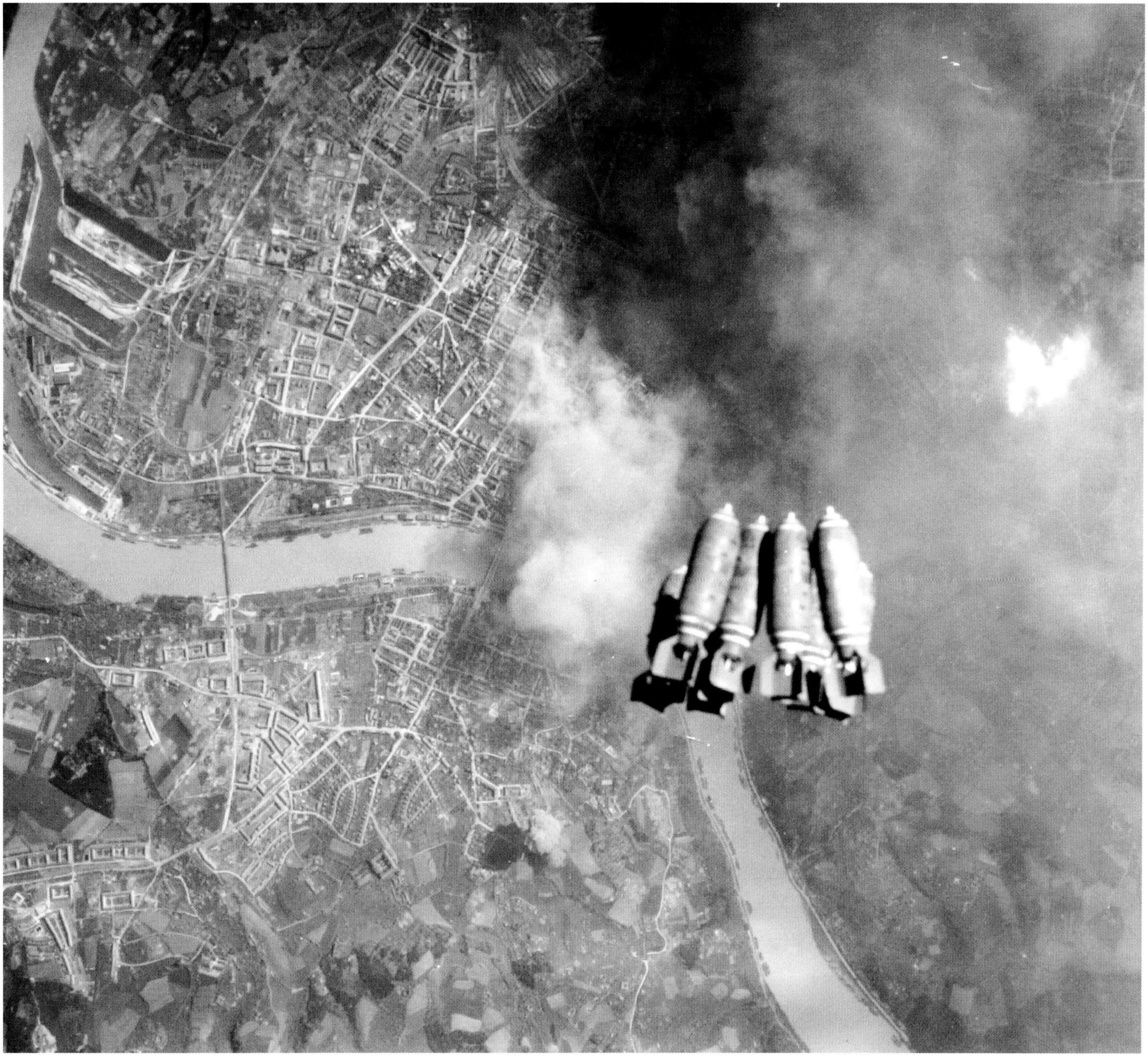

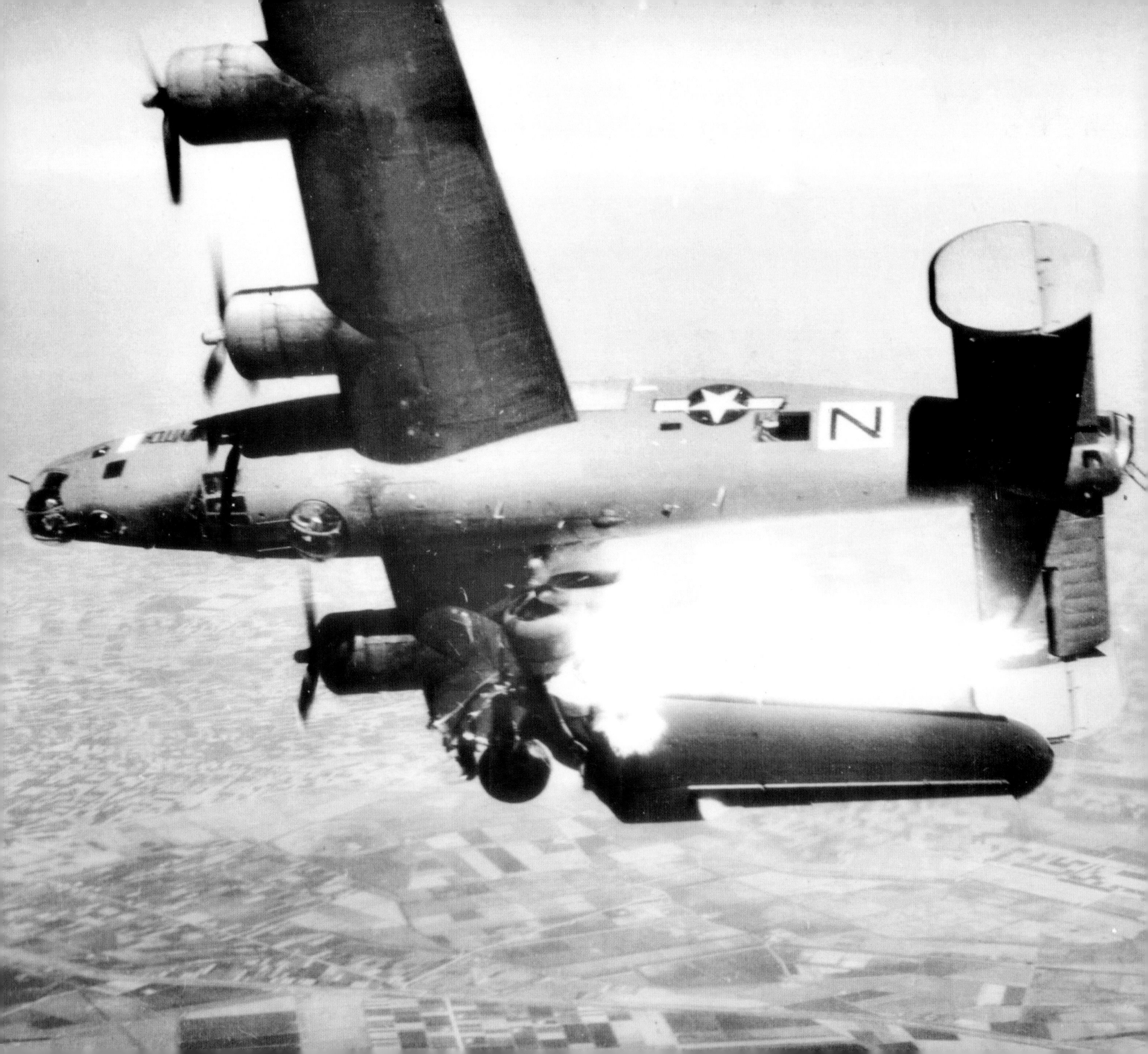
N

Opposite page: *Stevenovich II,* also known as *Black N,* of the 464th Bomb Group hit by flak over northern Italy on April 10, 1945. All but one crewman perished.

Right: A B-17 from the 419th Bomb Squadron, 301st Bomb Group, taxies prior to takeoff for a mission to bomb a railroad bridge at Bressanone, Italy, April 8, 1945.

day following the Linz mission, a 460th Bomb Group B-24 shot down by flak during the attack on Klagenfurt's marshalling yards on April 26. Only one combat box of the group was able to locate Klagenfurt, and although crews reported only slight flak, some of it did find one plane, a Liberator nicknamed *Seldom Available,* flown by the crew of 1st Lt. Paul O'Connell. Two engines were set afire and had to be feathered. The Liberator began to descend and slowly spiraled from the formation, flying for about ten miles until the crew began to bail out. All of the crew got out of the aircraft in good order, but Austrians on the ground saw the parachute of one, Sgt. Edward Kovaleski, collapse in the air, and he plummeted to the ground and was killed. German troops quickly rounded up the rest of the crew, but Allied troops liberated them on May 5.[cxxvii]

continued on page 229

Left: Flying Fortresses leave contrails behind them as they fly toward Bologna to bomb in support of Allied ground forces in mid-April 1945.

Opposite page: Smoke rises from the German vehicle depot at Osoppo, Italy, as B-24s from the 465th Bomb Group head for home in the waning days of the war in Italy.

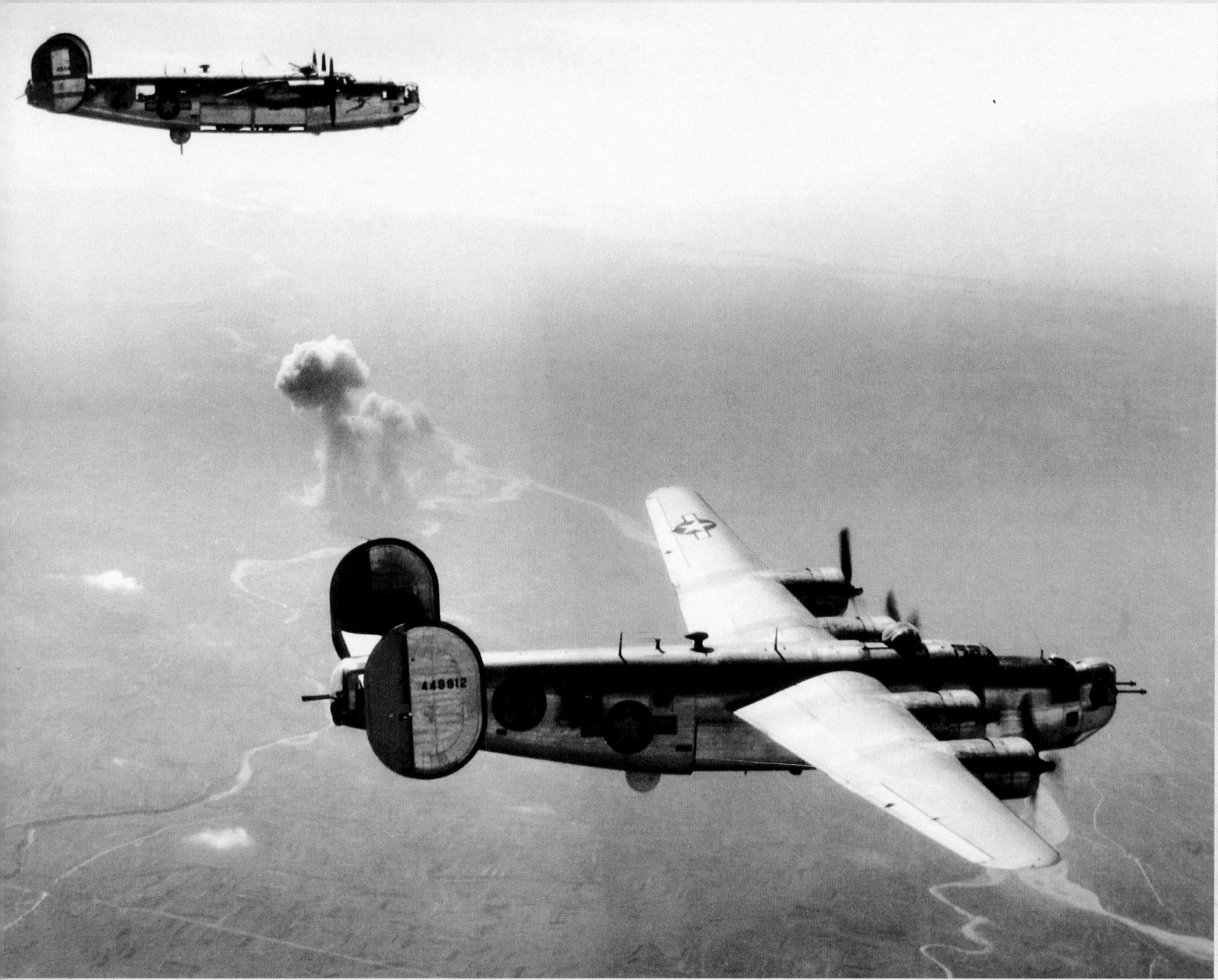
449912

Above: 5th Bomb Wing B-17s fly over the north Adriatic on their way to bomb the Southern Ordnance Depot in Vienna on February 13, 1945.

Left: A P-38 Lightning of the 1st Fighter Group takes off from its base in Salsola, Italy. Lightnings not only acted as fighter escort, but also carried out many bombing missions for the Fifteenth Air Force.

Above: Major General Nathan Twining, commander of the Fifteenth Air Force. He later became chairman of the Joint Chiefs of Staff in the late 1950s.

Right: A 5th Bomb Wing B-17 flies past a flag at half-mast to honor President Roosevelt after his sudden death on April 12, 1945.

continued from page 225

Miss Lace and *Seldom Available* were the last bombers lost on the last combat missions flown by the Fifteenth Air Force. These final missions were, in many ways, like the first major raid flown by the Fifteenth, when Lieutenant Jeffries and his crew went down (see chapter 4). Although the Luftwaffe had disappeared, flak remained a ubiquitous peril, responsible for the loss of both these bombers. The loss of the crewmen killed on *Seldom Available* was undoubtedly felt as keenly by their squadron mates as was the loss of the crew of Seitz's bomber at the beginning of the campaign, yet throughout it the airmen of the Fifteenth never wavered from flying the next mission, regardless of losses. Their campaign, flown over the nations of southern, central, and eastern Europe by the crews of the Fifteenth, was part of a unique period in military history, when armadas of aircraft covered the skies of Europe.

NOTES

i.   Missing Air Crew Report (MACR) 14019.

ii.   Boylan, *Long-Range Escort Fighter*, 158-60; McFarland and Newton, *To Command the Sky*, 196.

iii.   Norris, *Combined Bomber Offensive*, 83–84; 15th Air Force Narrative, 280; Stormont, *Combined Bomber Offensive*, 44, 96; Boylan,194, 199, 202–203.

iv.   Schmid, *Employment of German Luftwaffe*, 3, 7–8, 144; McFarland and Newton, 79.

v.   Encounter Reports, 325th Fighter Group, January 1944, 325th Fighter Group Combat Reports, Box 3350.

vi.   "Story by Captain Robert G. Zimmerman who was shot down over Bulgaria on 14 April 1944" in 14th Fighter Group Narrative Report, October 1944, 14th Fighter Group history files, reel B0080.

vii.   MACRs 1992, 4232; Escape Statement of Major Homer Hanes, May 31, 1944, Fifteenth Air Force Escape and Evasion Reports, reel A6544A.

viii.   Statement of John G. Karle, 2nd Lieutenant, Upon Return to His Organization, June 25, 1944, 52nd Fighter Group History, June 1944; 52nd Fighter Narrative Mission Report Number 16 for 31 May 1944, 52nd Fighter Group history, May 1944; both in 52nd Fighter Group history files, reel B0148.

ix.   Blake and Stanaway, *Adorimini*, 198–200; 14th Fighter Group Narrative Mission Report, 22 July 1944 in 14th Fighter Group history files, reel B0080; Lambert, *The 14th Fighter Group* 102–103; 82nd Fighter Group Mission Narrative Report, August 4, 1944, in 82nd Fighter Group history files, reel B0169; "Narrative of Captain White concerning his Mission to Russia," 14th Fighter Group History, September 1944, in 14th Fighter Group history files, reel B0080.

x.   Encounter Reports, 325th Fighter Group, October 1944, June 1944, 325th Fighter Group Combat Reports, box 3350; 325th Fighter Group Narrative Mission Report, October 16, 1944 in 325th Fighter Group history files, reel B0277.

xi.   "Story by Second Lieutenant Lorenz E. Weiglein who bailed out over the Adriatic Sea on 17 December 1944—returning to the Squadron on 23 December 1944" in 14th Fighter Group Escape Statements, 14th Fighter Group history files, reel B0080; MACR 10672; 14th Fighter Group Narrative Mission Report No. 232, December 17, 1944, 14th Fighter Group history files, reel B0080.

xii.   325th Fighter Group Narrative Mission Report, March 14, 1945, Reel B0276; Encounter Reports, 325th Fighter Group, March 1945, 325th Fighter Group Combat Reports, box 3350.

xiii.   Statement of Lieutenant Alvin N. Temple, 99th Fighter Squadron, 332nd Fighter Group, "Jet-Propelled A/C Activity—Period 1 December to 15 December," Special Intelligence Report No. 85, Headquarters, Fifteenth Air Force, December 22, 1944, p. 6.

xiv.   Statement of Lieutenant Edward M. Thomas, 99th Fighter Squadron, 332nd Fighter Group, "Jet-Propelled A/C Activity—Period 1 December to 15 December," Special Intelligence Report No. 85, Headquarters, Fifteenth Air Force, December 22, 1944, p. 6., reel A6543, Fifteenth Air Force, "Special Intelligence Reports."

xv.   Statement of Lieutenant Edward J. Williams, 302nd Fighter Squadron, 332nd Fighter Group, "Jet-Propelled A/C Activity—Period 1 December to 15 December," Special Intelligence Report No. 85, Headquarters, Fifteenth Air Force, December 22, 1944, p. 7, reel A6543, Fifteenth Air Force, "Special Intelligence Reports."

xvi.   Statement of Lieutenants Robert W. Williams and Samuel W. Watts Jr., MAAF Weekly Intelligence Summary, No. 13, April 2, 1945, p. 36, reel A6085, Mediterranean Allied Air Force, "Air Intelligence Weekly Summary."

xvii.   Statement of Lieutenant Joseph E. Chineworth, MAAF Weekly Intelligence Summary, No. 13, April 2, 1945, pp. 36–37, reel A6085, Mediterranean Allied Air Force, "Air Intelligence Weekly Summary."

xviii.   Statement of Lieutenant Charles V. Brantley, ibid.

xix.   Statement of Lieutenant Reid E. Thompson, ibid.

xx.   Statement of Lieutenant Roscoe C. Brown, ibid.

xxi.   Statement of Captain Edward M. Thomas; Lieutenant Vincent L. Mitchell, ibid.

xxii.   Statement of Lieutenant Earl R. Lane, ibid., 38–39.

xxiii.   Statement of Flying Officer Thurston L. Gaines, ibid., 35–36.

xxiv.   "Jet Propelled A/C Activity—Period 1 December to 15 December," Special Intelligence Report no. 85, December 22, 1944, reel A6543, Fifteenth Air Force, "Special Intelligence Reports"; MAAF Weekly Intelligence Summary, No. 13, April 2, 1945; 332 FG Mission Narrative Report, March 24, 1945, reel A6085, Mediterranean Allied Air Force, "Air Intelligence Weekly Summary."

xxv.   Encounter Reports, 325th Fighter Group, January 1944, 325th Fighter Group Combat Reports, Box 3350.

xxvi.   MACR 1306.

xxvii.   Fifteenth Air Force Special Intelligence Report No. 4, June 29, 1944, and No. 22, reel A6543, Fifteenth Air Force, "Special Intelligence Reports"; 14th Fighter Group Narrative Report, June 1944, 2–3, 14th Fighter Group history files; Special Intelligence Report, January 1944, 14th Fighter Group, January 1944, 14th Fighter Group history files, reel B0080.

xxviii.   52nd Fighter Group Narrative Mission Report, 3 September, 1944, 52nd Fighter Group history files; Ivie and Ludwig, 135–137.

xxix.   Missing Air Crew Reports, 8979 and 8983; Escape Statement of Second Lieutenant Andrew Marshall, 332nd Fighter Group Escape Statements; 332nd Narrative Mission Report, October 6, 1944, 332nd Fighter Group history files, reel B0280.

xxx.   MACRs 11916, 11817, 11818, 11819, 11820, 11821; 31st Fighter Group Mission Report, February 2, 1945, 31st Fighter Group history files, reel B0111.

xxxi.   MACR 1303.

xxxii.   MACR 1615.

xxxiii.   MACRs 2726, 2696; 15th Photo Reconnaissance Squadron Report, February 23, 1944, 15th Photo Reconnaissance Squadron Combat Reports, Box 3873.

xxxiv.   MACR 2075; 301st Bomb Group Mission Narrative, February 25, 1944, 301st Bomb Group history files, reel B0208.

xxxv.   MACR 3355; 99th Bomb Group Mission Narrative Report, March 18, 1944, 99th Bomb Group history files, reel B0199.

xxxvi.   MACR 4663; 454 BG Mission Diary for May 1944 and Escape Statement of Second Lieutenants Thomas Kerrigan and Thomas Muirhead, 454th Bomb Group Escape Statements, 454th Bomb Group history files, reel B0601.

xxxvii.   Lipfert, *The War Diary*, 117–118; MACR 6425.

xxxviii.   MACR 4608; 449th BG Mission Report, May 5, 1944, 449th Bomb Group history files, reel B0573.

xxxix.   MACR 7358; 325th Fighter Group Mission Summary, August 3, 1944, 325th Fighter Group history files, reel B0277; 465th Bomb Group Mission Narrative Report, August 3, 1944, 465th Bomb Group history files, reel B0616.

xl.   MACR 8766.

xli.   "Ruhland—or Sitting in Berlin's Back Yard," Major John Reardon, 2nd Bomb Group Special Accounts, March 1945, 2nd Bomb Group history files, reel B0043.

xlii.   MACR 13244; "Interrogation of 2nd Lieutenant C. L. Robinson and Crew," Escape and Evasion Reports, March–May 1945, 2nd Bomb Group history files reel B0043.

xliii.   Westermann, *Flak*, 157.

xliv.   MAAF Weekly Intelligence Summary 92, p. 19, Mediterranean Allied Air Force, "Air Intelligence Weekly Summary," reel A6085.

xlv.   Mediterranean Allied Air Force, *Air Power in the Mediterranean*, 33.

xlvi.   MACR 1143; 98th Bomb Group Sortie Report, November 2, 1943, 98th Bomb Group Mission Reports, Box 707.

xlvii.   MACRs 6315, 6892; 450th Bomb Group Mission Narratives, May 30 and July 3, 1944, 450th Bomb Group history files, reel B0593.

xlviii.   MACR 6972; Escape Statement of Second Lieutenant Lewis Nixon, 21 August 1944, Fifteenth Air Force Escape and Evasion Reports, reel 6544.

xlix.   MACR 9047.

l.   MACR 9889; Moxley, *Missing in Action*, 116, 118.

li.   MACR 2395.

lii.   MACR 2395, 2397; BG Special Mission Report, February 14, 1944, 97th Bomb Group history files, reel B0196.

liii. MACR 1308; 99th Bomb Group Mission Report, November 24, 1943, 99th Bomb Mission Reports, reel B0201.
liv. MACR 6955.
lv. Statement of Sergeant James Mund, MACR 8764.
lvi. MACRs 8764, 9971; Bohnstedt, *460th Bomb Group History*, 110–111.
lvii. Gulley, *The Hour Has Come*, 231–32; 97th Bomb Group Battle Casualty Report, April 6, 1945, 97th Bomb Group history files, reel B0195.
lviii. MACR 9297; Escape Statement of Second Lieutenant John Polando, et al., December 23, 1944, Fifteenth Air Force Escape and Evasion Reports, reel AA6544; 455th Bomb Group Mission Narrative, October 14, 1944, 455th Bomb Group history files, reel B0603.
lix. "Crash landing in Russia," 2nd Bomb Group Escape and Evasion Reports, January 1945, 2nd Bomb Group history files, reel B0042; Amos, *Defenders of Liberty*, 283–284.
lx. Consolidated Narrative Statement of First Lieutenant Eugene Bull et al., 2nd Bomb Group Escape and Evasion Reports, reel B0042; 2nd Bomb Group Special Mission Narrative Report, February 21, 1945; 2nd Bomb Group history files, B0043; and MACR 10732.
lxi. McCarty, *Coffee Tower*, 57–58.
lxii. Special Acounts, 97th Bomb Group History, July 1944, 97th Bomb Group history files, reel B0194.
lxiii. Press Release account about Goesling crew, 483rd Bomb Group History, July 1944, 483rd Bomb Group history files, reel B0642.
lxiv. MACR 5831; Amos, *Defenders of Liberty*, 229–230; Escape Statement of Sergeant Harold Bolick, 2nd Bomb Group Escape and Evasion Reports, 2nd Bomb Group history files, Reel A0042.
lxv. Statement of Lieutenant Franklin Christianson, MACR 8446.
lxvi. MACR 8446; 376th Bomb Group Crew Interrogation of Aircraft No. 515, September 8, 1944, 376th Bomb Group History, September 1944, 376th Bomb Group history files, reel B0353.
lxvii. McCarty, *Coffee Tower*, 52–53.
lxviii. Statement by Sergeant Charles W. Stuckert, MACR 11278.
lxix. MACR 11278; "Account of three men who returned to base," 483rd Bomb Group Escape and Evasion Reports, undated, 483rd Bomb Group history files, reel B0642.
lxx. MACR 11274; Escape Statement of Second Lieutenant Perry Hackett, et al., January 31, 1945, 454th Bomb Group Escape and Evasion Reports, 45th Bomb Group history files, reel B0601.
lxxi. Special Account "15th AAF in Italy," 97th Bomb Group, November 1944; 97th Bomb Group Mission Narrative Report, November 6, 1944 in 97th Bomb Group History files, reel B0194.
lxxii. Statement of Lieutenant John Wood, MACR 2070.
lxxiii. MACRs 2398, 2070.
lxxiv. Special Account "15th AAF in Italy," 97th Bomb Group History, April 1945, 97th Bomb Group history files, reel B0195.
lxxv. MACRs 1820, 1830, 1831, 1832, 1833, 1834, 2027, 2028.
lxxvi. "Flight Mission Over Germany—Alone!," Special Accounts, 2nd Bomb Group History, November 1944; 2nd Bomb Group Supplement and Special Narrative Mission Report, November 12, 1944, 2nd Bomb Group history files; Amos, *Defenders of Liberty*, 275.
lxxvii. "Solo Sortie," Special Accounts, 455th Bomb Group History, December 1944; December 12th 455th Bomb Group Mission Narrative Report, December 12, 1944, 455th Bomb Group history files, reel B603; GO 373, 15th Air Force, January 25, 1945, Fifteenth Air Force General Orders, reel A6423.
lxxviii. 15th Photo Reconnaissance Squadron Combat Report, March 15, 1944, 15th Photo Reconnaissance Squadron Combat Reports, box 3873.
lxxix. "Encounters with Jet-Propelled Aircraft," 5th Photo Group Monthly History, December 1944, 5th Photo Group History, reel B0752.
lxxx. Ibid.
lxxxi. 5th Photo Group Monthly History, "The Jet and Photo Reconnaissance," 5th Photo Group History, July 1945, 5th Photo Group history files, reel B0752; Foreman and Harvey, *Messerschmitt Combat Diary*, 241; MACR 10079.
lxxxii. "Encounters with German Jet-Propelled Aircraft," 5th Photo Group History, December 1944, 5th Photo Group history files, reel B0752.
lxxxiii. Ibid.

lxxxiv. "Encounter with ME 262s," Special Intelligence Report No. 82, December 6, 1944, Fifteenth Air Force "Special Intelligence Reports," reel A6543; "Jet Propelled A/C Activity—Period 1 December to 15 December," Special Intelligence Report No. 8, December 22, 1944, Fifteenth Air Force "Special Intelligence Reports," reel A6543.

lxxxv. Special Intelligence Report No. 86, 15th Air Force, December 30, 1944, Fifteenth Air Force "Special Intelligence Reports," reel A6543.

lxxxvi. 154th Weather Reconnaissance Squadron Monthly Historical Report, October 1944, 154th Weather Reconnaissance Group history files, reel A0919.

lxxxvii. Narrative History of Escape and Evasion, Fifteenth Air Force, Reel A6544, 1–2.

lxxxviii. 2nd Bomb Group Narrative History, February 1944, 293–294, 2nd Bomb Group history files, reel B0041.

lxxxix. Ibid, 293–298.

xc. MACR 1514; 2nd Bomb Group Narrative History, December 1944, 2nd Bomb Group history files, reel B0041.

xci. Diary of Staff Sergeant Franklin Grubaugh, February 25–April 6, 1944, 449th Bomb Group History, reel A6544D.

xcii. Ibid.

xciii. Ibid.

xciv. MACRs 2063, 2695, 3472; Diary of Staff Sergeant Franklin Grubaugh, 25 February–6 April 1944, Reel A6544D; 15th Air Force Escape and Evasion Interrogation Lists, List of Evaders Interrogated, April 8 and 15, 1944.

xcv. Narrative History of Escape and Evasion, Fifteenth Air Force, Reel A6544, 4–5.

xcvi. MACR 9666; Escape Statement of Sergeants Thurston Medlin and Jack Cooke, December 28, 1944, Fifteenth Air Force Escape and Evasions Reports, Reel A6544B.

xcvii. MACR 10896; Escape Statement of Vincent Fagan, et al., February 19, 1945, Fifteenth Air Force Escape and Evasions Reports, reel A6544C.

xcviii. MACR 1821; Escape Statement of Major Horace Hanes, March 22, 1944, Fifteenth Air Force Escape and Evasions Reports, reel A6544A.

xcix. MACR 8623; Escape Statement of Lloyd Hargrave, September 18, 1944, Fifteenth Air Force Escape and Evasions Reports, reel A6544A.

c. MACR, 6398; Escape Statement of Edward N. Donatelli and Frank W. Fuquay, October 8, 1944, Fifteenth Air Force Escape and Evasion Reports, reel A6544A.

ci. MACR 6818; Escape Statement of Frank C. Soltesz, October 8, 1944, Fifteenth Air Force Escape and Evasion Reports, reel A6544A.

cii. MACR 6590; Escape Statement of George Winberg, et al., October 8, 1944, and John J. Schiana, undated, Fifteenth Air Force Escape and Evasion Reports, reel A6544A.

ciii. MACR 6371; Escape Statement of Gerald E. Rothermel and Robert J. Flaherty, September 18, 1944, and Maurice Terry et al., October 8, 1944, Fifteenth Air Force Escape and Evasion Reports, reel A6544A.

civ. MACR 15225; Escape Statement of Ralph F. Fuchs and Clyde Thomas, October 8, 1944, and Walter Leach and Delos Miller, September 18, 1944, Fifteenth Air Force Escape and Evasion Reports, reel A6544A.

cv. Escape Statement of Paul C. Reinhart, September 18, 1944, Fifteenth Air Force Escape and Evasion Reports, reel A6544A.

cvi. Ibid.

cvii. Amos, *Defenders of Liberty*, 266; Escape Statements of Robert W. Hare, October 9, 1944, William N. Spruce, October 8, 1944, Paul C. Reinhart, September 18, 1944, and Henry E. Tennyson, October 8, 1944, Fifteenth Air Force Escape and Evasion Reports, reel A6544A.

cviii. Escape Statement of Ethan Smith Jr., October 9, 1944, Fifteenth Air Force Escape and Evasion Reports, reel A6544A.

cix. Report: Evacuation of Airmen from Tri Duby, Headquarters Fifteenth Air Force, September 18, 1944, and Incoming Message No. 7, from Dawes to Jakes and Deranian, September 20, 1944, Fifteenth Air Force Escape and Evasion Reports, reel A6544; Coalman Mission Summary, 5th Bomb Wing History, reel B0899; Operational History, Dawes and Associated Teams, Headquarters, 2677th Regiment (Provisional), Office of Strategic Services, January 27, 1945, Record Group 226, entry 190, box 22, folder 1; Fred Ascani, "More on the Secret Mission to Slovakia," 483rd Bomb Group Association (H) Newsletter, July 1986, p. 5; Short Report on the American Mission to the Czechoslovak Forces of the Interior at Banska Bystrica: September–October 1944, RR226, entry 143, box 12, folder 149.

cx. Bohnstedt, *460th Bomb Group History*, 57–60, MACR 6394; Escape Statement of Sergeant Leonard Bernhardt, March 10, 1945, Fifteenth Air Force Escape and Evasion Reports, reel A6544B.

cxi. Statement by Lieutenant Colonel James A. Gunn, 454th Bomb Group Escape Statements, p. 3–4, reel B0601

cxii. Ibid., 36–38.

cxiii. Mahoney, *Fifteenth against the Axis* 221, 223.

cxiv. MACR 14024; "Report of Pilot Returned from Enemy Territory," Fifteenth Air Force Escape and Evasion Reports, reel A6544C.

cxv. Affidavit of First Lieutenant Robert N. Lambert, September 24, 1945, Case No. 15-38, box 261, entry 2339, Untried War Crimes Cases, Record Group 594.

cxvi. Affidavit of Joseph Nargiso, February 1, 1946, Case No. 15-38, box 261, entry 2339, Untried War Crimes Cases, Record Group 594.

cxvii. MACR 11699; Case No. 15-38, Box 261, Entry 2339, Untried War Crimes Cases, Record Group 594; Amost, *Defenders of Liberty*, 246.

cxviii. Affidavit of Edward O. Grant, April 21, 1947, Case No. 8-10, Box 34, Entry 2338, Untried War Crimes Cases, Record Group 594.

cxix. MACR 9592; Case No. 8-10, Box 34, Entry 2338, Untried War Crimes Cases, Record Group 594.

cxx. Affidavit of Robert W. Zinn Jr., May 14, 1945, Case No. 5-34, box 5, entry 2339, Untried War Crimes Cases, Record Group 594.

cxxi. MACR 14060; Case No. 5-34, box 5, entry 2339, Untried War Crimes Cases, Record Group 594.

cxxii. MACR 9349; Case No. 5-113, box 3, entry 2338, Cases Tried, Record Group 594.

cxxiii. MACRs 12514, 12476; 450th Bomb Group Mission Narrative Report, February 28, 1945, 450th Bomb Group history files, reel B0594; 456th Bomb Group Narrative Mission Report, February 28, 1945, 456th Bomb Group history files, reel B0603.

cxxiv. MACR 12453; 484th Bomb Group Mission Narrative Report, February 21, 1945, 484th Bomb Group history files, reel B0643.

cxxv. MACR 14058.

cxxvi. 461st Bomb Group Mission Narrative, April 25, 1945, 461st Bomb Group history files, reel B0610.

cxxvii. MACR 14080; Bohnstadt, *460th Bomb Group History*, 150–151.

BIBLIOGRAPHY

Official Documents

Air Material Command. "History of the 15th Air Force, Narrative and Appendices." December 1946. Library of Congress, Microform Publication No. 1742, reel 6.

Fifteenth Air Force. Escape and Evasion Reports. National Archives and Records Administration, Record Group 342, United States Air Force, entry 1006B, reels A6544–A6544c.

_____. "List of Evaders Interrogated," 15th Air Force Escape and Interrogation Lists. National Archives and Records Administration, Record Group 342, United States Air Force, entry 6, box 16.

_____. "Narrative History of Escape and Evasion." National Archives and Records Administration, Record Group 342, United States Air Force, entry 1006B, reel A6544.

_____. "Special Intelligence Reports," December 1943–April 1945. National Archives and Records Administration, Record Group 342, United States Air Force, entry 1006B, reel A6543.

_____. "Weekly Summary of Operations," November 1943–May 1945. National Archives and Records Administration, Record Group 342, United States Air Force, entry 1006B, Box 173, reels A7379–A6389.

Fifteenth Air Force General Orders, Fifteenth Air Force. Record Group 342, United States Air Force, entry 1006B, reel A6423.

Mediterranean Allied Air Force, "Air Intelligence Weekly Summary," Nos. 58–128. National Archives and Records Administration, Record Group 342, United States Air Force, entry 1006B, reel A6085.

Missing Air Crew Reports. National Archives and Records Administration, Record Group 92, Office of the Quartermaster General. Microfilm Publication M1380. (Note: The Name Index to this series is also available on microfilm. The majority of these reports, but certainly not all, are also available online at www.Fold3.com.)

Operational History, Dawes and Associated Teams, Headquarters, 2677th Regiment (Provisional), Office of Strategic Services, January 27, 1945. National Archives and Records Administration, Record Group 226, Entry 190, Box 22, Folder 1.

"Short Report on the American Mission to the Czechoslovak Forces of the Interior at Banska Bystrica: Sept.–October 1944." National Archives and Records Administration, RR226, Entry 143, Box 12, Folder 149.

Untried War Crimes Cases. National Archives and Records Administration, Record Group 594, Entry 2339, boxes 5, 34, and 261. Cases Tried, Record Group 594, Entry 2338, box 3.

Official Wing and Group Histories

2nd Bomb Group history files. National Archives and Records Administration, Record Group 342, United States Air Force, entry 1006B, reels B0040–0043.

5th Bomb Wing History. National Archives and Records Administration, Record Group 342, United States Air Force, entry 1006B, reel B0899.

5th Photo Group history files. National Archives and Records Administration, Record Group 342, United States Air Force, entry 1006B, reel B0752.

14th Fighter Group history files. National Archives and Records Administration, Record Group 342, United States Air Force, entry 1006B, reels B0079–0080.

15th Photo Reconnaissance Squadron Combat Reports. National Archives and Records Administration, Record Group 18, US Army Air Force WWII Combat Operations Reports, Entry 7, Box 3873.

31st Fighter Group history files. National Archives and Records Administration, Record Group 342, United States Air Force, entry 1006B, reels B0110A–0011.

52nd Fighter Group history files. National Archives and Records Administration, Record Group 342, United States Air Force, entry 1006B, reels B0146–0148.

82nd Fighter Group history files. National Archives and Records Administration, Record Group 342, United States Air Force, entry 1006B, reels B0167–0169.

97th Bomb Group history files. National Archives and Records Administration, Record Group 342, United States Air Force, entry 1006B, reels B0194–0196.

98th Bomb Group history files. National Archives and Records Administration, Record Group 342, United States Air Force, entry 1006B, reel B0197–0199.

99th Bomb Group history files. National Archives and Records Administration, Record Group 342, United States Air Force, entry 1006B, reels B0199–0201.

301st Bomb Group history files. National Archives and Records Administration, Record Group 342, United States Air Force, entry 1006B, reel B0208.

325th Fighter Group history files. National Archives and Records Administration, Record Group 342, United States Air Force, entry 1006B, reels B0275–0277.

325th Fighter Group Encounter Reports, 325th Fighter Group Combat Reports, May 1943–April 1945. National Archives and Records Administration, Record Group 18, US Army Air Force WWII Combat Operations Reports, Entry 7, Box 3350.

332nd Fighter Group history files. National Archives and Records Administration, Record Group 342, United States Air Force, entry 1006B, reels B0279–0280.

376th Bomb Group history files. National Archives and Records Administration, Record Group 342, United States Air Force, entry 1006B, reels B0237–0238.

449th Bomb Group history files. National Archives and Records Administration, Record Group 342, United States Air Force, entry 1006B, reel B0752.

450th Bomb Group history files. National Archives and Records Administration, Record Group 342, United States Air Force, entry 1006B, reels B0593–0594.

454th Bomb Group history files. National Archives and Records Administration, Record Group 342, United States Air Force, entry 1006B, reels B0600–0601.

455th Bomb Group history files. National Archives and Records Administration, Record Group 342, United States Air Force, entry 1006B, reels B0601–0602.

456th Bomb Group history files. National Archives and Records Administration, Record Group 342, United States Air Force, entry 1006B, reel B0603.

460th Bomb Group history files. National Archives and Records Administration, Record Group 342, United States Air Force, entry 1006B, reel B0609.

461st Bomb Group history files. National Archives and Records Administration, Record Group 342, United States Air Force, entry 1006B, reel B0610.

465th Bomb Group history files. National Archives and Records Administration, Record Group 342, United States Air Force, entry 1006B, reels B0616–0617.

483rd Bomb Group history files. National Archives and Records Administration, Record Group 342, United States Air Force, entry 1006B, reel B0642.

484th Bomb Group history files. National Archives and Records Administration, Record Group 342, United States Air Force, entry 1006B, reel B0643.

Official Studies

Boylan, Bernard. "Development of the Long-Range Escort Fighter." USAF Historical Division, USAF Historical Study No. 136.

Mediterranean Allied Air Force. "Air Power in the Mediterranean: November 1942–February 1945." February 21, 1945.

Norris, Joel L. "Combined Bomber Offensive: 1 January–6 June 1944." April 1947. AAF Historical Office, USAF Historical Study No. 122.

Schmid, Josef. "The Employment of the German Luftwaffe against the Allies in the West, 1943–45." Vol. 3. AAF Historical Office, USAF Historical Study No. 58–60.

Stormont, John W. "Combined Bomber Offensive: April through December 1943." March 1946. AAF Historical Office. USAF Historical Study No. 119.

United Stated Air Force. "USAF Credits for the Destruction of Enemy Aircraft, World War II." USAF Historical Study No. 85.

Published Group Histories

Amos, Robert F. *Defenders of Liberty: 2nd Bombardment Group/Wing 1918–1993*. Paducah, KY: Turner, 1996.

Blake, Steve, and John Stanaway. *Adorimini ("Up and at 'Em!"): A History of the 82nd Fighter Group in World War II*. Boise, ID: 82nd Fighter Group History, 1992.

Bohnstedt, Duane and Betty. *460th Bomb Group History*. Dallas, TX: Taylor, 1992.

Foreman, John, and S. E. Harvey. *Messerschmitt Combat Diary Me.262*. New Malden, Surrey, Great Britain: Air Research Publications, 1990.

Grimm, Jacob, and Vernon Cole. *Heroes of the 483rd*. Rev. ed. 483rd Bombardment Group Association, 2004.

Gulley, Thomas. *The Hour Has Come: The 97th Bomb Group in World War II*. Dallas, TX: Taylor, 1993.

Hill, Michael, and Betty Karle. *The 464th Bomb Group in World War II: In Action over the Third Reich with the B-24 Liberator*. Atglen, PA: Schiffer Military History, 2001.

Hill, Michael. *The 451st Bomb Group in World War II: A Pictorial History*. Atglen, PA: Schiffer Military History, 2001.

Lambert, John W. *The 14th Fighter Group in World War II*. Atglen, PA: Schiffer Military History, 2008.

McCarty, Lyle. *Coffee Tower: A History of the 459th Bomb Group*. Paducah, KY: Turner, 1997.

99th Bomb Group Historical Society, *The Diamondbacks: The History of the 99th Bomb Group (H)*. Paducah, KY: Turner, 1998.

General Published Works

Dorr, Robert F. *B-24 Liberator Units of the Fifteenth Air Force*. Oxford, UK: Osprey, 2000.

Drain, Richard E. *5th Bomb Wing: History of Aircraft Assigned*. 1992.

Lipfert, Helmut, and Werner Girbig, *The War Diary of Hauptman Helmut Lipfert: JG 52 on the Russian Front, 1943–1945*. Atglen, PA: Schiffer Publications, 1993.

McFarland, Stephen L. and Wesley F. Newton. *To Command the Sky: The Battle for Air Superiority over Germany, 1942–1944*. Washington, DC: Smithsonian Institution Press, 1991.

Mahoney, Kevin A. *Fifteenth Air Force against the Axis: Combat Missions over Europe during World War II*. Lanham, Toronto: Scarecrow Press, 2013.

Moxley, Gene F. *Missing in Action*. n.p: Gene F. Moxley, 2002.

Rust, Ken. *Fifteenth Air Force Story*. Temple City, CA: Historical Aviation Album, 1976.

Westermann, Edward B. *Flak: German Anti-Aircraft Defenses 1914–1945*. Lawrence, KS: University of Kansas Press, 2001.

Articles

Ascani, Fred. "More on the Secret Mission to Slovakia." *483rd Bomb Group Association (H) Newsletter*, July 1986.

Internet Sources

Ancestry.com. *U.S. Rosters of World War II Dead, 1939–1945*. Provo, UT: Ancestry.com Operations Inc., 2007. (Original data: US Army, Quartermaster General's Office. *Rosters of World War II Dead (all services)*. Washington, DC: US Army.)

Register of WWII Burials and Memorializations complied by the American Battlefield Monuments Commission and available online at the Commission's website, www.abmc.gov. It only lists those buried overseas or whose remains were never recovered.

World War II Prisoners of War Data File, December 7, 1941–November 19, 1946. National Archives. aad.archives.gov

INDEX

Page numbers in italics indicate an item in a photograph or caption.